GCSE French

Ziggy Kambuts
Will Wilson

DP Publications Ltd
Aldine Place
142/144 Uxbridge Road
Shepherds Bush Green
London W12 8AA

1989

A CIP catalogue record for this book is available from the British Library

ISBN 1 870 941 25 X

PageSet by Kai Typesetters in Souvenir on Apple Macintosh.

Printed by The Bath Press
Lower Bristol Road
Bath BA2 3BL

ACKNOWLEDGEMENTS

The authors wish to thank the following for permission to reproduce copyright material:

France

L'Evènement du jeudi -
article on Washington; interview with Mme Gentzbittel

Groupe Progrès -
Pas de vacances pour le Syndicat d'Initiative

Le Monde -
Le Prince Randolph

Rouen, S.I. -
Les Voiles de la Liberté

Sud Ouest -
Première vague de retours; Prudence sur les routes; météo headlines

Télé 7 jours -
article on Ruth Rendell and P.D. James; TV programmes

Great Britain

London & East Anglian Group
(East Anglian Examinations Board; London Regional Examining Board; University of London School Examinations Board)

Midland Examining Group
(East Midlands Regional Examinations Board; Oxford & Cambridge Schools Examination Board; Southern Universities' Joint Board for School Examinations; West Midlands Examinations Board; University of Cambridge Local Examinations Syndicate)

Northern Examining Association
(Associated Lancashire Schools Examining Board; Joint Matriculation Board; Yorkshire & Humberside Regional Examinations Board)

Northern Ireland Schools Examination Council

Southern Examining Group
(The Associated Examining Board; Oxford Delegacy of Local Examinations Board; Southern Regional Examinations Board; South-East Regional Examinations Board; South-Western Examinations board)

Welsh Joint Education Committee

Cathérine Lawry for advice and help on language and listening items.

Photographs

Will Wilson took the Scottish photographs in *Self, house, home and family.*
Cover and all other photographs are by Ziggy Kambuts.

Illustrations

Map of Bordeaux by David Nunn; school lessons by Roger Laughton.

CONTENTS

PREFACE

AIM

The primary aim of this book is to provide all the support needed for a course in GCSE French.

The way the book is set out also makes it ideal for students revising independently.

APPROACH

The book is structured around the Topics and Settings prescribed by the Boards. The ten Topic Areas (part 2 of the book) form the core teaching and practice material for all the syllabuses, in the four skills and for basic and higher levels.
Topics which may be listed separately by some boards are represented under settings within this book.

Emphasis throughout is on authentic, up-to-date situations and materials; and on practical, effective communication.

To this end, the authors have given particular attention to the notional and functional approach to language learning/teaching, by providing a *Starter Kit*.
This is a unique feature of the book. It identifies and groups together - for easy reference - the 'top' 45 key notions and functions - ones which occur with regular frequency across all Topics or Settings. *(A complete list of these will be found in the Boards' syllabuses)*.

Together with easy practice tasks, notes, examples and structures, students and teachers will find the *Starter Kit* invaluable in one, or both, of these ways:

- at the start of each Topic Area, in the context of key speaking tasks: to obtain practice and confidence in formulating questions and making statements.

- as a consolidation and final revision module, just prior to the oral/conversation examination.

A FREQUENCY GRID is provided to enable students and teachers to identify, check off, and gain practice in referring to notions and functions as an aid to effective communication.

HOW TO USE THIS BOOK

This book is arranged in four sections:

Part 1:   Starter Kit
Part 2:   Topics Areas
Part 3:   Grammar Sections
Part 4:   Answers and Listening Scripts

TOPIC AREAS (PART 2)

The following notes may be helpful when planning a lesson or programme of revision, for each *Topic Area*. These have been arranged to a similar pattern, beginning in every case with key speaking tasks. The Topic Areas can be taken in any order; the authors have placed the topic of HOLIDAYS first, because it may be a natural topic to start with at the beginning of any term.

1.   **Establish** recall and knowledge of essential vocabulary through *key speaking tasks*. These are placed at the beginning of each *Topic Area* to enable students to check and gain confidence in using essential vocabulary which is common to both basic and higher level.

Practice Tasks, which have been collated from past papers and authors' own experience, are given:

- in English: where a straightforward exchange of vocabulary is required; e.g. numbers, names of places, buildings.

- as visual material: where this is more appropriate to the topic or setting; e.g. buying food, looking at menus.

- in French: where a personalized response is needed, and where no single 'answer' is correct.

The *key speaking tasks* are set notionally/functionally, and as questions/statements - to enable students to identify exactly what they want to say, and how to go about it. Additional help is given in the *Starter Kit*.

2.   **Consolidate** and **Extend** spoken language through *reading practice*. The selected texts and documents are intended to be teaching and learning materials. Students are advised to exploit these fully - for recognition and extension of vocabulary. The reading practice items are numbered in order of ascending difficulty. Generally, basic level reading tasks require students to elicit information from a text; higher level items suppose a greater range of vocabulary - in a longer text; they will also ask students to form opinions or draw conclusions, again firmly based on the text.

The range - and number - of texts and documents selected by the authors will enable teachers to use these models for higher speaking and writing tasks, in particular.

3.   **Progress** to use of language, at higher level, for *conversation or role-play*, as required by the nature of the topic or setting.

The practice tasks here are given, generally, in French: as questions or statements, with sample 'answers'. Teachers and students will need to personalize these as appropriate to their own situation; e.g. talking about where you live; family; hobbies and leisure.

4.   **Integrate** all the previous skills into the *written form*.

Writing tasks, representative of all the boards, are given as appropriate to the topic or level (eg. lists, notes, messages, forms, diaries, postcards, informal letters; formal letters, responding to formal/informal letters). The *Starter Kit* provides useful information and hints on writing holiday postcards, and writing for information.

5.   **Check** understanding of spoken language through *listening items*. Levels (basic/higher) are shown on the contents page of each *Topic Area*. Generally, basic level items cover understanding of vocabulary, and numbers in all their guises: time, cost, quantity, length of stay, number of people, telephone numbers. This is thoroughly covered in the *Starter Kit*. Higher level items additionally test a more extended vocabulary, in longer sequences. Students will need to identify attitudes, opinions - as in the higher reading items. It is suggested that teachers make tapes from the material in this section, for classroom use. (See also part 4).

Vocabularies.

Each *Topic Area* closes with vocabulary lists; differentiated into basic and higher levels. Key verbs precede each level - to highlight their importance in all the four skills. Other vocabulary has been grouped by settings, where appropriate. Where the levels differ from Board to Board, the authors have inflated the 'basic' lists. Teachers and students should also note that the Boards do not publish full vocabulary lists, and specify that about 15% vocabulary will remain unspecified!

GRAMMAR SECTION (PART 3)

This sets out in full, all the grammatical structures needed for both levels, as published in the Boards' syllabuses.

In order to promote the use of grammar as an aid to practical communication, the authors have given particular weighting to the 1st and 2nd person usage - in the examples and notes.

Some tables - especially for verbs and pronouns (for example) - have been set out to highlight usage, rather than 'grammar'.

Explanations - given as 'key notes, examples' have been kept to a minimum, and given with the French usage as a starting point. English language usage is given first only when it acts as a serious deterrent to French usage: eg. I like reading (in French: **j'aime lire**).

Students and teachers are enabled, through the notes and examples, to deduce and infer good practice.

ANSWERS AND SCRIPTS (PART 4)

This section provides listening scripts, with answers; and answers to other practice tasks - where clear and unambiguous answers are possible.

Starter Kit

STARTER KIT

CONTENTS

Frequency grid by *Topic Area*

The frequency grid columns (left to right): HOLIDAYS, TRAVEL, ENVIRONMENT, SHOPS, SERVICES, FOOD, HEALTH, SELF, LEISURE, SCHOOL

QUESTION FORMS
by notion and function

Note   1. *A simple, and correct, way to ask a question is by tone - by raising your voice at the end of what you say.*
2. *Some question forms can be made up with est-ce que - this is shown by* **
Note, however, **quand est-ce que**.

EXISTENCE

		Examples
is there? are there?	**il y a ..?	est-ce qu'il y a un marché par ici?

LOCATION, DIRECTION, POSITION, DISTANCE

where?	où?	où se trouvent les toilettes?
far? near?	**c'est près/loin?	c'est loin, la gare?

AVAILABILITY

have you got?	**vous avez..?	vous avez des journaux anglais?

QUANTITY, NUMBER, COST

how much?	combien?	
how many?	combien de..?	vous êtes combien de personnes?
how much is it?	c'est combien?	c'est combien, le jambon?

TIME; point in time, frequency, duration

when?	**quand est-ce que?**	**quand est-ce vous partez?**
when - at what time?	**à quelle heure..?**	**c'est à quelle heure, le train?**
how often/how many times?	**combien de fois..?**	**combien de fois êtes - vous allé en France?**
how long?	**combien de temps..?**	**vous apprenez l'anglais depuis combien de temps?**

CHARACTERISTICS

what colour?	**de quelle couleur?**	**une robe de quelle couleur?**
what sort of..?	**quelle sorte de..?**	**quelle sorte de films aimez-vous?**
what size?	**quelle taille?**	**vous avez quelle taille?**
shoe size?	**quelle pointure?**	**chaussures? quelle pointure?**

POSSIBILITY

can I?	****je peux?**	**je peux vous aider?**
can you?	****vous pouvez?**	**pouvez-vous m'indiquer la route?**

OBLIGATION

have I got to..?	****je dois..?**	**est-ce que je dois attendre longtemps?**

ORIGIN

where...from?	**d'où?**	**vous êtes d'où?**

IDENTIFYING

who?	qui?	c'est qui, ton prof. de maths?
what?	qu'est-ce que...?	qu'est-ce qu'il y a?
which?	quel/quelle/quels/quelles?	quelle voie? quels livres?

DESCRIBING

what's (it) like?	c'est comment..?	elle est comment, ta mère?

KEY NOTIONS
use and practice

EXISTENCE

KEY ENGLISH	KEY FRENCH	KEY STRUCTURES
if there is...	**il y a...par ici?**	gender number & indefinite articles; simple question forms
if there are...nearby		
what there is in the way of...	**qu'est-ce qu'il y a comme..?**	

LOCATION, DIRECTION, POSITION, DISTANCE

KEY ENGLISH	KEY FRENCH	KEY STRUCTURES
where is...	**où est le/la/l'..?**	
	où se trouve le..?	gender; number & definite articles
where are...	**où sont les..?**	
	où se trouvent les..?	
how to get to...	**pour aller à/au/aux..?**	à + definite articles
it's 100 metres/kilometres away	**c'est à 100 mètres/kilomètres**	à + numbers to express distance away

PRACTICE TASKS

Use the illustrations to practice asking about these places - if there are any around; where they are, and how to get there.

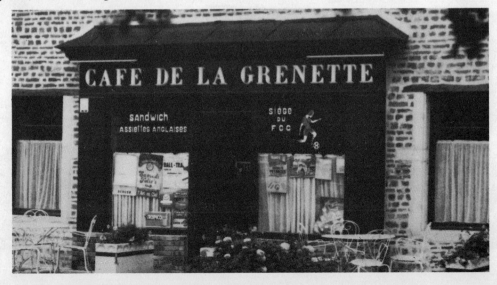

Prepositions to express location, position, direction, distance

			Examples
à	-	in; at; + names of towns & countries of m.gender	être/habiter/vivre à Paris; aux Antilles: au Japon
à	-	to; + verbs of motion	aller au cinéma; courir à la gare
à droite	de	on the right	à droite de la porte
au bord	de	by; on the edge	au bord de la mer
au bout	de	at the end/back	au bout de la rue
au centre	de	in the centre	au centre de la ville
au coin	de	on the corner	au coin de la grande rue
à côté	de	next door; next to	à côté du Monoprix
de l'autre côté	de	on the other side	de l'autre côté du trottoir
au delà	de	beyond	au delà de la ville
au fond	de	at the back	au fond du magasin
à la fin	de	at the end	à la fin de cette rue
à gauche	de	on the left	à gauche des toilettes
au milieu	de	in the middle	au milieu du quartier
après	-	after	après la gare
autour	de	round	autour de la place
avant		before	avant de prendre la 2e rue
contre	-	against	contre le mur
dans	-	inside; in	dans le magasin
derrière	-	behind	derrière l'immeuble
devant	-	in front	devant la pharmacie
en bas	de	down there; at the bottom	en bas de l'étagère
en face	de	opposite	en face de la mairie
en haut	de	up there: at the top	c'est tout en haut
entre	-	between	entre deux grandes maisons
jusqu'à	-	as far as: until	jusqu'aux feux rouges
le long	de	along	le long des quais
loin	de	far	loin du centre

parmi		- amongst	parmi mon courrier
près	de	near	près du garage
sous		- under	sous le pont
sur		- on top; on	sur la place
tout droit		- straight on	allez tout droit
vers		- towards	vers la R.N.7
chez		- No Direct Equivalent	chez moi
		at someone's	chez moi; chez les
		house/home/place	voisins; etc
No Direct Equivalent		up	
use verbs		down	
		go up the road	montez la rue
		go down the road	descendez la rue

Practice Tasks

Get to know these prepositions thoroughly: they are the absolute minimum needed.

en face de	opposite
devant	in front
derrière	behind
à gauche de	left of
à droite de	right of
près de	near to
loin de	far from
à côté de	next to
au coin de	on the corner of

Look back to the photos in *Location* (p 7), and practice using the prepositions to locate the places illustrated,

eg. **La boucherie se trouve en face du coiffeur.**

Pour aller à..? Où se trouve..?

Look at the plan of the citadel of St. Malo (called **"intra muros"**) to explain the whereabouts of places: sometimes you can be quite specific, sometimes more vague -

eg. **la piscine se trouve sur la plage de Bonsecours**
eg. **la Chapelle St. Sauveur se trouve pas loin de la plage du Môle.**

1.	**l'Aquarium**	12.	**la Galerie**
2.	**la bibliothèque**	13.	**le Musée**
5.	**la Cathédrale**	17.	**la Piscine**
6.	**la Chapelle St. Sauveur**	18.	**la poste**
7.	**le Théâtre**	19.	**l'hôtel de police**
9.	**le collège**	20.	**le camping de Nielles**

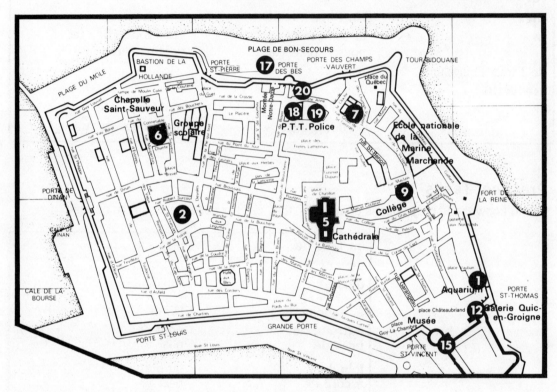

AVAILABILITY

KEY ENGLISH	KEY FRENCH	KEY STRUCTURES
if they've got...	**est-ce que vous avez..?**	**avoir; rester;** partitives; negatives of verbs;
if they've got any left...	**vous n'avez plus de..?** **il ne reste plus de..?**	negatives followed + **de**

QUANTITY, NUMBER, COST

KEY ENGLISH	KEY FRENCH	KEY STRUCTURES
How much...	**combien?**	numbers: weights & measures;
how much is that	**ça fait combien?**	demonstrative adjectives and pronouns.
how much do I owe you?	**je vous dois combien?**	
how much would you like?	**combien vous en voulez?**	

Practice Tasks

Go to the market - buy some fruit and vegetables; ask if they've got items you can't see displayed; ask the price. (Refer to the vocabulary of Topic Area 4: *Shops and Shopping,* if you need to.

NUMBERS

Cardinal

0	zéro	40	quarante	80	quatre-vingts
1	un	41	quarante et un	81	quatre-vingt-un
2	deux	42	quarante-deux	82	quatre-vingt-deux
3	trois	43	quarante-trois	83	quatre-vingt-trois
4	quatre	44	quarante-quatre	84	quatre-vingt-quatre
5	cinq	45	quarante-cinq	85	quatre-vingt-cinq
6	six	46	quarante-six	86	quatre-vingt-six
7	sept	47	quarante-sept	87	quatre-vingt-sept
8	huit	48	quarante-huit	88	quatre-vingt-huit
9	neuf	49	quarante-neuf	89	quatre-vingt-neuf
10	dix	50	cinquante	90	quatre-vingt-dix
11	onze	51	cinquante et un	91	quatre-vingt-onze
12	douze	52	cinquante-deux	92	quatre-vingt-douze
13	treize	53	cinquante-trois	93	quatre-vingt-treize
14	quatorze	54	cinquante-quatre	94	quatre-vingt-quatorze
15	quinze	55	cinquante-cinq	95	quatre-vingt-quinze
16	seize	56	cinquante-six	96	quatre-vingt-seize
17	dix-sept	57	cinquante-sept	97	quatre-vingt-dix-sept
18	dix-huit	58	cinquante-huit	98	quatre-vingt-dix-huit
19	dix-neuf	59	cinquante-neuf	99	quatre-vingt-dix-neuf
20	vingt	60	soixante	100	cent
21	vingt et un	61	soixante et un	101	cent un
22	vingt-deux	62	soixante-deux	102	cent deux etc
23	vingt-trois	63	soixante-trois	200	deux cents
24	vingt-quatre	64	soixante-quatre	201	deux cents et un etc
25	vingt-cinq	65	soixante-cinq	1000	mille
26	vingt-six	66	soixante-six	1,000,000	
27	vingt-sept	67	soixante-sept		un million
28	vingt-huit	68	soixante-huit	1,000,000,000	
29	vingt-neuf	69	soixante-neuf		un milliard
					(a billion in English)
30	trente	70	soixante-dix		
31	trente et un	71	soixante et onze		
32	trente-deux	72	soixante-douze		
33	trente-trois	73	soixante-treize		
34	trente-quatre	74	soixante-quatorze		
35	trente-cinq	75	soixante-quinze		
36	trente-six	76	soixante-seize		
37	trente-sept	77	soixante-dix-sept		
38	trente-huit	78	soixante-dix-huit		
39	trente-neuf	79	soixante-dix-neuf		

Ordinal

first	1st	**premier, première**	**1er**	**1ère**
second	2nd	**deuxième**	**2e**	
third	3rd	**troisième**	**3e**	
fourth	4th	**quatrième**	**4e**	
fifth	5th	**cinquième**	**5e**	
sixth	6th	**sixième**	**6e**	
seventh	7th	**septième**	**7e**	
eighth	8th	**huitième**	**8e**	
ninth	9th	**neuvième**	**9e**	
tenth	10th	**dixième**	**10e**	

To express age

avoir 18 ans	to be 18	**mon frère a 20 ans**
avoir la vingtaine/ trentaine/quarantaine	about 20/30/40; in their twenties/etc.	**elle doit avoir la trentaine**

To express the date and dates

le 1er mars	March 1st	the French way of writing the date is invariable
le 2 juin	2nd June	
le 3 août	August 3rd	
le 4 mai	4th of May	
les années 30/60	the Thirties/Sixties	**la mode des années 20**
dans les années 50	in the Fifties	

To express fractions; decimals; percentages

un quart	a quarter	**un quart de vin**
un/e demi	half	**un demi-litre**
		une demi-heure
un tiers	a third	**le Tiers Monde**
10,8 (dix virgule huit)	10.8 (ten point eight)	use of the comma in French
% (pour cent)	% (percent)	

Telephone numbers

21.68.09.72	In France telephone numbers have 8 digits, and are written - and said - in pairs of numbers

Expressing the time

Note   always start with the hour

il est une heure/deux heures/...	it's 1 o'clock/2 o'clock
à trois heures/quatre heures/...	at 3 o'clock/4 o'clock

Then, add the rest, like this

... et quart	quarter past	
... et demie	half past	**demie**
... dix/vingt etc	ten/twenty past	numbers only
... moins deux/cinq	two minutes to/five minutes to	
... moins le quart	quarter to	
midi	12 o'clock, midday	
midi et demi	12.30, midday	**demi**
minuit	12 o'clock midnight	
minuit et demi	12.30 midnight	
... du matin	a.m.	
... de l'après-midi	p.m. in the afternoon	
... du soir	p.m. in the evening	

Note   the 24 hour clock is always used in local or international timetables: frequently in banks, shops, businesses etc, to show opening & closing times.

PRACTICE TASKS

Try saying, and writing out, these numbers and times

CALENDAR

Days/**Les Jours**	Months/**Les Mois**	Holidays/**Les Fêtes**	
1. **lundi**	1. **janvier**	**01.01:**	**le jour de l'an**
2. **mardi**	2. **février**		
3. **mercredi**	3. **mars**		
4. **jeudi**	4. **avril**	**Pâques**	
5. **vendredi**	5. **mai**		
6. **samedi**	6. **juin**	**l'Ascension**	
7. **dimanche**	7. **juillet**	**14.07:**	**la Fête Nationale**
	8. **août**	**15.08:**	**l'Assomption**
	9. **septembre**		
	10. **octobre**		
	11. **novembre**	**1.11:**	**la Toussaint**
		11.11:	**l'Armistice**
	12. **décembre**	**25.12:**	**Noël**

KEY EXPRESSIONS		KEY STRUCTURES
a week	**huit jours/une semaine**	
a fortnight	**quinze jours; une quinzaine**	
today	**aujourd'hui**	
morning	**le matin**	
afternoon	**l'après-midi (m)**	
evening	**le soir**	
night	**la nuit**	
summer holidays	**les grandes vacances**	
Christmas holidays	**les vacances de Noël**	
day off	**un jour de congé**	
Bank holiday (equivalent of)	**un jour férié**	
the (whole) morning	**la matinée**	
the (whole) evening	**la soirée**	
in (the) winter	**en hiver**	
in (the) summer	**en été**	
in (the) autumn	**en automne**	
in (the) spring	**au printemps**	
tomorrow	**demain**	future tense
day after tommorrow	**après-demain**	
next Monday/Tuesday	**lundi/mardi prochain**	
next week/year	**la semaine/l'année prochaine**	
yesterday	**hier**	
yesterday morning	**hier matin**	
last night	**hier soir**	perfect tense
day before yesterday	**avant-hier**	imperfect tense
the next day	**le lendemain**	
last week/year	**la semaine/l'année dernière**	
every day	**tous les jours**	
every week	**toutes les semaines**	
monthly	**mensuel**	**une revue mensuelle**
yearly	**annuel**	**une publication annuelle**

TIME

Point in time

KEY ENGLISH	KEY FRENCH	KEY STRUCTURES
at what time	**à quelle heure..?**	clock
when	**quand est-ce que..?**	calendar

Duration

how long	**combien de temps..?**	clock; calendar
how long for/since	**depuis/depuis combien de temps..?**	- use of **depuis** with present tense
during	**pendant**	
in (a month's time)	**dans (un mois)**	- use of future tenses with **dans**

Frequency

how many times	**combien de fois..?**	adverbs
how often		**par jour, par semaine etc**
		use of **tout** as in **tous les jours** etc.

Beginning

at the beginning (of September)	**au début (de septembre)**
from 10 a.m. onwards	**à partir de (10h)**
starting from today/now	**dès aujourd'hui/ maintenant**

COUNTRIES

Destination, origin, languages

Habiter	Aller	Être	Parler
l'Allemagne	en Allemagne	Allemand/e	l'allemand
l'Angleterre	en Angleterre	Anglais/e	l'anglais
les Antilles	aux Antilles	Antillais/e	**l'anglais
la Belgique	en Belgique	Belge	le flamand
le Canada	au Canada	Canadien/ne	**l'anglais
la Chine	en Chine	Chinois/e	**le mandarin
le Danemark	au Danemark	Danois/e	le danois
l'Écosse	en Écosse	Écossais/e	**l'anglais
les États-Unis	aux États-Unis	Américain/e	**l'anglais
la France	en France	Français/e	le français
l'Espagne	en Espagne	Espagnol/e	l'espagnol
la Grèce	en Grèce	Grec/Grecque	le grec
l'Hongrie	en Hongrie	Hongrois/e	l'hongrois
la Guyane	en Guyane	Français/e	le français
l'Irlande	en Irlande	Irlandais/e	**le gaëlique
l'Italie	en Italie	Italien/ne	l'italien
le Japon	au Japon	Japonais/e	le japonais
le Maroc	au Maroc	Marocain/e	l'arabe
la Norvège	en Norvège	Norvégien/ne	le norvégien
le Pays de Galles	au Pays de Galles	Gallois/e	**le gallois
le Portugal	au Portugal	Portugais/e	le portugais
la Suède	en Suède	Suédois/e	le suédois
la Suisse	en Suisse	Suisse	**le français
la Tunisie	en Tunisie	Tunisien/ne	l'arabe
l'U.R.S.S.	en U.R.S.S.	Russe	**le russe
la Vénézuela	en Vénézuela	Vénézuelien/ne	l'espagnol
la Yougoslavie	en Yougoslavie	Yougoslave	**le serbe

Note 1. *Countries have gender!*
2. *Destination (going to... sending letters to... spending holidays in...) expressed as in column 2 - according to gender.*
3. *Note use of capital letter for expressing* <u>nationality only</u>.
4. ***denotes that more than one language spoken.*

COLOURS

Table of adjectives

1. Invariable; no changes

SINGULAR		PLURAL		
M	F	M	F	
marron	-	-	-	chestnut
noisette	-	-	-	hazel
orange	-	-	-	orange

2. Some changes in spelling; none in pronunciation

rouge	rouge	rouges	rouges	red
jaune	jaune	jaunes	jaunes	yellow

3. Changes in spelling; none in pronunciation

noir	noire	noirs	noires	black
bleu	bleue	bleus	bleues	blue

4. Changes in spelling and in pronunciation

vert	verte	verts	vertes	green
gris	grise	gris	grises	grey
brun	brune	bruns	brunes	brown

5. Big changes

blanc	blanche	blancs	blanches	white
violet	violette	violets	violettes	violet

Note   1. *Colours, like all adjectives, take the gender and number of the noun they describe, unless invariable like 1 above. Other adjectives, in full, are in the Grammar section.*
    2. *They follow the noun they describe.*
        eg   **un poisson rouge**   *goldfish*
               des cheveux gris   *grey hair*
               une voiture blanche   *a white car*

Hair and eye colour

Note the use of these colours, and their spelling, for hair and eye colour.

Avoir	To have
les cheveux châtains	brown hair
les cheveux châtain clair	fair hair
les cheveux châtain foncé	dark brown hair
les cheveux châtain roux	auburn
les cheveux roux	red hair
les cheveux blonds	really blond hair
Avoir	To have
les yeux noisette	hazel eyes
les yeux marron	brown eyes

PRACTICE TASKS

Describe yourself - and several other people:-

• age; date of birth
• height (in centimetres)
• colour of hair; eyes

KEY FUNCTIONS
use and practice

WANTS

		EXAMPLES
je voudrais	I'd like	**je voudrais 2 kilos de poires**
		je voudrais partir tout de suite
donnez-moi	give me	**donnez-moi 200 grammes de fraises**
je prends	I'll have	**je prends le plat du jour**
vous prenez?	will you have?	**vous prenez le dessert ou le fromage?**
vous désirez?	what would you like?	**vous désirez, madame?**

PRACTICE TASKS

Say what you'd like for breakfast from this menu; and buy some fruit at the market.

Petit-Déjeuner au choix

Grand café noir
ou
Grand café lait
ou
Grand chocolat
ou
Thé lait
ou
Thé citron
***
Pain beurre confiture
***
Un croissant

Prix: **22,50 f**

LIKES

		KEY STRUCTURES
1. in general	**aimer**	use following verb/s in the
2. quite like; be fond of	**aimer bien**	infinitive; nouns;
3. very much	**aimer beaucoup**	direct object pronouns
4. madly	**adorer**	
5. love	**aimer**	

	EXAMPLES
1. I like reading I like dogs	**J'aime lire** **J'aime les chiens**
2. I'm quite fond of walking I do like my job	**J'aime bien marcher** **J'aime bien mon métier**
3. I very much like swimming I like winter a lot	**J'aime beaucoup nager** **J'aime beaucoup l'hiver**
4. I adore Wagner; I'm a fan	**J'adore Wagner!**
5. I love my wife	**J'aime ma femme**

DISLIKES

		KEY STRUCTURES
1. fairly strongly	**ne pas aimer**	use following verb/s in the
2. not all that much	**ne pas aimer tellement**	infinitive; nouns; direct
3. intensely	**détester**	object pronouns
4. cannot stand, loathe	**ne pas pouvoir supporter**	

	EXAMPLES
1. I don't like doing housework	**Je n'aime pas faire le ménage.**
2. I don't like cheese all that much.	**Je n'aime pas tellement le fromage.**
3. I hate getting up early.	**Je déteste me lever tôt.**
4. I can't stand that woman.	**Je ne peux pas supporter cette femme-là.**

Note *also these free-standing expressions:*

not a lot	**pas beaucoup**
not much	**pas tellement**
not at all	**pas du tout**

PRACTICE TASKS

Refer to the Topic Areas on Food & Drink; Entertainment, and say to what degree you like/dislike different foods, TV programmes etc.

DESCRIBING PEOPLE

Characteristics and qualities

ADJECTIVE	ENGLISH EQUIVALENT	EXAMPLES
affreux	awful, frightful	**elle est affreuse**
agréable	pleasant, nice	**une personne agréable**
aimable	nice	**il est très aimable**
bien	good	**une personne vraiment bien**
bizarre	wierd, odd	**quelqu'un très bizarre**
chic	super	**un chic type; une fille chic**
correct	punctilious, proper	**des enfants corrects**
désagréable	unpleasant	**une copine désagréable**
difficile	difficult	**une personne difficile**
drôle	amusing, funny	**un garçon drôle**
dynamique	energetic	**un cousin dynamique**
ennuyant	someone who is a bore	**des voisins ennuyants**
ennuyeux	boring	**elle est ennuyeuse**
fier	proud	**elle est fière**
formidable	splendid	**une tante formidable**
généreux	generous	**quelqu' un de généreux**
gentil	nice - kind	**une personne gentille**
honnête	honest	**une personne honnête**
insupportable	unbearable, ghastly	**des collègues insupportables**
magnifique	superb	**une tante magnifique**

malin	clever-cunning	**une personne maligne**
moyen	mediocre	**des professeurs très moyens**
nerveux	highly strung	**une dame nerveuse**
névrosé	neurotic	**un garçon névrosé**
odieux	hateful, despicable	**un monsieur odieux**
paresseux	lazy	**elle est paresseuse**
ponctuel	very proper, correct	**un jeune homme poncteul**
rancunier	spiteful; bears grudges	**une personne rancunière**
sensationnel	marvellous	**une copine sensationnelle**
sérieux	serious-hard working	**des gens sérieux**
soigneux	meticulous	**une personne soigneuse**
spécial	special (good); special (odd)	**quelqu' un très spécial**
sympathique	understanding, good	**des copains sympathiques**

See adjective tables in the Grammar section for gender and number in full.

Size

For colour of hair and eyes, refer back to the notion of Colour

bien portant	well-built	**il était plutôt bien portant**
chauve	bald	**un homme chauve**
court	short (with hair only)	**elle avait des cheveux courts**
grand	tall; big	**un grand garçon**
gros	fat	**un gros monsieur**
long	long (with hair only)	**il avait des cheveux longs, blonds**
maigre	thin	**une personne maigre**
mince	slim	**une jeune fille mince**
de taille moyenne	medium height & size	**quelqu'un de taille moyenne**
petit	small; short	**c'était un homme petit**

Appearance

l'air malade	unhealthy looking	il avait l'air malade
beau	beautiful, handsome	un bel homme
élégant	elegant, chic	une dame élégante
jeune	young	une jeune personne
joli	pretty	un joli enfant
minable	shabby	une dame un peu minable
moche	shoddy, ugly-looking	un monsieur plutôt moche
vieux	old	une vieille dame
laid	ugly	un jeune homme plutôt laid

See adjective tables in Section III for gender and number in full.

KEY STRUCTURES
Present and imperfect tenses of **avoir** and **être**

QUANTIFIERS

These are words used to emphasise - or qualify - descriptions. These are the most useful ones.

	ENGLISH EQUIVALENT	EXAMPLES
assez	fairly; quite	elle est assez grande
bien	a lot	il est bien difficile
plutôt	rather	un voisin plutôt désagréable
tellement	so (much)	une copine tellement drôle
pas tellement	not all that...	il n'est pas tellement généreux
très	very	très malin
pas très	not very	un garçon pas très sérieux
pas du tout	not at all	pas du tout fière
vraiment	really	elle est vraiment odieuse
pas vraiment	not really	pas vraiment bien

PRACTICE TASKS

1. Go over the examples and make sure you understand the meaning and use.
2. List all the adjectives you would use to describe two people - one man, one woman - you don't like very much. Refer to the adjective tables in *Section III* to check gender and spelling.
3. List the adjectives you would use to describe two people (man, woman) you like enormously.
4. How would you describe your boss? your teacher/s? someone in your family? yourself?
5. Ask a friend or colleague to describe their family/friend/neighbour etc.

DESCRIBING BUILDINGS AND PLACES

*Note adjectives marked ** can also be used to describe people*

ADJECTIVE	ENGLISH EQUIVALENT	EXAMPLES
aménagé	restored - done up	**un appartement aménagé**
ancien	ancient	**une maison ancienne**
bruyant**	noisy	**une ville très bruyante**
commerçant	busy - shopping type	**une rue commerçante**
délabré	run-down	**un quartier délabré**
élégant**	elegant	**une cathédrale élégante**
ensoleillé	sunny	**une chambre ensoleillée**
étroit	narrow	**une rue étroite**
gênant**	awkward	**parking gênant**
gratuit	free of charge	**entrée gratuite**
historique	historic	**des monuments historiques**
imposant**	imposing	**un bâtiment imposant**
impressionnant**	impressive	**un musée impressionnant**
large	wide	**une rue très large**
luxueux	luxurious	**un hôtel luxueux**
moche**	shabby	**un quartier moche**
moderne	modern	**un théâtre moderne**
modernisé	modernised	**un immeuble modernisé**
neuf	brand new	**un appartement neuf**
nouveau**	new - different	**un nouvel appartement**

ombragé	in the shade	**une place ombragée**
pittoresque**	colourful	**un village pittoresque**
pratique**	handy, practical	**une cuisine pratique**
rénové	restored	**une église rénovée**
sale**	dirty	**une voiture sale**
sauvage	undomesticated	**un jardin sauvage**
simple**	plain	**une chapelle simple**
tranquille**	quiet	**un endroit tranquille**
vide	empty	**un quartier vide**
vieux**	old	**une vieille maison**
vivant**	lively	**un quartier vivant**

See adjective tables in the Grammar section for gender and number in full.

PRACTICE TASKS

Identify the buildings & places first; then desribe them briefly:
> eg. **un château simple mais élégant.**

There may be more than one illustration of each.

DESCRIBING FOOD

FRENCH	ENGLISH EQUIVALENT	EXAMPLES	
appétissant	appetising	**ça a l'air appétissant**	looks appetising
bon	good; nice	**les pommes sont bonnes**	apples are nice
brûlant	burning	**un thé brûlant**	a very hot tea
chaud	hot	**plats chauds**	hot dishes
dégoûtant	disgusting	**c'est dégoûtant!**	it's disgusting!
délicieux	delicious	**un repas délicieux**	delicious meal
doux	mild; sweet	**un vin doux**	sweet wine
fort	strong; spicy	**une moutarde forte**	hot mustard
frais	cool, cold	**des boissons fraîches**	cold drinks
mauvais	bad, not good	**des fruits mauvais**	bad fruit
salé	salty	**un poisson salé**	salty fish
sec	dry	**un vin sec**	dry wine
succulent	tasty	**un plat succulent**	delicious dish
sucré	sweet	**une boisson sucré**	sweet drink
tiède	warm, tepid	**une salade tiède**	warm salad

PRACTICE TASKS

How would you describe
- **les pêches?**
- **le raisin?**
- **le chou-fleur?**
- **les épinards?**
- **le poisson? (la sole? les huîtres? les moules?)**
- **les fromages? (le Camembert? le Cheddar? le Brie?)**

PREFERENCE

Préféfer; aimer mieux: to prefer; to like better

Note   the variety of structures you can use to express preference.

Key structures	Examples	
Using nouns	**je préfère la campagne**	I like the countryside better
	je préfère les maths.	I prefer maths.

Using verbs	**je préfère rester chez moi**	I prefer staying at home
	j'aime mieux sortir	I prefer going out

Using demonstrative adjectives	**j'aime mieux ce livre-ci/cette chemise-là**	I prefer this book/that shirt

See full table in Part III

Using demonstrative pronouns	**j'aime mieux celui-ci/ceux-là**	I prefer this one/those over there better

See full table in Part III.

Using interrogative pronouns	**laquelle des deux chemises tu préfères?**	which one of the two shirts do you prefer?

See full table in Part III.

Making comparisons using verbs	**je préfère marcher plutôt que de courir**	I prefer walking to running
	j'aime mieux rester à la maison plutôt que de sortir	I like staying in better than going out

| Making comparisons: using all other above structures | je préfère la ville à la campagne; le camping à l'hôtel, le français aux maths

cette robe-ci à celle-là | I prefer the town to the countryside; camping to a hotel; French to maths.

this dress to that one |

PRACTICE TASKS:

Lequel vous préférez?

State your preferences - choose! - in food; sport; TV and film; tapes; reading; activities. Your starter kit:

- **le poulet ou l'agneau?**
- **les frites ou les pommes à l'anglaise?**
- **le potage ou les crudités?**
- **du thé ou du café?**
- **le cricket ou le tennis?**
- **la gymnastique ou la danse?**
- **les feuilletons ou les films?**
- **les romans ou les policiers?**
- **lire ou dessiner?**
- **sortir, ou rester à la maison, ou recevoir?**
- **nager ou marcher?**
- **jouer du piano ou jouer au football?**
- **faire une promenade à pied ou à velo?**

INTEREST

Note   the use of comparatives to express interest or lack of interest (full table in section III)

Key structures

plus intéressant que	more interesting than
moins facile que	less easy than; not as easy as
aussi odieux que	as odious as; just as odious as

SOCIALISING

Attracting attention, for service - in the café, restaurant, shop etc.

FRENCH	ENGLISH EQUIVALENT	NOTES
monsieur!	none	polite to address people
madame!	none	as Monsieur, etc.
mademoiselle!	none	
s'il vous plaît!	none	
garçon!	waiter!	

Attracting attention in the street - to ask directions etc.

pardon... pour aller à...?	excuse me, how do I get to...	

Greeting friends

salut!	hi!	
bonjour!	hello!	an all-day greeting
bonsoir!	hello!	evening greeting

Greeting other people

bonjour, M/Mme/Mlle	good morning; good afternoon	
bonsoir, M/Mme/Mlle	good evening	

Making introductions, and being introduced

voici Alain	this is Alain	
voici Martine	this is Martine	
je <u>te</u> présente Alain/Martine	may I introduce Alain/Martine	introducing someone to a friend or family
je <u>vous</u> présente Alain..	may I introduce Alain..	introducing someone to other people, more formally
enchanté/e!	pleased to meet you	

Saying goodbye to friends

au revoir!	'bye!
à bientôt!	see you soon!
à demain!	see you tommorrow!
à la prochaine fois!	till the next time!

Saying goodbye to other people

au revoir, Monsieur/Madame/ Mademoiselle!	goodbye	always add the M/Mme/Mlle part

Thanking people

merci!	thanks/thank you!	
merci bien!	thank you very much!	
merci beaucoup!	thanks a lot/thank you very much!	
merci, M/Mme/Mlle		when thanking people other than friends

Responding to thanks

de rien!	not at all!	a friendly, casual response
je vous en prie!	not at all!	more formal, correct
à vous!	thank you!	

Expressing good wishes on birthdays etc.

bon anniversaire!	happy birthday!
bonne journée!	have a nice day!
bonne soirée!	have a nice evening!
bon voyage!	have a good journey!
bonnes vacances!	happy holidays!
bonne année!	happy new year!

bon appétit!		said at the beginning of meal
joyeux Nöel!	merry Christmas!	
meilleurs voeux	best wishes	use on greeting cards
félicitations!	congratulations!	
bon séjour!	have a pleasant stay	
bonne chance!	good luck!	

Making invitations and paying for others

je t'invite		I'm paying!
je vous invite!		
je vous invite à prendre un café	come & have a coffee	

Accepting

je veux bien!	yes please!
volontiers!/très volontiers!	willingly!
avec plaisir!	with pleasure!

Refusing

merci, non	no, thank you	say "merci" before "non"

Apologising

oh! pardon!	oops! sorry!
excusez-moi!	sorry!
je regrette, mais...	I'm sorry, but...

WRITING FORMALLY

BEGINNINGS AND ENDINGS

Writing business-type letters in French requires certain standard set phrases, including beginnings and endings. Here are the ones you are most likely to need.

BEGIN

La Direction,
Hôtel Marigny
24 rue Thiers,
76000 Rouen.

3 Main Road
Alton,
York YO4 8JN

le 23 juin

Monsieur,

Je vous serais .....

END

Veuillez agréer, Monsieur, l'expression de mes sentiments distingués.

Your signature

Your name, printed clearly

KEY NOTES	
Your address	top right
their address & title	top left
postal code (see map)	include, and write clearly
date	top left, under your address, in numbers and letters
leave space	after date line
"Monsieur" etc	slightly in the middle
begin letter	on left

KEY EXPRESSIONS

Dear Sir,	**Monsieur,**
Dear Madam,	**Madame,**
Dear Sir/Madam,	**Monsieur, Madame,**
could you please (send me; tell me)	**pourriez-vous (m' envoyer; me dire)**
I would be grateful	**je vous serais reconnaissant/e**
if you could send me	**de bien vouloir m'envoyer**
if you would let me know	**de me faire savoir**
if I can (reserve; hire...)	**si je peux (réserver; louer...)**
if you can (change dates...)	**s'il vous serait possible de (changer de dates)**
from... to...; including	**du... au...; inclus**
instead of	**au lieu de**
I'm writing to let you know - that we are arriving on the...	**j'écris pour vous dire - que nous arrivons le...**
I am sorry (we cannot; I must)	**J'ai le regret de vous dire (que nous ne pouvons pas; je suis obligé/e de)**
change the booking/flight	**changer de réservation/de vol**
in reply to your letter of the...	**en réponse à votre lettre du...**
I am interested in	**je suis intéressé/e par**
the job/the course	**le poste/le stage**
the following information	**les renseignements suivants**
all further details (about)	**tous renseignements complémentaires (sur)**
prices and cost	**les conditions et tarifs**
I enclose	**veuillez trouver ci-joint/je joins**
an international reply coupon	**un coupon-réponse international**
a stamped s.a.e.	**une envelope timbrée (*** french stamp)**
as quickly as possible	**très rapidement**
hoping to hear from you soon	**dans l'attente de vous lire très prochainement**
thanking you in advance	**en vous remerciant d'avance**
with thanks	**avec mes remerciements**

PRACTICE TASKS

Pick out the phrase(s) you would use to:
- indicate you'd appreciate a quick reply
- confirm a reservation
- apologize for changing a booking
- request specific details
- request further information in general
- enquire about prices
- make sure you've booked up to and including 27 August

Writing to an Office du Tourisme

Ask that they send you a town plan, a hotel list and any other information about the area. Enclose a reply coupon, and sign off correctly.

Writing to a hotel

Say that you would like to book for 5 people: from 18th-23rd August (inc); you want 2 double rooms and 1 single. Ask them also to send you a general price list. Say you'd like to have an early reply, and sign off appropriately.

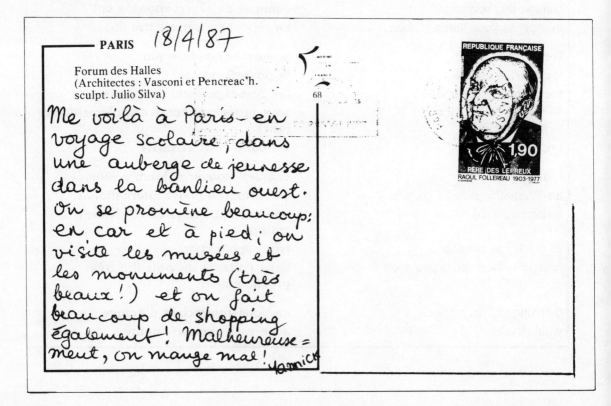

WRITING A HOLIDAY POSTCARD

Within the limited space of a postcard there are still a fair number of things you can say. Here are some key expressions.

KEY ENGLISH	KEY FRENCH	NOTES
hi! hello!	**Salut! Bonjour!**	

Saying where you are

here I am	**me voici/me voilà**	for brevity, avoid
here we are	**nous voici/nous voilà**	verbs in full
in Scotland	**en Ecosse**	**en/au** + name of country
in Nice/in Brighton	**à Nice/à Brighton**	**à** + name of town
near/not far from	**près de/pas loin de**	
Bordeaux/York	**Bordeaux/York**	
by the sea	**au bord de la mer**	
in the countryside	**à la campagne**	
in the Alps/Pyrenees	**dans les Alpes/Pyrénées**	
in the North/South/East/	**dans le nord/sud/l'est/**	lower case for **nord** etc
West of the	**l'ouest du pays**	
North/South/East/West of	**au nord/au sud/à l'est/à**	
Montpellier	**l'ouest de Montpellier**	

Saying where you're staying

in a hotel	**dans un hôtel**	use **être** if you need a verb
camping	**dans un camping**	
with friends	**chez des amis**	
in a holiday cottage	**dans un gîte**	

Saying something about the weather

good	**il fait beau/très beau**
poor	**il fait mauvais/très mauvais**
warm; hot	**il fait chaud; très chaud**
raining	**il pleut**
snowing	**il neige**

Saying what you do

going for walks	**faire des promenades à pied**	remember to change **"faire"** for change
cycling	**faire des promenades à vélo**	of subjects, eg.
horse-riding	**faire des promenades à cheval**	**je fais des promenades; mon frère fait ... etc.**
taking boat trips	**faire des promenades en bateau**	
taking trips by car	**faire des promenades en voiture**	
going swimming	**se baigner; nager**	use **"se baigner"** for casual, carefree splashing about in the sea
sightseeing	**visiter les sites et monuments**	
eating out	**sortir manger**	unnecessary to add "in restaurants"
going to a disco	**aller à une discothèque**	

Saying when

in the morning	**le matin**	do *not* use **"dans"** to mean "in" - it doesn't
in the afternoon	**l'après-midi**	
in the evening	**le soir**	

Saying with whom

with friends	**avec des copains**	**"copines"** if girl friends only
with my family	**avec ma famille**	
with an organised tour	**en voyage organisé**	
on a school journey	**en voyage scolaire**	

Commenting on food

food's good	**on mange bien**	do *not* use
food's bad	**on mange mal**	**"nourriture"** to mean
to like French/	**aimer la cuisine**	"food" - it's more like
English food	**française/anglaise**	"feed"

Signing off

	amitiés	a nice, friendly term
love 'n' kisses	**grosses bises**	very familiar; for family

PRACTICE TASKS

Pick out the phrases to say that -

1. you're staying with friends in St. Malo
2. you're in a hotel, on a package tour, in Paris
3. you're camping, not far from St. Tropez
4. you're staying in a holiday cottage in the countryside, near Macon
5. you spend the mornings going for walks, and the afternoons swimming
6. you go out to eat in the evenings with friends
7. you're taking trips round the countryside by car

FRANCE - LES DÉPARTEMENTS (administrative regions)

In 1789 the **départements** replaced the provinces as administrative areas. Belfort became a **département** in 1922.

The postal code adds three 000 to the department number; eg. Rouen 76000.

Paris et la région parisienne

The departments are numbered alphabetically: eg.

01 = **Ain**
02 = **Aisne**
89 = **Yonne**

The administrative capitals of the **département** are in capital letters eg. BORDEAUX is the prefecture of the Gironde.

There are 5 DOM **(départements d'Outre Mer) - Guadeloupe; Martinique; Guyane; la Réunion; and Saint-Pierre et Miquelon.**

The numbering of the Paris region was added later, as Paris grew; and so is out of step.

Topic Areas

TOPIC AREA 1

HOLIDAYS, ACCOMMODATION AND ACTIVITIES

SETTINGS

Staying in a hotel, holiday cottage and campsite, youth hostel. Fetes, fairs and festivals. Sightseeing: taking trips by car, coach, boat. Making the most of the area.

KEY NOTIONS AND
FUNCTIONS
(refer to Starter Kit)

Availability; location; wants. Describing.

KEY STRUCTURES
(refer to Grammar Section)

Revision/consolidation of gender, number. Using the perfect tense.

CONTENTS

KEY SPEAKING TASKS

Practise asking questions and making statements. Write them out if it will help you to remember. Refer to the *Starter Kit* for additional help with language and structures.

1 At the hotel

Availability and wants

ASK IF
they have a room free/a room with a shower/a family room

if the rooms have television/if there is a lift/if they serve breakfast in your room
they would like breakfast in the dining room/dinner in the hotel

SAY
you would like a single room/double room/a room for three people/a room with a bath/a room on the first floor
you will take the room

you would like dinner; breakfast in your room

Number

FIND OUT
how long they want to stay
how many people is it for

SAY
it's for three nights/two nights/one week
there are four of you/two adults and two children

Cost

FIND OUT
the cost per night of a single room/a double room with no shower
if breakfast is included

SAY
it's 150F per day/210F per night

a double room with a bath costs 225F per night

Time

ASK
what time breakfast/dinner is served

SAY
that breakfast is served from eight till ten

Location

FIND OUT	SAY
where the dining-room/games room/telephone/lift is	over there on the right/in the basement next to the toilets

2. At the campsite

Availability and wants

ASK IF	SAY YOU WOULD LIKE
they have room for a caravan/a play area for children/shop/a swimming pool	a pitch for two tents/one tent and a car/a car and a caravan

Number

ASK	SAY
how many people there are	there are three of you/two adults
how long they want to stay	three children/two girls and two boys
	say you have a car/a motorbike
	you would like to camp for five/six nights
	say it's for one night only

Cost

ASK	SAY
the price per night per person/per adult/per child	it's 30F per person/20F per child

Location

FIND OUT	SAY
where the toilets/telephones/dustbins/showers/washing facilities are	100 metres to the left near the entrance
where you can buy gas	there is a gas depot in the village

3 At the youth hostel

Availability and wants

ASK IF

there are any places left

there is room for four people/two
people/one girl and one boy

ask if you can eat in the hostel

SAY

you would like to hire a sleeping bag/a pair
of sheets

Number

ASK

how long they want to stay

SAY

it's for four nights

there are two/four/five of you/two boys
and two girls/two adults and one child

Location

FIND OUT

where the kitchen/boys' dormitory/girls'
dormitory is

SAY

it's upstairs on the second/third floor

Time

ASK WHAT TIME

the hostel closes

you must leave in the morning

reception opens/the shop closes

SAY

at midnight/23.000

before midday

at 9.15

Obligation

ASK IF

you must help in the kitchen/do the
dishes/tidy the dormitory

you should pay now/leave a deposit

READING PRACTICE

1 Quel hôtel?

Which hotel/s -

1. have a restaurant?
2. are in the town centre?
3. offer parking facilities?
4. are in the countryside?
5. are near the station?
6. are by the seaside?
7. are open all year round?
8. are near the motorway?
9. are in a quiet location?
10. Which would you recommend to friends who want off-street parking, and be in the town centre, and peace and quiet?

A

HOTEL DE LA GARE**
son restaurant
Mme BON propriétaire
Chambres tout confort
bains-douches-w.c.
21500 MONTBARD

ouvert toute l'année

B

SERMIZELLES-HOTEL
Route de Vézelay — 89200 Givry

Au calme, hors du pays
Les rivières, la forêt
Cure de repos et de plein-air
Chasse et pêche

C

HOTEL-RESTAURANT
DE LA COTE-D'OR
G. et M. REMILLET
21140 SEMUR-EN-AUXOIS
Sortie A6 Bierre-les-Semur à 6 km

D

LA CLOSERIE ***
Hôtel sans restaurant
Logis de France

Route d'Autun

Piscine climatisée · Jardin
PARKING FERMÉ

E

HOTEL DU COMMERCE
RESTAURANT *
21320
POUILLY-EN-AUXOIS

24 chambres tout confort
Cuisine soignée
MAZALLY Propriétaire

F

Hôtel Régina ★ NN
Classé - Calme - 20 chambres
Parking - Plein Centre Ville
91. Grande-Rue - BESANÇON - Tél.: 81.81.50.22 - 81.81.49.74

G

Hôtel★★★NN Restaurant
les ormes
77, bd de la plage
33120 ARCACHON
Tél. 56 83 09 27

Les pieds dans l'eau

OUVERT TOUTE L'ANNÉE

H

HOTEL DE ★★★ N.N.
CHAMPAGNE
Centre ville
Ouvert nuit et jour
à proximité des caves de champagne
Téléphone en direct des chambres
et télévision couleur - Minitel au service clientèle
30, rue Eugène Mercier - 51200 Epernay
Tél.: 26.55.30.22 - Télex 842 068

29
B/3
Verso

2 Pension ou location?

A	B	C
PENSION COMPLETE	**DEMI-PENSION**	**LOCATION**
En surplomb du port de plaisance et directement sur la mer, la maison de vacances l'Oasis est un ensemble d'une vingtaine de chambres confortables de 1,2 ou 3 lits avec, pour certaines, sanitaires complets et pour d'autres lavabo (w.c. à l'étage).	L'hôtel (40 chambres) est situé sur le lagon le plus important, le plus sauvage et le plus beau de l'île Maurice, à 15 mn de l'aéroport. Ambiance décontractée et jeune.	Le Moulin à Vent à 500 m de la Roque sur Pernes (20 bungalows) est bâti sur une colline, dans un site calme, en face du mont Ventoux. Deux-pièces pour 4 ou 5 personnes et trois-pièces pour 6 personnes, simples mais confortables, avec sanitaires complets et kitchenette équipée. Linge non fourni (possibilité de location de draps).
Salle à manger panoramique, salon télévision, bibliothèque. Ménage à votre charge, linge de toilette non fourni.	Chambres reparties dans 3 bâtiments de style mauricien, avec salle de bains (lavabo, douche et w.c.) et ventilateur. Cuisine familiale. Boisson non incluse.	

1. Which one would you recommend to friends who:
   - want all their meals laid on for them
   - want to be totally independent
   - would prefer half-board
2. What are:
   - the main accommodation facilities in each place
3. Which place would you recommend to friends who:
   - want a sea-view
   - like mountain country
   - want to go to a French-speaking country, but not France itself.

3 Équipement et confort

Find the French for the English phrases (write them out in matched pairs), and then tick off which of the facilities are available on each site.

CAMPINGS

CAMPING COMMUNAL "LES PEUPLIERS"*** 160 emplacements
Tél. 85 30 33 65
Situé au bord de la Saône. Sports nautiques, Boules, Volley, Jeux pour enfants, Pêche.

A Approvisionnement sur place. Restaurant à proximité.

CAMPING "AUX RIPETTES" à 01190 SAINT-BENIGNE
Tél. 85 30 36 86
25 Emplacements - Location d'une caravanne équipée - Douches chaudes - Salle commune - Produits fermiers - Piscine privée - Boules - Volley-ball.

B Propriétaire : M. Roger PONCET

CAMPING "LES VERNETTES" à 01560 ST JEAN SUR REYSSOUZE
Tél. 74 52 65 42
Ferme équestre - 6 Emplacements - Douches chaudes - Equitation.

C Propriétaire : Mme Rose-Marie BERTHILLER

	A	B	C
bowls			
caravan hire			
common room			
farm produce			
fishing			
food on site			
games			
horseriding			
hot showers			
pitch (number)			
restaurant nearby			
swimming pool			
water sports			

4 Section caravaning-camping ***NN

DÉSIGNATION	TARIF JOURNALIER TTC
Adultes, Enfants + de 10ans	10,50
Enfants - de 10 ans	6,15
Visiteurs (+ de 2 heures) Adultes, Enfants - de 10 ans	10,50
Visiteurs (+ de 2 heures) Enfants - de 10 ans	6,15
Caravane + véhicule ou Tente + Véhicule (emplacement 200 m^2 environ avec borne électrique 10 ampères)	31,85
Chiens	8,50

How much does this campsite cost:

1. For each adult and child over 10
2. For children under 10
3. For friends who come and spend a day with you
4. What facilities do you get for 31F 85?

Work out how much these people would need to budget for each day:

5. A family of 2 adults and a boy of 9, with a car and caravan
6. A family of 1 adult and 2 children: a boy of 13 and a girl of 8, with a car and tent.
7. Three friends of 16, 18, 17, with a car and tent.
8. A single adult whose 2 friends came to stay for the afternoon, with their dog.

5 Faites la fête!

Scan the four posters (A B C D) advertising local fetes, and list the activities they have in common, under these headings:

1. Ball games
2. Water sports
3. Competitions
4. Races
5. Music & Dance
6. Food & Drink

Write down what the activities are, in English.

Some activities may qualifiy under more than one area.

A

SAMEDI 15 AOUT

10 h. 00 : **GRAND RAID DE PLANCHE A VOILE**
11 h. 00 : **Ouverture de la fête**
11 h. 30 : **Messe en plein air sur l'esplanade et bénédiction des disparus en mer. Envoi d'un bouquet de fleurs.**
12 h. 00 : **Ouverture du restaurant animée par les bandas "LA LANTONAISE" et les "KANAR" de Vic-Fezensac.**
14 h. 30 : **GRAND CONCOURS DE PÉTANQUE** patronné par la Société RICARD.
15 h. 30 : **Jeux divers, rugby sur la vase, tir à la corde et jeux de plage animés par** la Société RICARD.
17 h. 30 : **DANSES ET CHANTS FLAMENCO AVEC Henrique de SOLEDA et ses guitaristes.**
19 h. 30 : **Ouverture du restaurant avec les bandas "LA LANTONAISE" et les "KANAR" de Vic-Fezensac.**
21 h. 00 : **SOIRÉE FLAMENCO** avec **Henrique de SOLEDA et ses guitaristes.**
22 h. 00 : **GRAND BAL DISCO avec NRJ**

DIMANCHE 16 AOUT

11 h. 00 : **Ouverture de la fête.**
12 h. 00 : **Ouverture du restaurant animée par les bandas "LA LANTONAISE" et les "KANAR".**
14 h. 00 : **Jeux de plage sous le haut patronage de** la Société RICARD.
Courses de trottinettes organisées par l'Amicale des Sapeurs-Pompiers d'ARÈS.
14 h. 30 : GRAND CONCOURS DE PÉTANQUE animé par la Société **RICARD.**
15 h. 00 : **COURSES AUX ANES**
19 h. 30 : **Ouverture du restaurant animée par les bandas "LA LANTONAISE" et les "KANAR".**
23 h. 00 : **GRAND FEU D'ARTIFICE** offert par l'Office Municipal de Tourisme d'ARÈS.
24 h. 00 : **GRAND BAL DISCO avec STUDIO 33**

B

PROGRAMME

MARDI 14 AOUT

10 H 30 - VISITE CIRCUIT RICARD : COURSE AUTOMOBILE (RENDEZ-VOUS À L'ACCUEIL)
17 H 00 - MATCH WATER POLO FRANCO ANGLAIS   ENFANTS ET ADULTES
    1 MATCH FEMME - 1 MATCH HOMME

22 H 00 SOIREE DANSANTE : SPECTACLE : GROUPE ARGENTIN

MERCREDI 15 AOUT

17 H 00 CONCOURS DE BOULES
17 H 00 DISCO ENFANTS
17 H 30 JEUX PISCINE + WATER POLO
22 H 00 DISCOTHEQUE

JEUDI 16 AOUT

17 H 30 JEUX PISCINE
18 H 30 CONCOURS DE CARTES
20 H 00 SOIREE ANGLAISE : SPECTACLE DE PIANO BAR
22 H 00 DISCOTHEQUE

VENDREDI 17 AOUT

10 H 30 VISITE CIRCUIT PAUL RICARD
17 H 00 JEUX PISCINE + CONCOURS DE NATATION
18 H 00 COURSES DE RELAIS : FRANCO - ANGLO - BELGES (JUNIORS - SÉNIORS)
22 H 00 DISCOTHEQUE

SAMEDI 18 AOUT

17 H 00 CONCOURS DE BOULES
17 H 30 JEUX PISCINE
21 H 00 SOIREE DANSANTE   "ECOLE DES FANS"
21 H 30 DANSES PROVENCALES

VOTRE ANIMATEUR,

LAUZUN

6 · 7 · 8 · AOUT

GRANDE FÊTE VOTIVE

organisée par le comité des Fêtes qui vous souhaite la Bienvenue ...

3 GRANDS BALS

animés par **HIFI 2000** - **DISCO DANSE LIGHT** - **PASCALY**
(SAMEDI 6 AOUT)   (DIMANCHE 7 AOUT)   (LUNDI 8 AOUT)

6 AOÛT	21 h.	CONCOURS de BOULES
7 AOÛT	10 h 30	JEUX pour ENFANTS
	15 h 00	GRANDE COURSE de LEVRIERS championnat de France . 10.000 F de prix .
	24 h 00	GRAND FEU d'ARTIFICE
8 AOÛT	9 h 00	CONCOURS de BELOTE
	15 h 00	COURSE CYCLISTE U.F.O.L.E.P.

Attractions Foraines . Manège . Tir . Auto scooter . Tir à l'ARC . Buvette ~

CREDIT AGRICOLE

C

Château du Champ de Bataille
Le Neubourg (Eure)
(20 km d'Evreux)

Ouvert tous les jours, sauf le mardi, de 10 h 30 à 19 heures

LES ACTIVITÉS

Visite avec guide écrit des Salons

Promenades en voiture à cheval
Dans le parc, les samedis et dimanches après-midi. En semaine, sur demande pour groupes

Initiation au golf

Jeux de croquets et de boules

Animations musicales
Le samedi et dimanche après-midi (concerts de musique baroque)

Salon de thé dans le château

D

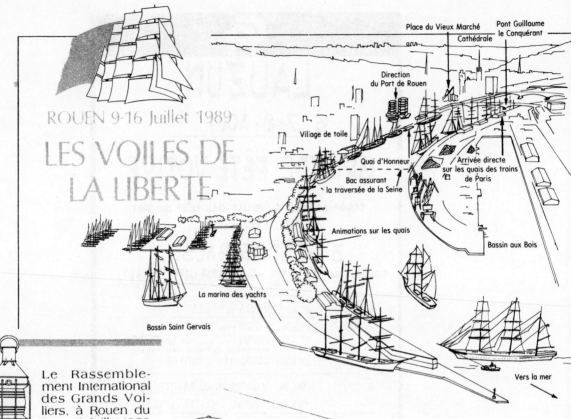

ROUEN 9-16 Juillet 1989

LES VOILES DE LA LIBERTE

Place du Vieux Marché
Pont Guillaume le Conquérant
Cathédrale
Direction du Port de Rouen
Village de toile
Quai d'Honneur
Arrivée directe sur les quais des trains de Paris
Bac assurant la traversée de la Seine
Animations sur les quais
Bassin aux Bois
La marina des yachts
Bassin Saint Gervais
Vers la mer

Le Rassemblement International des Grands Voiliers, à Rouen du 9 au 16 Juillet 1989 sera incontestablement l'une des manifestations les plus prestigieuses du bicentenaire de la Révolution et de la Déclaration des Droits de l'Homme et du Citoyen.
Un événement maritime également exceptionnel.
Aucun rassemblement d'une telle ampleur n'a jamais été organisé en France et il faut remonter à 1976, aux fêtes qui ont célébré à New York l'Indépendance Américaine, pour retrouver une concentration aussi importante de Grands Voiliers. Plus de 15 trois et quatre mâts, dépassant les 70 m et rivalisant de hauteur avec la flèche de la cathédrale, seront présents à Rouen avec des centaines d'anciens voiliers de toute l'Europe.

C'est au cœur même de la vieille ville de Rouen, que les Grands Voiliers viendront accoster le long de 6 km de quais juste en amont du dernier pont, le bassin St Gervais, rive droite étant transformé en port de plaisance.
Sur les terre-pleins, les tentes du village accueilleront les animations, les expositions et abriteront les restaurants, les tavernes tandis que sur le vaste plan d'eau du fleuve se dérouleront de multiples régates, des défilés nautiques et les meilleurs groupes européens feront connaître les chansons de marin traditionnelles pleines d'entrain et de nostalgie, sur des barges sonorisées, gigantesques scènes flottantes.

Vers 10 heures, le 16 juillet 1989, un coup de canon annoncera l'appareillage du port de Rouen, de tous les voiliers géants à 3 et 4 mâts pour la Grande Parade dans la vallée de la Seine jusqu'à la mer.

Toutes les dispositions seront prises pour faciliter l'accès de Rouen pendant la semaine des VOILES DE LA LIBERTE. De vastes parkings, aux portes de la ville seront directement reliés au port par des navettes et des trains spéciaux au départ de la gare St Lazare à Paris, amèneront les visiteurs jusqu'au quai des Grands Voiliers.

6 Les voiles de la liberté

1. What event does the gathering of the Tall Ships celebrate?
2. Which country held an event of similar size: when; and why?
3. Why is a maritime celebration appropriate to Rouen's history?
4. How many ships are there at the celebrations?
5. Name 3 events put on to entertain the public, along the quays.
6. What facilities are available to people arriving at Rouen by car?
7. For people arriving from Paris by train?
8. For people arriving by boat or yacht?
9. How is the closing Grand Parade signalled?
10. What is the end-destination of the Tall Ships in the Grand Parade?

SPEAKING PRACTICE

1 Mes vacances (higher level)

Holidays are the most obvious - and sensible! - topics you are likely to need to talk about; either in a narrative, or in a conversation where you will need to relate to questions.

Prepare an adequate vocabulary, and particularly *verbs*.

Remember:

* that when talking about a *past* holiday you will need to use *past* tenses (the perfect), to describe *past* activities.
* The thirteen verbs (see *Grammar Section*) which use **être**; they are marked here with two asterisks**

Here is a verb starter-kit for this holiday (*MEG joint examination 1986*)

avoir un accident

** **aller à la plage/au marché**

faire un pique-nique/des excursions/beau temps

** **partir de Newhaven; partir pour Blois**

passer trois jours/une soirée ensemble

prendre le bateau/l'avion/un repas/des bains de soleil

quitter Dieppe/la ville

** **rester à Blois/à Bordeaux**

traverser la Manche

visiter la ville/les vignobles/les châteaux

voir

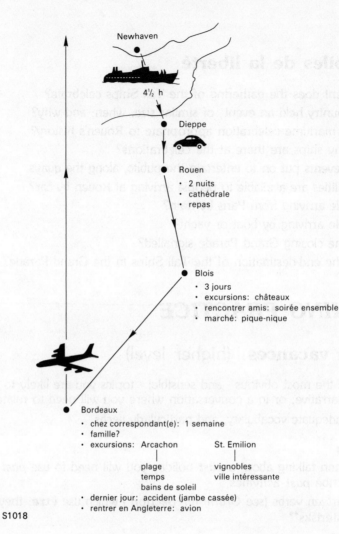

Newhaven

4½ h

Dieppe

Rouen
- 2 nuits
- cathédrale
- repas

Blois
- 3 jours
- excursions: châteaux
- rencontrer amis: soirée ensemble
- marché: pique-nique

Bordeaux
- chez correspondant(e): 1 semaine
- famille?
- excursions: Arcachon   St. Emilion

  plage   vignobles
  temps   ville intéressante
  bains de soleil
- dernier jour: accident (jambe cassée)
- rentrer en Angleterre: avion

S1018

WRITING PRACTICE

1   L'année dernière (higher level)

Write up this holiday, as if you had taken it last year:
l'année dernière...

2 Lettre à la direction (basic level)

The following letter contains several numbered spaces. Using the list below the letter, write out in French the words which would apply to your own circumstances.

Londres............(1)..............

Monsieur,

       Je voudrais passer ....(2).................. avec ....(3)......... **dans votre hôtel.**

       Pouvez-vous me réserver une chambre ....(4) .... avec douche **et une chambre à deux personnes avec ....(5) ...., pour** **les nuits ....(6) .... Est-ce qu'il y a ....(7)** **....................... dans toutes les chambres? Nous préférons être au ....** **(8).....................**

       Je voudrais <u>savoir</u> aussi s'il est possible de ....(9) .... **à l'hôtel, et si l'hôtel se trouve ....(10)....................**

       Je vous prie d'agréer, Monsieur, mes sentiments distingués.

       ....(Signature)

Answers

1. (today's date).....................................
2. (how long?)...
3. (who is accompanying you?)................
4. (what kind of room?)..........................
5. (washing facilities?).............................
6. (dates?) ....
7. (some extra facility) ....
8. (which floor).......................................
9. (eating arrangements)..........................
10. (situation?)...

(L.E.A.G. specimen paper)

LISTENING PRACTICE

1 Tour du Golfe du Morbihan

You're taking a boat trip round the Golfe du Morbihan. The guide gives an introductory talk.

1. How long will the boat trip last?
2. How long is the stop-over at the Ile aux Moines?
3. What is noteworthy about this island?
4. How big is the Golfe du Morbihan?
5. Most of the Islands are: (choose ONE):-
   inhabited/not inhabited/private property/bird sanctuaries
6. What does *Morbihan* mean, as the guide explains it?
7. Note down the two characteristics about the tides which make swimming dangerous.
8. What two features of the environment make the area attractive to migrating birds?
9. The area is world famous for what?
10. What is the connection between the town of Auray and Benjamin Franklin?

VOCABULARIES

Basic vocabulary

KEY VERBS

accepter	to accept	**payer**	to pay
acheter	to buy	**porter**	to wear; to carry
aimer	to like	**pouvoir**	to be able
aller	to go	**préférer**	to prefer
appuyer	to press (a button)	**prendre**	to take
arriver	to arrive	**prendre l'avion/le bateau/le train**	
		to take the plane/boat/train	
avoir	to have	**préparer**	to prepare
camper	to camp	**regretter**	to be sorry
chercher	to look for	**remplir**	to fill in
coûter	to cost	**réserver**	to reserve
débarquer	to disembark	**rester**	to stay
déjeuner	to have lunch	**s'amuser**	to enjoy oneself
descendre dans un Hôtel		**se baigner**	to go for a swim
to stay in a Hotel			
dîner	to have dinner	**se détendre**	to relax
écrire	to write	**se faire bronzer**	to go and sunbathe
embarquer	to embark	**se laver**	to wash
envoyer	to send	**se mettre en route**	to start out
être en vacances	to be on holiday	**se trouver**	to be situated
louer	to hire	**servir**	to serve
mettre	to put	**trouver**	to find
monter	to put up	**visiter**	to visit
nager	to swim	**voir**	to see
partir	to leave	**vouloir**	to want
passer	to spend (time)	**voyager**	to travel

faire la cuisine/la vaisselle   to do the cooking/washing up

faire de la voile/du ski/du ski nautique/de la planche à voile
to go sailing/skiing/water skiing/windsurfing

faire des promenades à cheval/en bateau/à pied/à velo/en voiture/en car
to go horse-riding/boating/walking cycling/for a car trip/coach trip

All settings

	à l'étranger abroad	f	montagne mountain
f	agence de voyages travel agency	m	monument monument
	agréable pleasant	m	musée museum
m	anorak anorak	m	parapluie umbrella
m	appareil photo camera	m	pays country
	au bord de la mer at the seaside	f	pêche fishing
m	bateau à voile yacht	m	phare lighthouse
	beau nice, fine	f	photo photo
f	brochure brochure	m	pique-nique picnic
m	bureau de tourisme tourist office	f	piscine swimming pool
f	campagne countryside	f	piste ski run, dance-
f	carte postale postcard	f	plage beach
m	centre de vacances holiday centre	m	plan plan, map
m	château castle	m	port port, harbour
f	chaussures de ski ski boots	m	prix price
m	chèque de voyage traveller's cheque	m	quinze jours fortnight
m	coquillage shell	f	région region
m	coup de soleil sun-stroke	m	renseignements information
f	crème solaire sun cream	f	rivière river
f	excursion trip	m	séjour stay
f	falaise cliff	f	semaine week
f	forêt forest	m	sports d'hiver winter sports
f	grandes vacances summer holidays	m	syndicat d'initiative tourist information office
m	groupe group	m	touriste tourist
f	hospitalité hospitality		typique typical
m	intéressant interesting	m	village village
f	liste list	f	ville town
f	mer sea	m	voyage journey
m	mois month		

Accommodation

1. Hotel

ƒ	**arrhes** deposit		ƒ	**nuit** night
m	**ascenseur** lift		m	**numéro** number
m	**bagages** luggage			**occupé** engaged, occupied
m	**bain** bath		m	**passeport** passport
ƒ	**chambre** room		ƒ	**pension complète** full board
	cher expensive		m	**petit déjeuner** breakfast
ƒ	**clé/clef** key			**poussez!** push!
	complet full, no vacancies			**privé** private
ƒ	**demi-pension** half board		ƒ	**réception** reception
	compris included		ƒ	**réceptionniste** receptionist
	confortable comfortable		m	**restaurant** restaurant
ƒ	**date** date		m	**rez-de-chaussée** ground-floor
	directeur/trice manager		ƒ	**salle à manger** dining room
ƒ	**douche** shower			**sans** without
ƒ	**entrée** entrance		ƒ	**sortie (de secours)** (emergency) exit
m	**escalier** stairs		m	**sous-sol** basement
m	**étage** floor		m	**téléphone** telephone
ƒ	**fiche** form		ƒ	**télévision** television
m	**garçon** bell-hop			**tirez** pull
m	**hôtel** hotel		ƒ	**toilettes** toilets
	libre free, not occupied		ƒ	**valise** suitcase
	moderne modern		ƒ	**vue** view
ƒ	**note** bill			

2. Campsite

m/ƒ	**adulte** adult			**gardé** supervised
m	**arbre** tree		m	**gardien** warden
m	**bac à vaisselle** washing-up facilities		ƒ	**glace** ice (-cream)
m	**bloc sanitaire** washroom and toilets		m	**jeu** game
ƒ	**bouteille de gaz** bottled gas		m	**lavabo** washhand basin
m	**campeur** camper		ƒ	**machine à laver** washing machine
m	**camping** camping, campsite			**municipal** municipal
ƒ	**caravane** caravan		m	**plats cuisinés** take-away food
ƒ	**cuisinière à gaz** gas cooker		m	**sac de couchage** sleeping bag
m	**dépôt de butane** bottled gas depot		ƒ	**salle** room

f	**eau potable** drinking water		*f*	**tente** tent
	électrique electric		*m*	**terrain de camping** campsite
m	**emplacement** site, pitch		*f*	**véhicule** vehicle
m	**enfant** child			

3. Youth hostel

f	**auberge de jeunesse** youth hostel		*f*	**poubelle** dustbin
f	**carte** card		*m*	**repas** meal
f	**cuisine** kitchen		*m*	**sac à dos** rucksack
m	**dortoir** dormitory		*f*	**salle de bains** bathroom
m	**drap** sheet		*f*	**salle de jeux** games room
m	**lit** bed		*m*	**tarif** tariff, price list
f	**paire** pair			**toute l'année** all year
	par jour/nuit/ personne per day/night/ person		*m*	**visiteur** visitor
f	**place** room			

Additional higher vocabulary

KEY VERBS

balayer to sweep		**s'en aller** to go away
déranger to disturb		**s'informer** to get information
indiquer to point out		**se plaindre** to complain
ranger to tidy		**se souvenir** to remember
remplacer to replace		

All settings

aménagé   equipped

m   **bruit**   noise

bruyant   noisy

f   **carte d'adhérent**   membership card

f   **couverture**   blanket

f   **électricité**   electricity

m   **endroit**   place

m   **guide**   guide

historique   historic

f   **installations sanitaires**
washrooms and toilets

m   **congé**   holiday

léger   light

m   **linge**   linen

lourd   heavy

m   **matelas pneumatique**   air bed, lilo

m   **matériel de camping**   camping equipment

m   **Michelin Rouge/Vert**
Michelin red/green guide

f   **pellicule**   film (for a camera)

f   **prise de courant**   socket

m   **reçu**   receipt

m   **règlement**   rules

m   **responsable**   person in charge

satisfait   satisfied

m   **son et lumière**   son et lumiere show

m   **spectacle**   show

m   **tourisme**   tourism

TOPIC AREA 2 TRAVEL AND TRANSPORT

| SETTINGS | Finding your way. Using public and private transport. Road accidents. |

KEY NOTIONS AND
FUNCTIONS
(refer to Starter Kit)

Time: frequency, duration, point in time. The 24 hour clock. Asking for repetition and clarification. Need; obligation; forbidding.

KEY STRUCTURES
(refer to Grammar Section)

Consolidation of present tense, including commands and negatives. Adverbs. More use of the perfect tense - in conversation and in describing past journeys.

CONTENTS

KEY SPEAKING TASKS

Practice asking questions and making statements. Write them out if it will help you remember. Refer to the *Starter Kit* for additional help.

1 Finding the way

Location and distance

ASK
how to get to the bus-stop/station/bus station/airport
if these places are far

SAY
cross the bridge and take the first street on the left
ten minutes on foot/straight on/2 kms away

2 Using public transport

Availability and existence

FIND OUT
if there is a train to Rouen this morning/ coach to Paris this afternoon/plane to Madrid tomorrow evening

SAY
the next one is this afternoon/this evening/ tomorrow morning

Wants and costs

ASK
for two single tickets to Newhaven a return to Avignon/two return tickets to Rennes
the cost of a single/a return/a reservation
if there is a supplement/reduced rate (**un tarif réduit**) for students

SAY
you would like to reserve 1/2/3 seats
20.00F/54.00F/138.00F

Time

ASK
what time the train/ferry/coach leaves/arrives

SAY
it leaves/arrives at 11.15/23.10/6.45am.

Obligation

ASK IF
you have to change trains
you have to book seats

SAY
no, it's straight through/must change
a reservation for the TGV is compulsory

3 Using private transport

Location and Distance

ASK
how to get to the motorway/town
centre/tourist office
if this is the right road to the
coast/Strasbourg/Montpellier
if there is a service station nearby

SAY
go straight down this road

turn right at the lights and it's13 kilometres
away

Wants and Availability

ASK
the attendant to fill the tank/check the
tyres/oil/water
for 160F of 4 star/30 litres of 2 star/
3 litres of two stroke/a litre of oil
if there are any toilets
if they sell newspapers/maps/postcards/
sweets/cold drinks

SAY
certainly, sir/madam

sorry, but we have none left

over there, by the door

READING PRACTICE

1 Titres de transport

Which ticket/s would have enabled you to:
1. Take an airport shuttle?
2. Go by bus?
3. Take a boat trip?
4. Go on a coach trip?
5. Board a plane?
6. Park your car?
7. Take the train?
8. Use the underground?

A

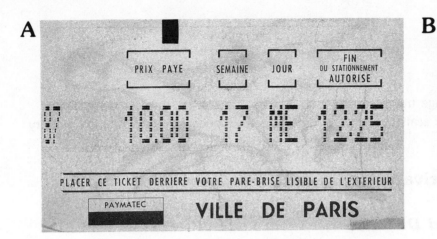

PRIX PAYE SEMAINE JOUR FIN DU STATIONNEMENT AUTORISE

87 10.00 17 ME 12:25

PLACER CE TICKET DERRIERE VOTRE PARE-BRISE LISIBLE DE L'EXTERIEUR

PAYMATEC VILLE DE PARIS

B

127014

VEDETTES DU PONT-NEUF
PLEIN TARIF 15 F

VEDETTES DU PONT-NEUF

PARIS 1er
Tél. : 633-98-38

PLEIN TARIF
15 F

127014

C

AIR FRANCE
CARTE D'ACCES A BORD

AVANT DE LA CABINE

ARRIERE DE LA CABINE

3

D

RATP
AUTOBUS

20

002D5D170

CE TICKET DOIT
ETRE OBLITERE
AUSSITOT APRES L'ACHAT

E

France
vacances **Pass**

SNCF

CRÉDIT-VOYAGE 4 JOURS/15 JOURS
TRAVEL CREDIT 4 DAYS/15 DAYS – REISEKREDIT 4 TAGE/15 TAGE

N° 068054

PREMIER JOUR
1st DAY · 1. TAG

DAY MONTH YEAR
24 08 87

POSITION 17 2cl

JOUR MOIS ANNÉE

DERNIER JOUR
LAST DAY · LETZTER TAG

07 09 87

TAG MONAT JAHR

M.J 2 R RAMBUS

PAYS DE RÉSIDENCE UK.
CONTRY · HEIMATLAND

F

007654

VEDETTES BLANCHES

RETOUR

Passage de St-MALO
Péage perçu pour la douane

MOORE·PARAGON · ARGENT

ALLER

Passage de St-MALO

VEDETTES BLANCHES

007654

G

AEROPORT INTERNATIONAL DE BORDEAUX

Chambre de Commerce et d'Industrie

_ NAVETTE _

Aérogare
Centre _ Ville
Gare St Jean

N⁰ 45286

Ce billet doit être détaché et oblitéré devant le passager. Il doit être conservé pour contrôle.
This ticket must be detached and stamped in the passenger's presence. It must be kept for any subsequent checking.

Date & Heure

TRAJET SIMPLE
20 francs

H

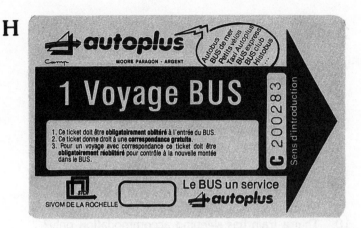

autoplus
MOORE PARAGON - ARGENT

1 Voyage BUS

1. Ce ticket doit être obligatoirement oblitéré à l'entrée du BUS.
2. Ce ticket donne droit à une correspondance gratuite.
3. Pour un voyage avec correspondance ce ticket doit être obligatoirement réoblitéré pour contrôle à la nouvelle montée dans le BUS.

Sens d'introduction 382002

Le BUS un service autoplus
SIVOM DE LA ROCHELLE

I

VILLE DE SAINT CYR SUR MER

DROIT DE STATIONNEMENT
DEMI-JOURNÉE : **10 f.**
soit de 8 h. à 13 h. 30 ou de 12 h. à 19 h.

N⁰ 004713   **B**

Placer ce ticket derrière votre pare-brise, lisible de l'extérieur
IMP. CENTRALE - 83500 LA SEYNE

J

CARS PANSART, St-Malo - 99.40.85.96

CAP FREHEL

Nombre de places : 1   Prix : 80 fs.
Départ : 14h15 le Samedi
N° 33   20 Aout,
N⁰ 000025

IMP. DE LA GARE - ST-MALO

K

965 Q
C 2
RATP
SECTION URBAINE
RER METRO AUTOBUS
70869

2 A la gare

Which notice advises you:
1. To keep your ticket?
2. Of car hire?
3. Push to open?
4. Where to go to send luggage on?
5. Of connecting services?
6. That a machine is out of order?
7. Of long distance tickets?
8. Of the Lost Property Office?
9. Of the emergency exit?
10. That a train has sleeping accommodation only?

Which notice forbids you to:
11. Lean out.
12. Stick posters.
13. Park.
14. Go in
15. Open

A.	ENREGISTREMENT DE BAGAGES
B.	SORTIE DE SECOURS
C.	HORS SERVICE
D.	CORRESPONDANCES
E.	POUR OUVRIR APPUYER
F.	CE TRAIN NE COMPORTE PAS DE PLACES ASSISES
G.	BILLETS GRANDES LIGNES
H.	CONSERVEZ VOTRE BILLET
I.	OBJETS TROUVES
J.	LOCATION DE VOITURES
K.	NE PAS OUVRIR
L.	NE PAS SE PENCHER AU DEHORS
M.	DEFENSE D'AFFICHER
N.	ENTREE INTERDITE
O.	DEFENSE DE STATIONNER

What are the 3 ways in which a notice forbidding something is written?

3 Voyages et excursions en autocar

LE GOLFE DU MORBIHAN
QUIBERON - CARNAC **140 F**
* Traversée non comprise
Les Alignements Mégalithiques

A

| JUILLET - AOUT | | | | | | | | | | | Mardi |

LE MARCHÉ DE DINAN **90 F**
ERQUY - CAP FRÉHEL - FORT LA LATTE

B

| MAI - JUIN | | | | | | | | | | Jeudi |
| JUILLET - AOUT - SEPTEMBRE | | | | | | | Jeudi |

LES CHAPELLES EN PAYS
MALOUIN **70 F**

C

| JUILLET - AOUT | | | | | | | | | | | Mardi |

LA CÔTE BRETONNE **130 F**
LA CORNICHE DES ROCHERS ROSES
PLEUMEUR BODOU - Station Spatiale

D

| JUIN | | | | | | | | | | les 17 et 24 |
| JUILLET - AOUT - SEPTEMBRE | | | | | | Vendredi |

LE CIRCUIT DES CHATEAUX
COMBOURG LA BOURBANSAIS **70 F**

E

| JUILLET - AOUT | | | | | | | | | | Lundi |
| SEPTEMBRE | | | | | | | | | | | Mardi |

You're spending a week near St. Malo, in August.

Which coach tour would you take:-

1. To go to a market?
2. To see some castles?
3. To see some churches?
4. To do the coastline?
5. To see some prehistoric monuments?
6. You're on holiday in June; which tours are available to you?
7. You're on holiday in August, but you've only got Thursday, Friday & Saturday; which tours are available to you then?

4 Une solution: le bus!

La circulation dans Besançon

Une solution, LE BUS !

La C.T.B., Compagnie des transports de Besançon, vous informe que :

- **Huit lignes régulières** relient entre eux les différents quartiers de Besançon, entre 6h et 20h, à des fréquences de 6 à 12 minutes.

Il existe même un réseau simplifié qui fonctionne en soirée jusqu'à minuit ainsi que le dimanche.

- **Un service de Minibus** assure des liaisons commodes à l'intérieur du Centre Ville. Ce réseau comporte deux lignes (31 et 32) qui desservent la Gare SNCF et les rues les plus animées du Centre Ville - de 7h à 19h30.

- **L'information** relative au transport public est affichée dans tous les abribus du réseau : Plan de ville - Lignes - Tarifs - Fiches horaires...

- **Les tickets** sont vendus, soit à l'unité par le conducteur, soit sous forme de carnets dans les bureaux de tabac arborant l'enseigne «tickets bus». Il existe également des formules d'abonnement mensuel.

- **La correspondance** est gratuite sur l'ensemble du réseau (ticket valable 1 heure).

1. When do the main services start and finish?
2. What kind of service operates till midnight?
3. What additional service is there in the town centre?
4. Where will you find bus timetables and prices?
5. You want to buy a booklet of tickets. Where should you go?
6. Under what conditions can you use 1 ticket several times?

5 Première vague de retours

ROUTES

Première vague des retours de vacances

Les « aoûtiens » commencent à rentrer chez eux

Première vague des retours de vacances, ce week-end. On attend près de trois millions de Français sur les routes ainsi que de nombreux touristes étrangers regagnant leur pays. La rentrée scolaire est en effet imminente chez la plupart de nos voisins européens.

Selon Bison futé le trafic devrait être dense dès cet après-midi en particulier sur l'axe Espagne-Bordeaux-Paris. Et la situation risque d'être encore un peu plus délicate demain samedi. Dimanche sera la journée idéale pour prendre la route, à condition d'éviter de rentrer des plages en fin d'après-midi.

Les endroits à éviter en priorité seront les abords de Bordeaux, spécialement sur les RN et A 10, aujourd'hui entre 11 et 14 heures et demain entre 10 et 14 heures, ainsi que la RN 10 entre Hendaye et Bayonne demain de 15 à 18 heures. Ce seront là les principaux points noirs dans notre région.

A tous les automobilistes, il est en tout cas recommandé de prendre garde à la signalisation plus importante sur les routes au mois d'août en raison de nombreux chantiers saisonniers. Un conseil qui s'ajoute à toutes les recommandations habituelles que « Sud-Ouest » et les organismes de sécurité routière prodiguent aux conducteurs depuis le début de l'été. A savoir boucler les ceintures, s'arrêter régulièrement, respecter les limitations de vitesse, garder ses distances...

1. Who is returning home from holiday, in addition to 3 million French?
2. Why?
3. Where are traffic conditions expected to be tricky on the Saturday morning?
4. Name the 2 roads which are expected to be black spots.
5. For what extra reason are motorists warned to take care?
6. What are the four pieces of advice given to drivers generally?

6 Accidents et pannes

Sur l'A6, deux femmes légèrement blessées dans une collision

1. Where was a motor cyclist injured?
2. What accident injured two women? Where?
3. What happened to the cyclist?
4. Where on the road were two people hurt?

Virage raté : deux blessés

Collision au carrefour : Un motocycliste blessé

Un cycliste renversé par une voiture

PANNE / ACCIDENT / MALAISE

Garez-vous sur la voie la plus à droite (bande d'arrêt d'urgence) en signalant bien votre voiture(feux de détresse et triangle de signalisation 200m à l'arrière) Rejoignez à pied, sans traverser, la borne d'appel téléphonique orangée la plus proche (1 km maximum). Elle vous mettra gratuitement en contact avec la gendarmerie qui vous situera grâce à votre appel et vous enverra les secours nécessaires.

Indiquez notamment la nature de la panne, la marque de la voiture.

DÉPANNAGE Si vous avez signalé une panne, un dépanneur agréé vous sera envoyé par la gendarmerie.

● Si le dépanneur peut réparer en moins de 30 minutes, il le fera sur place, et vous n'aurez à payer, en plus du forfait, que les pièces fournies.

● Si la réparation est plus longue, il vous remorquera jusqu'au garage d'accueil de votre choix.../...

If you have a breakdown, feel unwell on a motorway:-

5. Where should you park your car?
6. What should you display to indicate an accident/breakdown?
7. How far is the nearest emergency 'phone?
8. How much does a call cost?
9. What will the police do on your call?
10. In what circumstances will repairs be made on the spot?

SPEAKING PRACTICE

1 Comment venez-vous au collège; au bureau? (basic level)

The conversation

At higher level you need to move from practical, informational details to giving descriptions, preferences, and opinions and to using past tenses when talking about a past journey.

PREPARE by putting these key verbs into the present and perfect tenses (check against the verb tables in Part III). Two asterisks ** = **être** verb

**	**arriver**
	avoir
	être
	faire une promenade à pied/à velo/à bicyclette/à cheval
	faire une excursion en voiture/en autocar/en bateau
**	**partir de**
	penser de
	préférer
	prendre
	quitter
	mettre
**	**rentrer**
**	**venir**
	voyager

CHOOSE an adverb or phrase to describe what you do usually; when; how often.

Normalement	**tous les jours**	**une fois par jour**
généralement	**les matins**	**deux fois par semaine**
d'habitude	**les soirs**	**par mois etc**
	les dimanche	
	les samedi	
	toutes les semaines	

BACK UP your preferences - for a particular mode of transport e.g. because its more comfortable (plus); less dangerous (moins).

C'est plus/moins   **confortable**
                          rapide
                          pratique
                          intéressant
                          dangereux

PRACTICE QUESTIONS	SAMPLE ANSWERS
Comment est-ce que vous venez au collège/bureau?	Normalement, je viens à pied. J'habite pas très loin. Je viens par le train; j'habite assez loin..
Quel moyen de transport prenez-vous pour...?	Je prends le bus/la voiture...
Vous mettez combien de temps?	Je mets une demi-heure/vingt minutes, à peu près...
Il vous faut combien de temps?	Il me faut une heure normalement, parce que....
Qu'est-ce que vous préférez - le train ou la voiture?	Je préfère le train; c'est plus pratique; assez confortable....
Quand est-ce que - vous allez apprendre à conduire?	Je vais apprendre l'année prochaine/bientôt..
- vous avez appris à conduire?	J'ai appris il y a un an/trois ans/ longtemps; quand j'avais 18/20 ans.
Que pensez-vous des trains à grande vitesse?	Je suis pour: c'est une bonne idée; c'est rapide, confortable, pas très cher...
- du tunnel sous la Manche?	Je suis contre: c'est une mauvaise idée; c'est cher; cela pourrait être dangereux.....
Qu'est-ce que vous achèteriez comme voiture s'il ne vous manquait pas d'argent?	J'achèterais une Porsche/une Volvo.... Je n'achèterais pas de voiture - je suis écolo., les voitures c'est polluant.....
Quand est-ce que vous avez fait une grande promenade à pied?	C'était samedi/dimanche dernier; il y a une semaine... je suis parti/e seul/e; je suis allé avec des copains; nous nous sommes promenés dans le parc/la forêt à...

WRITING PRACTICE

1 Message (basic level)

Whilst staying in a Youth Hostel in France, you answer the 'phone (everyone else is out!)
The message is for Yannick, from Hervé. Hervé will phone again for a meeting, about the coach excursion next week.

Tick the right boxes on the message pad, and jot down the gist of the message.

```
╔══════════════════════════════════════╗
║  M    E    S    S    A    G    E      ║
╚══════════════════════════════════════╝

   date_____  heure_____

   pour M_____

   pendant votre absence

   M_____

   _____  tél. :_____

   ▨ a téléphoné  ▨ rappellera  ▨ pouvez vous rappeler

   ▨ est passé(e) vous voir   ▨ désire un rendez-vous

   message_____

   _____

   _____

   _____

   _____

   _____

   reçu par_____

                        EXACOMPTA réf. 5290
```

2 Rendez-vous à la gare (basic level)

A French friend, staying in London, is coming to stay with you in York. You're unable to reach her/him by 'phone - send a note by post! Tell them to get a single, 2nd class ticket from Paddington Station; to take the 17h 10 train (it's a fast train and cheaper than the 13h 05); the train arrives at 20h 15; that you'll be waiting at the exit.

3 Un petit mot (basic level)

Here is part of a thank-you letter to the family you stayed with in France. Fill in the dotted blanks with the right verb in the perfect tense.

Madame,

Un petit mot pour vous dire que .. 1 .. chez moi! .. 2 .. le TGV à Macon, comme prévu. Le train .. 3 .. à Paris sans que je m'en aperçoive, presque. A Paris .. 4 .. changer de gare. Une fois à la gare du Nord, .. 5 .. attendre quelque temps pour la correspondance. .. 6 .. le temps à acheter des magazines à lire. La traversée de la

Manche était fatigante - le ferry .. 7 .. presque 6 heures de Dieppe à Newhaven; mais de là, c'était plus facile: .. 8 .. seulement 2 heures pour rentrer chez moi enfin...

---

1. I've arrived
2. I caught
3. arrived
4. I changed
5. I had to
6. I spent
7. took
8. I took

LISTENING PRACTICE

1 Départs (basic level)

Scan the departure board for trains to Bordeaux, Fontenay le Comte, Paris and Poitiers. Which particular train is being announced?

Write down the *time* of the trains, in the order you hear them (1 to 5).

RITES	N°	DESTINATION	HEURES	QUAI	PARTICULARITES	N°	DESTI
21/9	340	NANTES	9ʰ16	1		6975	SAINTES
	122	PARIS	9ʰ39	2	CORAIL	6975	SAINTES
	4376	RENNES	11ʜ19	1	CORAIL	6876	NIORT
	3471	BORDEAUX	11ʰ23	2	Sꜰ D&F	990	FONTEN
	978	FONTENAY Lᴇ C	11ʰ25	CAR	Sꜰ D.F	992	FONTENA
	3473	BORDEAUX	12ʜ20	2	LE PALUDIER CORAIL	3499	TOULOU
	6969	SAINTES	12ʰ40	3	DU 26.6 AU 06.9	3533	LES Aꜰ
						5336	NANTES
						3892	POITIEꜰ
A	4365	ROCHEFORT	14ʜ23	2	DU 26.6 AU 06.9	5336	RENNES
	3886	PARIS	14ʜ32	1	DU 26.6 AU 06.9	343	VINTIM
	3475	TOULOUSE	15ʜ44	2		4384	QUIMPE
	4372	QUIMPER	16ʜ18	1		3525	NICE
	166	PARIS	16ʜ54	1	Sꜰ SA. CORAIL	3541	NICE
	984	LA ROCHE ꜱᴜʀ Yᴏɴ	17ʜ05	CAR	Sꜰ D.F	4358	PARIS
	3890	POITIERS	17ʜ11	1	SA.		
	6870	POITIERS	17ʜ20	3	D.F	3293	ROCHE
	6973	BORDEAUX	17ʜ29	1	Vᴇ	167	ROCHE
	986	FONTENAY Lᴇ C	17ʜ35	CAR	Sꜰ D.F	4360	PARIS
	988	LA ROCHE ꜱᴜʀ Yᴏɴ	17ʜ45	CAR	D.F		
	3450	PARIS	18ʜ00	2	Vᴇ.Dɪ.& 14.7 SF.12.31.7 & 07 14.21.28 , 8		

(Board title: EAU HORAIRE D)

2 Station announcements (basic level)

Attention! Attention!

 Which of these announcements:

A. Call for a tour leader?

B. Announce the arrival of a high speed train?

C. Announce the arrival of a train to Paris?

D. Is for parents of a child who's got lost?

E. Call for a porter?

F. Gives warning that the train is leaving?

G. Tells you that the train stops at all stations?

Match the number of the announcement to the alphabetical letter.

VOCABULARIES

Basic vocabulary

KEY VERBS

acheter to buy
aider to help
aller to go
amener quelqu'un en voiture
  to give someone a lift
annoncer to announce
arriver to arrive

attendre to wait
changer to change
chercher to look for
composter to validate ticket
comprendre to understand

continuer to continue
contrôler to check tickets
débarquer to disembark
déclarer to declare
déposer quelqu'un en voiture
  to drop someone off

descendre de to get off
descendre to go down
durer to last
embarquer to embark
entrer dans to go in

louer to hire
manquer to miss
marcher to walk

mettre trente minutes à
  to take thirty minutes to
monter dans to get in/on
monter to go up
ouvrir to open
partir (+ de) to leave
payer to pay

porter to wear; to carry
préférer to prefer
prendre to take
quitter to leave
rater to miss

rentrer to go home
réserver to reserve
revenir to come back
s'arrêter to stop
se dépêcher to hurry
se mettre en route to start out

se perdre to get lost
se renseigner to get information
se trouver to be (situated)
sortir (+ de) to go out
suivre to follow

tourner to turn
traverser to cross
vérifier to check
voyager to travel

Finding the way

à ... mètres metres away
à ... minutes... minutes away
à droite (to the) right
à gauche (to the) left
à pied on foot

m **agent de police** policeman
f **autoroute** motorway
m **centre-ville** town centre
m **chemin** way, road

là there
là-bas over there
m **nord** north
m **ouest** west
m **passant** passer-by

m **piéton** pedestrian
f **place** square
m **plan** (street) map
m **pont** bridge

m	**coin** corner		*m*	**port** harbour,port
m	**commissariat** police station		*f*	**poste** post office
f	**côte** coast			**pour aller à** how do I get to
f	**direction** direction			**premier** first
f	**distance** distance			**proche** near
m	**est** east			**puis** then
m	**feux rouges** traffic lights		*f*	**rue** street
m	**garage** garage		*m*	**sud** south
f	**gendarmerie** police station		*m*	**syndicat d'initiative**
				tourist information office
m	**hôpital** hospital		*f*	**usine** factory
	ici here			

Travel by public transport

	à destination de going to		*f*	**gare routière** bus station
	à l'heure per hour;on time		*f*	**guichet** ticket office
m	**aéroport** airport		*m*	**horaire** timetable
f	**affiche** notice, poster		*f*	**hôtesse de l'air** air hostess
m	**aller simple** single ticket			**libre** free, not occupied
m	**aller-retour** return ticket		*f*	**ligne** line
m	**arrêt** stop			**non-fumeur** non smoking
f	**arrivée** arrival			**obligatoire** compulsory
m	**autobus** bus			**occupé** occupied,engaged
m	**autocar** coach		*m*	**passeport** passport
m	**avion** plane		*f*	**place** square
m	**bagages** luggage			**ponctuel** punctual
f	**banlieue** suburbs		*m*	**port** harbour
m	**bateau** boat		*m*	**porteur** porter
m	**billet** ticket		*m*	**prix** price
m	**buffet** buffet			**prochain** next
m	**carnet** book of tickets		*m*	**quai** platform
m	**chemin de fer** railway		*m*	**rapide** fast train
	chez moi (at) home/my house		*f*	**réduction** reduction
f	**classe** class		*m*	**renseignements** information
m	**compartiment** compartment		*f*	**réservation** reservation
f	**consigne** left-luggage office		*f*	**salle d'attente** waiting room
f	**correspondance** connection		*f*	**sortie** exit
	de bonne heure early			**supplémentaire** supplementary
m	**départ** departure		*m*	**T.G.V.** high speed train
	direct straight-through		*m*	**ticket** ticket
f	**direction** direction			**toilettes** toilets
f	**douane** customs		*m*	**train** train
	en avance early		*f*	**valise** suitcase
	en provenance de arriving from		*f*	**voie** platform, track

	en retard late	
m	**express** express train	
f	**gare** station	

m	**vol** flight	
m	**voyage** journey	
m	**voyageur** traveller	

Travel by car, motorcycle, moped

f	**ambulance** ambulance
	arrière back (seat)
f	**assurance** insurance
f	**auto-école** driving school
m	**avant** front
f	**bicyclette** bicycle
m	**camion** lorry
f	**carte routière** road map
m	**casque** helmet
m	**chauffeur** driver
f	**chaussée** road surface
f	**clé de voiture** car key
m	**coffre** boot (of car)
m	**conducteur** driver
	crevé flat (tyre)
m	**deux-temps** two-stroke
f	**déviation** diversion
f	**eau** water
	en panne broken down
	en panne d'essence out of petrol
f	**essence** petrol
m	**essuie-glaces** windscreen wipers
m	**frein** brake
m	**gas-oil** diesel
	grave serious
f	**huile** oil
	interdit forbidden
m	**litre** litre
m	**mécanicien** mechanic
m	**moteur** engine
f	**moto** motorbike
m	**(moto-)cycliste** (motor-)cyclist

f	**obligatoire** compulsory
f	**ordinaire** 2 star petrol
m	**pare-brise** windscreen
m	**parking** carpark
m	**passage protégé** pedestrian crossing
m	**péage** toll
m	**permis de conduire** driving licence
m	**phare** headlight
m	**piéton** pedestrian
m	**pneu** tyre
m	**poids lourd** heavy vehicle
	pratique practical
f	**pression** pressure
f	**priorité** priority
	rapide fast
m	**rétroviseur** rear-view mirror
f	**route** road
m	**scooter** scooter
m	**siège** seat
f	**station de métro** tube station
f	**station-service** petrol station
m	**stationnement** parking
f	**super** 4 star petrol
m	**transport** transport
m	**travaux** roadworks
m	**trottoir** pavement
m	**vélo** bike
m	**vélomoteur** moped
m	**virage** bend (in road)
f	**vitesse** speed; gear
f	**voiture** car
f	**zone** area

Additional higher vocabulary

KEY VERBS

atterrir	to land	**rembourser**	to reimburse
circuler	to keep moving	**rester**	to stay
consulter	to consult	**retourner**	to return
décoller	to take off	**rouler**	to drive along
être de retour	to be back	**s'approcher**	to approach
oublier	to forget	**s'égarer**	to get lost
ralentir	to slow down	**voler**	to fly
remarquer	to notice		

All settings

m	**aéroglisseur** hovercraft	*m*	**lavage automatique** automatic car wash
f	**amende** fine	*m*	**moyen de transport** means of transport
	assuré insured	*m*	**papiers** papers, documents
m	**bâtiment** building	*m*	**passage à niveau** level crossing
f	**batterie** battery	*m*	**pilote** pilot
m	**carrefour** crossroads	*m*	**pompiste** forecourt attendant
f	**ceinture de sécurité** seat-belt	*f*	**portière** door(of car etc)
f	**couchette** couchette		**sens unique** one-way
f	**destination** destination		**vide** empty
f	**durée** duration	*f*	**voiture** carriage(of train)
f	**frontière** frontier	*m*	**volant** steering wheel
f	**horloge** clock	*m*	**wagon- restaurant** dining car
	immédiatement immediately		

Accidents

KEY VERBS

accuser	to accuse	**heurter**	to collide with
appeler	to call	**marcher**	to walk
avoir peur	to be afraid	**menacer**	to threaten
contacter	to contact	**oser**	to dare
courir	to run	**poser des questions**	to ask questions
crier	to shout	**ralentir**	to slow down
dépasser	to overtake	**renverser**	to knock over
écraser	to crush	**respecter**	to respect
étonner	to astonish	**s'excuser**	to apologise
faire attention	to be careful	**se mettre en colère**	to get angry
freiner	to brake	**tuer**	to kill

m	**accident** accident	m	**gendarme** policeman
f	**adresse** address	m	**hôpital** hospital
m	**agent de police** policeman	f	**marque** make (of car)
f	**auto** car	m	**médecin** doctor
	blessé injured	f	**pièce d'identité** identity card
f	**chaussée** road surface	m	**sapeur-pompier** fireman
m	**code de la route** highway code		**soudain** suddenly
f	**collision** collision		**tout à coup** suddenly
m	**constat** statement		**trop vite** too fast
m	**consulat britannique** british consulate		**urgent** urgent
m	**dommage** damage		
f	**faute** fault	f	**véhicule** vehicle

TOPIC AREA 3

THE ENVIRONMENT:
town, country, climate.

SETTINGS	Living in town or country; talking about where you live. Places of interest. Joining a conservation project. Washington, USA.
KEY NOTIONS AND FUNCTIONS *(refer to Starter Kit)*	Identifying, locating and describing places and buildings. Evaluating; recognising approval and disapproval.
KEY STRUCTURES *(refer to Grammar Section)*	Prepositions; commands; the infinitive as commands; present, perfect tenses; the future tense in forecasts.

CONTENTS

KEY SPEAKING TASKS

Look at the map of Bordeaux and practice:

ASKING the way to the places mentioned & finding out if they are far or near

STATING directions - as if you were standing at the Gare Citram

e.g.
- **la Place Gambetta**
- **la Maison du Vin**
- **le marché**
- **l'Office de Tourisme**
- **le Grand Théâtre**
- **la Garonne**

READING PRACTICE

1   Bordeaux: plan de ville

How much information can you put together about Bordeaux from a map?

Work out these details:-
1. The name of the station.
2. Where can you park a car?
3. Where will you find the Tourist Office?
4. Is there a car-free area, for some leisurely shopping?
5. Where might you go to have a picnic lunch?
6. Where should you go to get a taxi?
7. You collect stamps; where would you get them?

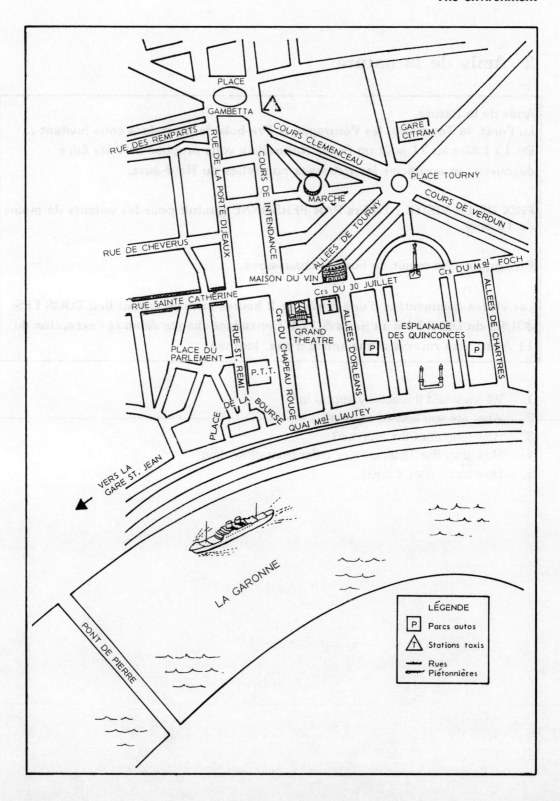

2 Amis de la nature

Amis de la Nature,
La Forêt, la Tourbière, les Pâturages et Pré-bois de Haut-Jura vous invitent ...
Du 15 juillet au 31 août un Guide Naturaliste vous propose de vous faire
découvrir et apprécier les richesses naturelles du Haut-Jura.

PRIX DE LA VISITE : 10 Frs PAR PERSONNE (gratuit pour les enfants de moins
de 13 ans).

Précaution : Se munir de bonnes chaussures.

Les visites commentées d'une durée de 2 heures environ auront lieu TOUS LES
JOURS du Lundi 14 h au Samedi 12 h Cependant chaque Jeudi (à l'exception du
11 Août) sera reservé à une sortie d'une journée.

---

1.   Whom would this activity appeal to?
2.   What are you advised to wear?
3.   How long does the tour last?
4.   How does the Thursday tour differ from other days?
5.   How much does it cost?

3 La Vallée du Dropt (Dordogne)

*Ses moulins, ses bastides**

* Bastides: fortified towns built in 13th-14th centuries, by French and English kings; all have large central square surrounded by covered arcades.

LA VALLÉE DU DROPT

Ses moulins, ses bastides

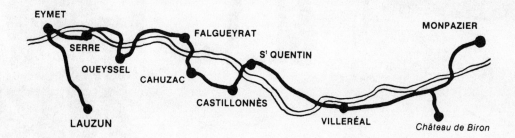

Au départ de LAUZUN, prendre la D 111 vers EYMET. Découvrez cette bastide fondée en 1270 par Alphonse de Poitiers, sa place des arcades, l'aspect médiéval, son château et son musée préhistorique. Quittez EYMET par la R 133 vers BERGERAC : ne pas franchir le Dropt, juste avant le pont qui l'enjambe, tournez à droite par SERRES ET MONTGUYARD.

Flâner sur la vieille route ombragée jusqu'à SERRES, là, bifurquez vers RAZAC, passez le Dropt et prenez à droite la D 25, en direction d'ISSIGEAC ; arrivé au niveau de la piscine du Cabanon, tournez à droite vers LAUZUN. Au passage, découvrez l'ancien moulin restauré. Tout de suite après, à gauche, allez vers QUEYSSEL : bien cachée, son église romane ô ! combien sereine. N'oubliez pas le moulin dans son écrin de peupliers. Remontez vers la D 25 jusqu'à FALGUEYRAT, engagez vous sur la D 288 jusqu'à CAHUZAC : comme La Rochefoucault aimait le faire, reposez vous un instant. Repartez vers CASTILLONNÈS. Après une visite à cette bastide, si vous ne craignez pas de vous perdre en campagne, partez à la découverte de S' DIZIER, par la D 121, puis par la D 250 vers DOUDRAC et VILLERÉAL. Ne quittez pas ce village sans voir la halle à piliers du XIII° siècle et l'église de même époque. Poussez vos périgrinations jusqu'à MONPAZIER par la D 104 en redécouvrant le Dropt et sa station de captage des eaux de la Brame. Accédez à la cité de MONPAZIER, bastide la mieux conservée de la région, et admirez ses portes fortifiées, son église, et à la saison... son marché aux cèpes, ou aux chataîgnes !

Which town would you stop at to see:

1. Castles?
2. Windmills?
3. Romanesque churches?
4. An arcaded square?
5. Bastide towns?
6. Where could you have a swim?
7. Whereabouts would you stop to stretch your legs and explore the countryside?
8. In what way is Montpazier outstanding?

4 Chantier des fouilles (Bretagne)

Concerned about the environment? Interested in the past? Join an archaeological dig (**des fouilles**); work out the practical details of this dig in Brittany.

A. Eligibility.
1. How old must you be?
2. How long are you expected to stay?
3. What are the health requirements?

B. The site.
1. How far is Locmariaquer from the nearest railway station?
2. When does the dig start, and end?

C. Board and lodging.
1. Where would you be lodged?
2. When is there a campsite available?
3. What should you bring with you?
4. Who pays for the food?

D. The working day.
1. When do you have time off?
2. How long is the working day?

Chantier de fouilles préhistoriques
LOCMARIAQUER (Morbihan)
Ensemble mégalithique
Table des Marchands - Grand Menhir

Nature du chantier : Opération de fouille préalable à la restauration de ce célèbre ensemble mégalithique.

Poursuite des fouilles sur le dolmen de la Table des Marchands.

Reprise des fouilles associé au Grand-Menhir.

Conditions générales d'admission : Age minimum : 18 ans

Bonne condition physique compatible avec un travail physique soutenu en plein air. Pas de régime alimentaire contraignant.

Dates de fonctionnement du chantier : Du 30 mars au 26 septembre

Situation-Accès : Locmariaquer est à 14 Km au sud d'Auray

Gare SNCF : Auray

Nourriture prise en charge par le chantier les jours de travail.

Hébergement : A l'ancien phare de Kerpenhir (lits fournis).

(En été, possibilité de camper sur le terrain jouxtant le bâtiment).

Apporter son couchage et éventuellement sa tente.

Présence minimale: 2 semaines complètes.

Horaires de travail: modulables selon les conditions climatiques sur la base de 7 heures de fouille effective par jour. Samedis et dimanches libres.

5   Tempête - catastrophe

TEMPETE

Une catastrophe sans précédent pour l'Ouest de la France

La tempête qui s'est abattue dans la nuit du 15 au 16 octobre dernier sur l'Ouest de la France a constitué une catastrophe sans précédent pour la forêt bretonne, les dégâts représentants au total l'équivalent de douze années de production.

Selon le directeur régional de l'agriculture qui effectuait un bilan chiffré vendredi soir au terme d'une reunion entre le préfet et les responsables des différents secteurs de Bretagne, 6,5 millions de m3 de forêts ont ainsi été touchés, soit 20 % de la forêt bretonne.

La perte directe s'élève à 650 MF auxquels il faut ajouter les crédits qui seront nécessaires pour dégager les routes forestières, récupérer le bois à exploiter et reboiser. Soit un total d'environ 2 milliards.

L'Etat de catastrophe naturelle, rappelle-t-on, a été constaté dans six départements les plus touches par la tempête : Côtes-du-Nord, Finistère, Morbihan, Ille-et-Vilaine, Manche et Calvados.

Vendredi soir, 14.400 foyers bretons étaient toujours privés d'électricité contre 650.000 au lendemain de la tempête. Quelque 1.500 hommes sont actuellement dans la région (pompiers, sécurité civile, armée) pour réparer les dégâts).

1.   What was the catastrophe?
2.   When did it strike?
3.   What did it flatten?
4.   What is the estimated direct loss in francs?
5.   What two additional tasks are going to increase the final cost?
6.   What was the effect on people, Friday evening?
7.   What organizations are on the spot, clearing up?

6 La météo 1 - hiver

> **Sur le sud-est le ciel sera très nuageux, avec quelques pluies sur les Alpes, et de la neige au-dessus de 900 m. Le matin il y aura beaucoup de brouillard des Pyrénées Orientales au Massif Central; mais de belles éclaircies se développeront l'après-midi. Sur la Bretagne un vent fort ne s'atténuera qu'en fin de soirée.**

Note down where - and for which part of the day - this is the weather forecast:

forecast	area	when
bright spells		
fog		
overcast		
rain		
snow		
windy		

La météo 2 - été

Note down the gist of these headlines about the weather.

Tiens, voilà le soleil !

Non, ce n'est pas un poisson d'août. Ne vous désespérez pas en voyant des nuages le matin. Ils céderont vite la place au soleil. Etonnant, non ?

De l'orage dans l'air

La foudre, les éclairs et les grosses pluies d'été vous feront la fête. Si vous ne restez pas chez vous, vous mouillerez le maillot immanquablement

Du plomb sur la tête

L'orage menace et les températures en profitent pour prendre la voie ascendante. On a dépassé la température du corps à Auch (39°) et à Bergerac (37°)

Le beau temps après l'orage

Prière de ne pas s'affoler et de ne pas désespérer. Les orages viennent faire trois petits éclairs puis s'en vont. Et le soleil revient. Quel soulagement !

30° à l'ombre

Les (très) légères brumes matinales ne doivent pas vous démoraliser. Aujourd'hui ça va encore cogner !

Orages, ô désespoir !

Ça ne pouvait pas durer ! Les nuages vont progressivement assombrir le ciel et notre humeur, jusqu'à ce que l'orage éclate en fin de journée

Sortez les parapluies

Comme si le temps orageux ne suffisait pas ! Voilà la pluie qui s'en mêle du Poitou-Charentes à l'Aquitaine

7 Washington, capitale

Washington

*Capitale
d'un pays blanc à 90%,
elle est noire aux trois quarts.
Dans cette ville
de dieux blancs
et de misère noire,
les Blancs monopolisent
l'avant-scène. Et cachent
au reste du monde
ses records en matière
de crime, de drogue
et de mortalité infantile.*

**DE NOTRE ENVOYÉ SPÉCIAL PERMANENT. C'est comme ça tous les quatre ans.
Quand Washington se prend pour le centre du monde et y réussit assez bien. Le
20 Janvier, sous un ciel sans doute clair et froid, les messieurs seront en
redingote et les femmes en vison. Le président prêtera serment sur la Bible.**

**C'est comme ça tous les quatre ans, quand Washington redécouvre ce qu'elle est:
une provinciale capitale, belle, froide, indigeste, au centre de la terre. Une ville
phare. Une ville culte.**

Les images mentent.

**Il y a deux Washington qui se croisent sans se voir. Une blanche et une noire.
Washington est le siège de toutes les administrations, de la CIA, du FBI, de la Food
and Drug Administration: de tous les lobbys - du lobby juif et du lobby antijuif (le
Liberty lobby), de la National Rifle Association (les amoureux des armes) et de
son contraire, la Handgun Control Association. Toutes les industries stratégiques
du pays, de l'armement à la pharmacie. y ont un bureau chargé de faire pression
sur les membres du Congrès. Les grosses entreprises françaises - Matra,
Thomson, etc., sont là aussi. Près du Capitole et de la Maison-Blanche, près des
grands networks de télévision.**

**Il faut donc voir Washington l'été. L'industrie du pouvoir a fermé ses portes,
fonctionnaires et grands commis sont allés retrouver leurs racines du côté de Los
Angeles ou de Whichita Falls. Le théâtre est fermé.**

Washington se donne alors aux quinze millions de touristes qui la visitent chaque année pour ce qu'elle est au fond: une ville noire, déjà sudiste.

Se rappeler alors qu'elle fut dessinée par un Français, Pierre Charles l'Enfant, qui mourut dans la misère et l'amertume bien avant de voir la première pierre s'élever.

C'est la ville de la Loi par excellence, et pourtant une des villes américaines où la loi souffre le plus.

- la mortalité infantile (21 pour 1,000) y est deux fois plus élevée que dans l'ensemble des Etats américains et dépasse même le taux de certaines régions du tiers monde!

- Tandis que les touristes s'émerveillent de la plus forte concentration de musées au monde, de la plus grande bibliothèque de la planète, la Library of Congress, on recense dans la capitale fédérale l'un des plus forts taux d'analphabétisme du pays.

- Tandis que Ronald Reagan ne cessait de faire de grandes déclarations sur la lutte contre la drogue, le crack envahissait la ville, traînant la violence derrière lui.

60% des homicides - ils ont doublé en trois ans - sont liés à la drogue. A quelques centaines de mètres du palais de l'homme le plus puissant de la terre, des crack houses se dressent impudemment, entre la 5e et la 14e Avenue. La place de Dupont Circle est devenue un marché de la drogue à ciel ouvert. Chaque jour, la police arrête cinq adolescents noirs pour trafic de drogue. L'an dernier, près de deux mille mineurs, la plupart noirs ont commis des meurtres, vols, agressions. Ainsi va, aussi, la vie à Washington, ville de hauts lieux et de basfonds, de dieux blancs et de misère noire.

L'EVENEMENT DU JEUDI - 9 AU 25 JANVIER 1989

1. What ceremony in Washington, U.S.A. has occasioned this article?
2. What is the percentage of black inhabitants in Washington? and in the U.S.A. altogether?
3. According to the author, in what three areas does Washington hold records?
4. Do you think the author is mostly sympathetic, or mostly unsympathetic, to the leading, white, community?
5. Name two administrative organizations, and two industries, which have their principal offices in Washington.
6. Give two reasons why this is so.
7. Name three areas of activity or people which shut shop in summer.
8. In what circumstances did Pierre Charles l'Enfant die?
9. What is his connection with Washington?
10. What statistics does the author give to support his argument that infant mortality is extremely high in Washington?
11. Why does he think it incongruous that Washington has one of the highest levels of illiteracy in the States?
12. What particular crime has doubled in three years? To what is it linked?
13. Where does drug dealing take place openly?
14. What other 2 crimes are committed by minors?

SPEAKING PRACTICE

1 Mon quartier (basic level/higher level)

The conversation : talking about where you live.

At higher level you need to give informational details (where? whereabouts? where exactly?) and then to move onto descriptive details (what's it like?) and a more varied vocabulary. The verb tenses will be in the present tense -the 'grammar' therefore is not difficult.

PRACTICE QUESTIONS	SAMPLE ANSWERS
Vous habitez **- quelle région?** **- quelle ville?** **- quel quartier?**	**J'habite (...) - une grande ville; à (...) -** **un petit village. Dans le nord/sud... de** **la G.B. Dans la banlieue. Au centre.** **Près de la côte. A la campagne.**
Décrivez-moi votre **- ville/village/ quartier**	**C'est petit/grand; c'est triste/vivant;** **c'est animé/morne...**
Q'est-ce qu'il y a **- à voir?** **- à faire?** **- à visiter?**	**Nous avons beaucoup de/plusieurs** **/très peu de:sites/monuments/** **châteaux/...** **On peut aller à /visiter/faire/...**
Qu'est-ce qu'il y a comme **- distractions?** **- loisirs?** **- commerces?** **- industries?** **- climat?**	**Pour se distraire il y a beaucoup** **de/très peu de: cinémas/théâtres/** **promenades/sports/concerts/....** **Pour les courses et pour les souvenirs** **il y a plusieurs/très peu de grands** **magasins/marchés/ supermarchés/** **boutiques**
Qu'est-ce que vous avez fait pour vous distraire samedi dernier? pendant les grandes vacances?	**Je suis allé à la pêche. Je me suis** **promené à pied/en voiture/.. Je n'ai** **rien fait - j'étais trop fatigué/e. Je suis** **partie à l'étranger: en France, au** **Portugal. Je suis resté chez moi.**
Quel pays aimeriez-vous visiter/voir - et pourquoi?	**J'aimerais aller au Canada/aux** **Antilles/en Suisse. Parce que je n'y** **suis jamais allé/e. Parce que j'aimerais** **voyager.**

WRITING PRACTICE

1 Une journée à Bordeaux (higher level)

The informal letter, or postcard

REFER to the *Starter Kit* (Writing) for key language on informal writing.

PREPARE by jotting down a suitable vocabulary, and especially verbs. Never leave blanks - try and remember something similar: you need to convey meaning, not a prose translation.

Write a brief letter (about 100 words) to a French friend - who does not know Bordeaux - about your day trip there. Say:

- how you went there (e.g. by car)
- how you spent the morning (eg. sightseeing); what you saw
- where you had lunch (eg. restaurant or picnic)
- what you did in the afternoon (eg. shopping: trip down the river)
- what presents or souvenirs of Bordeaux you bought
- give an opinion of the town, and your visit.

Here is a verb starter kit for the letter. (Two ** for **être** verbs in the perfect)

** **aller à Bordeaux: en voiture/en autobus: au marché**
  visiter
  voir
  prendre le déjeuner
  faire un pique-nique/une promenade à pied/en bateau; des courses
  acheter des cadeaux

---

2 Agenda (basic level)

The diary: places to see and visit, activities to do.

JOT verbs down in the infinitive.

AVOID full sentences.

PUT TOGETHER a suitable vocabulary: the 'instructions' are often open-ended and allow you to put together something suitable.

AVOID English - use the nearest French equivalent, or leave it out altogether and write down something you can remember!
VARY your vocabulary -places and verbs.

Complete this example for the rest of the week.

samedi matin : **sortir en ville**

soir : **rencontrer copains**

dimanche après-midi : **aller au centre sportif**

3 Mon pays (higher level)

The narrative, informal, letter.

In this kind of writing you need to initiate correspondence, or respond to a previous letter, wherein you describe fully - but succinctly - the area you live in.

BEAR in mind that the person you are writing to, for the first or second time, most probably does not know your part of GB at all. Where exactly is it ? How large or small is it ? What is there in the way of shopping, sports facilities ? Is it in the countryside, near the sea, mountains, a large town ? or is it a large town ? What is there to see and to do - for a visitor ? Are there any castles, historic houses, national parks, riverside walks to do and see?

What entertainment is available in the evenings: cinemas, youth clubs, theatres ?

FIND OUT what your area/home town has to offer, even if you haven't been there yourself.

PREPARE a presentation of your area: look up (beyond the scope of this book) what there is in the way of theme parks, race courses, historic houses, wildlife etc.

ALWAYS avoid English: don't just write down the English name of the Youth Club, the shopping mall - say what it is ! "**un centre commercial, un club des jeunes**", etc

FOR PRACTICAL, examination purposes (and in real life too!) don't burble on about one or two things only, if your correspondent wants to know about five or six.

Here are two extracts from letters from people in France, making contact for the first time, and describing the area they live in. The first person lives just outside Paris, in the suburbs; the second one in a small village in Brittany.

What does each of them say about :-

1. The location of their home town/area ?
2. Entertainment ?
3. Weather in the area ?
4. Public transport facilities ?
5. Shopping facilities ?
6. Special features/attractions of the area ?

J'habite à Bagneux: ce n'est pas tout à fait Paris - c'est dans la banlieu sud, dans le département des Hauts de Seine. C'est presque comme un petit village - il y a la place centrale, ou, tous les samedi, il y a a un marché - pas mal du tout. Il y a beaucoup de cafés, où on se rencontre entre copains, les soirs, et souvent à midi. Nous avons aussi 2 cinémas et un club des jeunes. Il n'y a pas de grands magasins - pour cela il faut aller à Paris. Ce qui est bien c'est que nous sommes vraiment pas loin de Paris; par le R.E.R. on peut arriver au centre même de Paris dans une demi-heure...

J' habite à Locqmariaquer - c'est un tout petit village dans le Morbihan en Bretagne. Ce qui est bien ici c'est la proximité de la mer, et le climat: nous bénéficions d'un climat très particulier, on appelle ça un 'microclimat' - cela veut dire que nous avons toujours du beau temps, même lorsqu'il fait froid, ou qu'il pleut, à quelques kilomètres à l'intérieur. C'est bizarre, mais moi, j'en profite, surtout en été, pendant les grandes vacances, pour aller à la plage, ou pour faire des promenades ou randonnées, soit à pied, soit à velo - parce que nous n'avons pas de transports publics bien développés.La gare la plus proche est à 14 kms, à Auray, et il n'y a pas de bus - correspondances que les jours de marché à Auray: les samedi et les mercredi. Si vous aimez la nature, c'est très bien ici. Pour les loisirs: rien ! sauf des réunions de copains dans le café principal! C'est pas mal, d'ailleurs...

WRITE a narrative letter, describing your home town/area.

4 Prévisions pour demain (basic level/higher level)

Ensure your future tenses! Put the verbs in brackets into the future.

A: regular verbs
B: **avoir; être; faire.**

A   1.   Les brouillards (se dissiper) vers la fin de matinée.
     2.   La tramontane (souffler) encore assez fort en Provence.
     3.   Les vents du nord-est (s'affaiblir) au cours de la journée.
     4.   Les pluies (tomber) sur la Bretagne.
     5.   De belles éclaircies (se développer) dans la journée.
     6.   Le ciel (se couvrir) au cours de matinée.

7. Des bruines (tomber) sur le Finistère.
8. Dans les Alpes, au-dessus de 800m il (neiger)
9. Des nuages orageaux (se développer) près de L'Atlantique.
10. Les averses (s'atténuer) vers la fin de soirée.

B   1. Il y (avoir) des nuages abondants.
      2. Le temps (être) généralement ensoleillé sur l'ensemble du pays.
      3. Les orages (être) violents, accompagnés de fortes rafales.
      4. Les températures (être) en baisse.
      5. Brumes et brouillards (être) très nombreux.
      6. Il (faire) très chaud, après dissipation des brumes matinales.
      7. Sur beaucoup de régions il y (avoir) des nuages.
      8. Le ciel (être) très chargé le matin, avec des ondées en montagne.
      9. Il y (avoir) de rares éclaircies.
    10. Il (faire) très doux pour la saison.

C   Now try your own weather forecasting; using a local or national newspaper, and over a period of months, put the weather forecasts into French. Remember not to translate, but to convey the meaning.

LISTENING PRACTICE

1 Tour de Bordeaux à pied (higher level)

You're on a coach party of mostly French-speaking tourists to visit Bordeaux. Your guide, Catherine, gives an introduction to the tour, in French.

Look at the map of Bordeaux (*see page 93*), to help you locate the places mentioned; then work out the main points of her introduction.

1. Give two details about the guide.
2. Where is the exact set-down point?
3. Give one detail about the Place Gambetta.
4. How are the 18th century houses on the Cours de l'Intendance presently used?
5. What is the connection between the town of Bordeaux and the painter Goya ?
6. What is the attraction of the rue Ste. Catherine for the tourist ?
7. Give one detail about the Place du Parlement.
8. What is specifically noteworthy about the Pont de Pierre ?
9. What is the main feature of the Esplanade des Quinconces ?
10. Where is the pick up point for the return journey ?
11. How much free time will you have ?
12. What time does the coach leave for the return journey ?

VOCABULARIES

Basic level vocabulary

Note   for adjectives describing buildings and places, and seasons, refer to the Starter Kit.

KEY VERBS

connaître	to know	**savoir**	to know
entrer dans	to go in	**se situer**	to be situated
(se) fermer	to close	**se trouver**	to be (situated)
(s') ouvrir	to open	**visiter**	to visit
protéger	to protect	**voir**	to see

All settings

m	**arbre**	tree	m	**lac**	lake
f	**autoroute**	motorway	m	**magasin**	shop
f	**banlieue**	suburbs	f	**maison**	house
m	**bâtiment**	building	f	**mer**	sea
m	**bois**	wood	f	**météo**	weather forecast
m	**bord**	edge	m	**monde**	world
f	**campagne**	countryside	f	**montagne**	mountain
f	**capitale**	capital	m	**mouton**	sheep
m	**carrefour**	crossroads	m	**musée**	museum
f	**cathédrale**	cathedral	m	**oiseau**	bird
f	**champ**	field	m	**parc**	park
m	**château**	castle	m	**pays**	country
m	**cheval**	horse	f	**piscine**	swimming pool
m	**ciel**	sky	f	**plage**	beach
f	**circulation**	traffic	f	**plante**	plant
m	**climat**	climate	m	**poisson**	fish
f	**côte**	coast	m	**pont**	bridge
m	**degré**	degree	m	**port**	harbour
f	**église**	church	f	**poule**	hen
m	**endroit**	place	m	**quartier**	district
m	**environnement**	environment	f	**région**	region; area
f	**espace**	space	f	**rivière**	river
f	**essence sans plomb**	lead-free petrol	f	**rue**	street
f	**ferme**	farm	f	**serpent**	snake
f	**fleur**	flower		**situé**	situated
f	**forêt**	forest	m	**stade**	stadium, sports ground
m	**habitant**	inhabitant	f	**température**	temperature
f	**herbe**	grass	f	**vache**	cow
m	**hôtel de ville**	town hall	f	**vallée**	valley
f	**île**	island	m	**village**	village

m	**hôtel de ville** town hall	f	**vallée** valley
f	**île** island	m	**village** village
m	**immeuble** block of flats	f	**ville** town
f	**industrie** industry	m/f	**voisin/e** neighbour
m	**jardin** garden	f	**vue** view

Weather words: all levels

VERB		NOUN	ADJECTIVE	
s'affaiblir	m	affaiblissement	-	to moderate, die down (winds)
s'améliorer	f	amélioration	-	to improve; improvement
s'atténuer	f	atténuation	-	to diminish:lessening
-	f	averses	-	showers
baisser		en baisse	-	to fall: falling (temperatures)
faire beau temps	m	beau temps	beau	to be fine: fine weather: fine
faire du brouillard	m	brouillard	-	to be foggy: fog
-	f	bruine	-	fine rain
-	f	brume	brumeux	(morning) mist:misty
faire chaud	m	chaleur	chaud	to be hot: heat: hot
changer	m	changement	-	to change: change
se couvrir		-	couvert	to cloud over: overcast
continuer	f	continuation	-	to continue: continuation
se dégager	m	dégagement	dégagé	to clear: clearing
se déplacer	m	déplacement	-	to move/shift: movement
se développer	m	développement	-	to develop: development
se dissiper	f	dissipation	-	to clear up (rain) dispersion
faire doux	m	douceur	doux	to be mild: mildness: mild
-	m	éclair	-	(flash of) lightning
s'éclaircir	f	éclaircies	clair	to brighten: bright spells: clear

éclater	m éclats	-	to break out: bursts
s'évoluer	ƒ évolution		to evolve:evolution/ development
fondre	-	fondu	to melt: melted
faiblir	-	faible	to weaken: weak
-	-	fort	strong
-	-	frais	cool
faire froid	m froid	froid	to be cold: cold: cold
geler	m gel	gelé	to freeze: frost: frozen
givrer	m givre	givrant	to ice up: frost: frosty
-	ƒ glace	-	ice
-	ƒ grèle		hail
-	ƒ humidité	humide	humidity: humid
inonder	ƒ inondations;ondées	inondé	to flood: floods: flooded
se limiter à	ƒ limitation	limité	to be confined to: restriction: restricted
-	-	lourd	close
-	m mistral	-	mistral (bitter wind in the Rhône valley)
neiger	ƒ neige	neigeux enneigé	to snow: snow: snowy snowed up
-	m nuages	nuageux	clouds: cloudy
faire de l'orage	m orages	orageux	storms: stormy
pleuvoir	ƒ pluie	pluvieux	to rain: rain: rainy
-	ƒ précipitation	-	rain/snow falls
prévoir	ƒ prévision	prévu	to forecast: forecast : forecast
-	ƒ rafales	-	strong gusts of wind
se rafraîchir	m rafraîchissement	rafraîchi	to get cooler: cooler spell:cooler
se refroidir	m refroidissement	-	to get colder: colder spells
-	ƒ sécheresse	sec	drought: dry
faire du soleil	m soleil	ensoleillé	to be sunny: sun: sunny
souffler	-	-	to blow
-	ƒ tempête	-	storm

-	*m* **tonnerre**	-	thunder
-	*f* **tramontane**	-	tramontane (bitter wind in Mediterranean area)
varier	*f* **variation**	**variable**	to change: change: changeable
faire du vent	*m* **vent**	**venteux**	to be windy: wind: windy
-	*m* **verglas**	**verglaçant**	ice: icy (on roads)
-	*f* **visibilité**	**visible**	visibility: visible

Additional higher vocabulary

KEY VERBS

croire to believe
en avoir marre to have had enough
exister to exist
paraître to appear

remarquer to notice
s'amuser to enjoy oneself
s'ennuyer to be bored
sembler to seem

All settings

autrefois formerly
m **bulletin météorologique** weather forecast
f **colline** hill
f **distractions** amusements
en plein air in the open air

entièrement entirely
m **environs** surrounding area
f **époque** time, period, age
m **évènement** event
m **insecte** insect
m **lieu** place

m **paysage** scenery
f **photo satellite** satellite photo

f **pression** pressure
f **randonnée** trip, excursion
m **siècle** century

m **sommet** top
m **terrain** ground
f **terre** earth

f **truite** trout
f **zone piétonne** pedestrian precinct

TOPIC AREA 4　　SHOPS AND SHOPPING

SETTINGS

Shopping for food and clothes in stores, shops; looking for special offers and sales.

KEY NOTIONS AND FUNCTIONS
(refer to Starter Kit)

Number: cost, quantity; weights and measures.
Colour, materials, suitability and quality.
Describing, comparing and expressing preference.
Satisfaction, dissatisfaction.

KEY STRUCTURES
(refer to Grammar Section)

Adjectival agreement; partitives; negatives; demonstratives; comparatives.

CONTENTS

KEY SPEAKING TASKS

1   Fruits et légumes

1. Identify the items.
2. Pick out the prices, per kilogram, and practise saying them.

3. Ask for a variety of weights.

Je voudrais un kilo de..
Donnez-moi un demi-kilo de…
Je prends 500 grammes de…
Je prends 250 grammes de…

4. Ask the cost/total price.

Ça fait combien?
C'est combien?
Je vous dois combien? en tout?

2 Boîte, bouteille, paquet, ou pot?

First - identify the items. What kind of packaging are they likely to be in? Ask for a variety.

Bonbons tendres aux fruits

READING PRACTICE

1 Le panier garni

Special offers at the supermarket!

1. What can you buy in tins?
2. In multiples of twenty four?
3. In units of the kilogram?
4. In multiples of twelve?
5. Singly?
6. How long for does the special offer last?
7. Spot the name of the supermarket chain!

2 Où est-ce que je peux acheter...?

1. Which shop/s should you go to in order to find:
   A. sticking plaster
   B. a selection of cheeses
   C. hardware
   D. women's clothes
   E. aspirin
   F. posters
   G. discount books
   H. cakes
   I. guide books
   J. chocolates
   K. post cards
   L. new books
   M. something for a child
   N. comic books

2. Write out: the name/type of shop for each of the items listed (A to N), and/or the item itself; to help you fix and memorize the written form.

1

2

3

ELLES

Régie d'édition
publicitaire

Editions de tous ;
☐ Guides
☐ Dépliants
☐ Affiches

8, rue de la Monnaie
39100 DOLE – 84 72 13 03

La Roberie

De la jeune fille à la femme

16, rue aux Cordiers - Tél.: 52.31.3

4

5

6

7

Pâtissier - Chocolatier - Glacier

G. BEREYZIAT

69, rue de Lattre-de-Tassigny
01190 **PONT DE VAUX**
Tél. 85.30.34.52

Les douceurs de mon Pays

8

3 Quelle taille?

When shopping by post/catalogue you need to indicate measurements.

1. Which two measurements do you need to show if you want a dress/suit/jacket/raincoat?
2. And in order to send off for a sweater?
3. And for a pair of trousers?
4. The French word **taille** has two separate meanings/words in English - what are they; working from this catalogue?
5. What is the advice they give you if you're not sure exactly of your clothes' size?

Si vous hésitez entre deux tailles, choisissez toujours la plus grande.

ROBES, ENSEMBLES, VESTES, IMPERMEABLES

1 Tour de poitrine en CM	86	89	92	95	99	102	108	114	120
3 Tour de bassin en CM	91	94	97	103	107	110	116	122	128
Taille à commander	38	40	42	44	46	48	50	52	54

CHEMISIERS PULLS

1 Tour de poitrine en CM	87	90	93	96	99	102
Taille à commander	38	40	42	44	46	48

PANTALONS

3 Tour de bassin en CM	89	92	95	98	101	104
2 Tour de taille en CM	56 à 60	60 à 64	65 à 68	69 à 72	73 à 76	77 à 80
Taille à commander	36	38	40	42	44	46

1 Tour de poitrine — **2** Tour de taille — **3** Tour de bassin

4 Soldes monstres et prix massacrés

Graffitti

1. What are the items on sale here?
2. When does the sale start?

Lovly

1. Why is this shop having a sale?
2. Name the three types of clothing it is selling off.
3. What kind of brand-names do you expect from **grandes marques**?
4. What's the least you expect to get off normal prices?
5. When will the sale end?

SPEAKING PRACTICE

1   **Vous avez autre chose?** (higher level)

Negotiation

Shopping is a basic task! At higher level you will also need to be able to negotiate: eg. wrong size? no change? different styles? none left?

Food

NOTION FUNCTION	KEY LANGUAGE	KEY STRUCTURES
preference	**Vous prenez les pommes ou les poires? celles-ci/celles-là?** **Vous préférez la robe verte ou la robe bleue?**	demonstratives - refer back to Starter Kit "preference"
non-availability	**Nous n'avons plus de raisin; vous voulez autre chose?** **Je n'ai pas de monnaie.**	negatives
access & non-access	**Le magasin est fermé/ouvert. Il ouvre/ferme à quelle heure?**	ouvert - ouvrir - s'ouvrir
quality	**Les pommes sont bonnes? Je voudrais un vin doux/un fromage sec/un melon pour demain.**	refer back to Starter Kit on describing food.
comparison	**Donnez-moi les pommes de terre les plus grandes;des tomates plus petites.**	comparatives

Clothes

suitability	**Ce livre est trop cher; ces chaussures sont trop grandes**	colours; sizes; materials. Prices.
satisfaction & dissatisfaction	**J'aime bien la couleur mais pas le modèle - vous avez autre chose en bleu/vert..?**	comparatives; demonstratives.
	C'est la mauvaise taille je voudrais échanger..	

WRITING PRACTICE

1   Chez le boulanger, à la boulangerie

Lists

The basic level tasks of list-writing is a neat way of checking up on grammar, and showing a range of vocabulary. The tasks here give practice in gender, partitive articles, adjectival agreement, and the use of **chez/à la**...

Complete this shopping list by filling in suitably the gaps marked X.

articles	boutique	personne (m)	personne (f)
1.du fromage	**à l'épicerie**	**chez l'épicier**	**chez l'épicière**
2. x x	**à la boucherie**	**x**	**x**
3. x pâté	**x**	**x**	**x**
4. de l'aspirine	**x**	**chez le pharmacien**	**x**
5. x x	**à la boulangerie**	**x**	**x**
6. x x	**x**	**x**	**chez la quincaillère**
7. x x	**à l'épicerie**	**x**	**x**
8. x poisson	**x**	**x**	**x**
9. x x	**à la crèmerie**	**x**	**x**
10. x x	**x**	**chez le confisier**	**x**

2 Taille, tissu, couleur

Make a list of 10 different clothing items to buy, showing colour and size (**grand; petit; moyen**). Refer to the Starter kit for colours. Note down also what material you'd like them in (**en coton**, etc.). One example is done for you.

article	couleur	taille	tissu
des mouchoirs	blancs	grands	en coton

3 Prenez l'habitude

Get into the habit of jotting down your own shopping lists in French!

LISTENING PRACTICE

1   A quel étage se trouve..? (basic level)

What are the items announced? What floor will you find them on?

Write down the items against the correct floor

FLOOR	ITEM/S
basement	
ground floor	
1st Floor	
2nd Floor	
3rd Floor	
4th Floor	
5th Floor	

2 *Je cherche le rayon pour...* (basic level)

 On which floor will you find these departments? Write in the number/name of the floor against the department.

DEPARTMENT	FLOOR
Children's wear	
D-I-Y	
Food	
Handbags	
Men's wear	
Perfumes	
Records & cassettes	
Toys and games	
Women's wear	

VOCABULARIES

Basic vocabulary

KEY VERBS

accepter to accept		**peser** to weigh	
acheter to buy		**montrer** to show	
aider to help		**ouvrir** to open	
aimer to like		**payer** to pay	
avoir besoin de to need		**porter** to wear; carry	
coûter to cost		**préférer** to prefer	
demander to ask for		**prendre** to take	
devoir to have to		**remercier** to thank	
désirer to want		**prêter** to lend	
emporter to take away		**(se) servir** to serve	
essayer to try (on)		**signer** to sign	
faire la queue to queue up		**trouver** to find	
faire les courses to do the shopping		**vendre** to sell	
fermer to close		**voler** to steal	
mettre to put (on)		**vouloir** to want	

Shops

f	**alimentation** foodstore	m	**libre-service** self-service
m	**argent** money	m	**magasin** shop
	bon marché cheap	m	**marchand de fruits** fruiterer
f	**boucherie** butchers'	m	**marché.** market
f	**boulangerie** bakers'	f	**monnaie** change
f	**boutique** shop	f	**parfumerie** perfume shop
f	**caisse** cash desk, check out	f	**pâtisserie** cake shop
m	**centre commercial** commercial centre	f	**pharmacie** chemists
f	**charcuterie** delicatessen	m	**plats cuisinés** take away food
m	**choix** choice	f	**poissonnerie** fish shop
m	**client** customer	m	**prix** price
m	**coiffeur** hairdresser	f	**qualité** quality
f	**confiserie** sweetshop	f	**quincaillerie** ironmongers
f	**crèmerie** dairy	m	**rayon** shelf; department
f	**épicerie** grocers'	m	**rez de chaussée** ground floor
f	**erreur** mistake	f	**solde** sale
m	**étage** floor	f	**sorte** sort, kind
m	**grand magasin** department store	m	**sous-sol** basement
	gratuit free	m	**supermarché** supermarket
m	**hypermarché** hypermarket	m	**tabac** tobacconist
f	**librairie** bookshop	m	**vendeur** sales assistant

Goods, containers, and quantities

m	**ananas** pineapple		f	**légume** vegetable
f	**aspirine** aspirin		f	**lentilles** lentils
f	**baguette** loaf		m	**livre** book
f	**banane** banana		f	**magazine** magazine
m	**beurre** butter		m	**médicament** medicine
f	**boîte d'allumettes** box of matches		m	**moins** less
f	**boîte** box, tin		m	**morceau** piece
f	**boîtes de conserves** tinned food			**ni repris/ni échangé**
				no refunds or exchange
m	**bonbon** sweet		m	**oeuf** egg
f	**bouteille** bottle		m	**oignon** onion
m	**bricolage** do-it-yourself		m	**pain** bread
m	**cachet** rubber stamp; seal of approval		m	**paquet** packet
m	**cadeau** present		m	**parfum** perfume; flavour
m	**café** coffee		f	**pâte** pasta
f	**carotte** carrot		f	**pêche** peach
f	**carte** card			**petits pois** peas
f	**carte postale** postcard			**plus** more
f	**cerise** cherry			**plusieurs** several
m	**chou** cabbage		m	**poids** weight
f	**confiture** jam		f	**poire** pear
m	**crayon** pencil		f	**pomme de terre** potato
m	**demi-kilo** half a kilo		f	**pomme** apple
f	**dentifrice** toothpaste		m	**pot** jar; tub
m	**disque** record		m	**produit** frozen food item
f	**douzaine** dozen		m	**raisin** grape
f	**eau minérale** mineral water		m	**sac** bag
f	**enveloppe** envelope		m	**saucisson** salami
m	**filet** net; filet steak		m	**savon** soap
f	**fraise** strawberry		m	**sel** salt
m	**fromage** cheese		m	**shampooing** shampoo
m	**gâteau** cake		m	**stylo** pen
m	**grammes** grams		m	**sucre** sugar
m	**haricot** bean		m	**thé** tea
m	**jambon** ham		f	**tomate** tomato
m	**journal** newspaper		f	**tranche** slice
m	**jus de fruit** fruit juice		f	**viande** meat
m	**lait** milk		m	**vin rouge/blanc** red/white wine
f	**laitue** lettuce		m	**yaourt** yoghurt

Additional higher vocabulary

KEY VERBS

aimer mieux	to prefer	**faire du lèche- vitrines**	to window shop
aller	to go	**offrir**	to offer
avoir honte	to be ashamed	**plaire**	to please
compter	to count	**recevoir**	to get receive
conseiller	to advise	**réclamer**	to complain
dépenser	to spend	**rembourser**	to reimburse
distribuer	to distribute	**remplacer**	to replace
échanger	to exchange	**rendre**	to give back
enlever	to take off	**se plaindre**	to complain
envelopper	to wrap up	**se vendre**	to be sold
faire des achats	to do some shopping		

All settings

	à carreaux	checked (eg.material)	m	**loisir**	leisure
f	**augmentation**	increase	m	**maquillage**	make-up
f	**carte bancaire**	bankers' card	m	**paiement**	payment
m	**chariot**	trolley	m	**panier**	basket
	clair	light (of colour)	m	**papier à lettres**	writing paper
m	**commerçant**	shopkeeper	m	**patron**	boss
m	**compte**	an account	f	**promotion**	special offer
m	**comptoir**	counter	f	**provisions**	food
f	**couture**	sewing		**rayé**	striped
m	**crédit**	credit	f	**réclamation**	complaint
m	**escalier roulant**	escalator	f	**taxe valeur ajouté (TVA)**	V.A.T.
f	**étagère**	rack, display shelves	m	**tricot**	knitted jumper
f	**faute**	fault	f	**vente**	sale
	foncé	dark (of colour)	f	**vitrine**	shop window
m	**gérant**	manager	m	**voleur**	thief
m	**jouet**	toy			

Clothes and materials

	assez quite; enough			
m	**maillot de bain** swimming costume	m	**lourd** heavy	
m	**blouson** jacket (casual)	m	**manteau** coat	
m	**bonnet** bonnet, cap	f	**mode** fashion	
f	**bottes** boots	m	**mouchoir** handkerchief	
			neuf new	
m	**chapeau** hat			
f	**chaussette** sock	f	**paire** pair	
f	**chaussure** shoe	m	**pantalon** trousers	
f	**chemise de nuit** nightshirt nightdress	f	**pantoufles** slippers	
f	**chemise** shirt	m	**parapluie** umbrella	
			petit small	
m	**chemisier** blouse			
	cher expensive	f	**poche** pocket	
m	**collant** tights	f	**pointure** size (of shoes)	
m	**costume** suit	m	**pullover** sweater	
f	**couleur** colour	m	**pyjama** pyjamas	
		f	**robe de chambre** dressing gown	
	court short			
f	**cravate** tie	f	**robe** dress	
f	**écharpe** scarf	f	**sandale** sandal	
	étroit narrow	m	**short** shorts	
m	**gant** glove	m	**slip** underpants	
		m	**tablier** apron	
	grand big			
m	**imperméable** raincoat	f	**taille** size(of clothes)	
m	**jean** jeans		**trop** too; too much	
f	**jupe** skirt	f	**veste** jacket	
	large wide	m	**veston** jacket	
	léger light	m	**vêtements** clothes	

en bois made of wood   **en métal** made of metal
en coton made of cotton   **en nylon** made of nylon
en cuir made of leather   **en plastique** made of plastic
en laine made of wool   **en soie** made of silk

TOPIC AREA 5 SERVICES

SETTINGS

Using the Post Office and telephone. At the Bureau de Tourisme. Getting things repaired and cleaned; dealing with lost property.

KEY NOTIONS AND
FUNCTIONS
(refer to Starter Kit)

Location, availability. Number: cost, time, duration.
Countries and destination. Describing. Possibility, access, need.

KEY STRUCTURES
(refer to Grammar Section)

Gender and agreement.
Present and perfect tense of key verbs; **pouvoir, devoir, avoir besoin.**

CONTENTS

KEY SPEAKING TASKS

1 At the Post Office

ASK FOR

these stamps. Say the number you want of each, and the denomination.

eg. **Deux timbres à 2F 20**

FIND OUT

the cost of a letter/post-card to: England/ Ireland/Portugal/America.

where the telephone is

how to telephone GB/Spain/Canada

when the Post Office closes in the evening

if you can change money at this Office

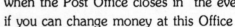

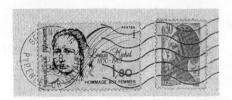

2 At the Tourist Information Centre

ASK FOR
a map of the area/a plan of the town/some leaflets on Paris
a list of hotels and campsites

ASK IF
they can recommend a good hotel in the town
there is a restaurant/campsite/toilet nearby

ASK
where the bank/Post Office/station is
how to get to the motorway/campsite/youth hostel/Hotel de la Paix
about tourist and sporting facilities

ASK IF
you can fish in the river
you can visit the castle/museum/today/tomorrow/Saturday
the Eiffel tower is open today

ASK HOW MUCH
it costs to go up the Eiffel tower/get into the castle/museum/swimming pool

ASK WHEN
the library/swimming pool/castle/sports centre/opens/closes

READING PRACTICE

1   Quelle boîte?

Which of these signs advises you of:

1. First-class post?

2. Collection times?

3. Local mail?

4. Second-class post?

5. Mail abroad?

6. Printed matter?

A	HORAIRES DES LEVEES
B	DEPARTEMENT
C	ETRANGER
D	IMPRIMES
E	TARIF NORMAL
F	TARIF REDUIT

Quel guichet pour..?

A	MANDATS
B	AFFRANCHISSEMENTS
C	TIMBRES DETAIL
D	PHILATELIE
E	COLIS
F	CHANGE

Which counter/window should you go to:

1. Get some stamps?

2. Change foreign money?

3. Get your mail weighed & stamped?

4. Send a parcel?

5. Buy a money-order?

6. Buy stamps for collection?

2 La Poste simplifie l'adresse

LA POSTE SIMPLIFIE L'ADRESSE

N'ÉCRIVEZ PLUS >

M. DUPONT
VOSNE ROMANÉE
21700 NUITS St GEORGES

MAIS ÉCRIVEZ >

M. DUPONT
21700 VOSNE ROMANÉE

Pour écrire dans 30.000 communes françaises, il fallait jusqu'à présent mentionner le nom de la commune de destination, le code postal et le bureau distributeur. Désormais, c'est plus simple: il suffit d'indiquer le code postal et le nom de la commune du destinataire.

LA POSTE ➤
BOUGEZ AVEC LA POSTE

EQVATEUR RCS PARIS B 304 457 917 DGP 01-89

Find the French for:-

1. Local sorting office.
2. District area.
3. Addressee.
4. Postal code.
5. What should you now omit when writing an address?

Petits conseils utiles

When should you dial:

1. 16, then 1, then 8 digits?

2. 8 digits only?

3. 16 followed by 8 digits?

Petits conseils utiles pour téléphoner

<u>De Paris ou de la région parisienne vers la province</u> : composer le 16 et les huit chiffres de votre correspondant.

Exemple : 16.83.00.00.00.

<u>De la province vers Paris/région parisienne</u> : composer le 16 puis l'indicatif (1) et les huit chiffres de votre correspondant.

Exemple : 16 (1) 46.51.01.11

<u>De province à province</u> : composer seulement les huit chiffres.

Exemple : 83.00.00.00

3 Information-services

1. What holiday period does this information relate to?

What are the services available on March 31 for the following?

Mark your answers as

- shut/not available
- open/available
- reduced
- additional

2. Banks

3. Department stores

4. Mail deliveries

5. Newspapers

6. Trains (local)

7. Trains (international)

8. Underground

PÂQUES
Les services ouverts ou fermés

PRESSE - Les quotidiens paraîtront normalement le lundi 31 mars.

BANQUES - Fermées du vendredi 28 mars à 12 heures (11 h 45 pour certaines), jusqu'au mardi 1 avril au matin.

BUREAUX DE POSTE - Pas de distribution de courrier à domicile les 30 et 31 mars. Seuls seront ouverts les bureaux fonctionnant le dimanche.

SNCF - Trains supplémentaires pour les départs grandes lignes les 30 et 31 mars. Pour le réseau banlieue, trafic réduit des dimanches et jours fériés.

RATP - Trafic réduit des dimanches et jours fériés les 30 et 31 mars

GRANDS MAGASINS - Tous fermés le lundi 31 mars.

Police-Secours
Pompiers
Gendarmerie
Hôtel de police
Hôpital Fleyriat
Medecin de garde
Taxis
Allocations Familiales
Assurance Maladie
A.N.P.E.

| E.D.F. | Renseignements |
| | Dépannages |

Mairie
Préfecture

| Téléphone | Renseignements |
| | Réclamations |

| S.N.C.F. | Renseignements |

Pour vos petites annonces
Voix de l'Ain
Pour votre publicité
Espace VA

Bloc-notes

You've hired a holiday cottage in France. The owners have left you a list of various phone numbers. Which of these services would you contact it you needed:

a. A doctor urgently
b. The fire brigade
c. To call a taxi
d. Information about trains
e. The Police (999)
f. Send a telegram
g. Place an advertisement in a paper
h. Get the electricity seen to.

4 Pressing de Paris; nettoyage

You need to get some dry-cleaning and laundry done.

1. How do they cost the laundry?
2. How long does it take?
3. If you brought the dry- cleaning in the morning,would it be ready the same day or the next?

What are all the items listed here?

NETTOYAGE	
jupe simple, non doublée	25 F
manteau	45 F
pantalon: homme, femme	23 F
pull à manches	18 F 50
robe simple, non doublée	29 F 50
veste, homme	35 F

5 Le nouveau télégramme

You're staying or travelling in France, and you need to send a telegram to cancel or confirm a reservation, meeting; to send greetings, etc.

1. You have access to a telephone - what number should you dial?

2. You have access to MINITEL - what number should you key in?

3. What information do you give before the text of the telegram?

4. You need to be sure your recipient **(le destinataire)** gets your message: how is this confirmed?

5. Six months later you need a copy of the telegram for your own reference. How do you get one?

**Mode d'emploi du
NOUVEAU TELEGRAMME**

Toutes les communications pour accéder par téléphone, par Minitel, par telex à ce service sont gratuites.

**Par Minitel: Faites le 36 56
Par téléphone: Faites le 36 55
Par telex: Faites le 214814**

A partir de n'importe quelle cabine publique avec une Carte Telecom. Par télécopie: Renseignez-vous au 36 55

**Pour toute demande d'information appelez le 36 55 Dictez (au téléphone) ou tapez (sur le clavier):
1. Vos propres coördonnées: nom, adresse, numéro de téléphoné.
2. Le nom, l'adresse, le numéro de téléphone, du telex ou de télécopie du destinataire.
3. Le texte du télégramme.**

Le prix vous est indiqué en fin de communication par Minitel ou telex... A l'arrivée le télégramme est transmis au destinataire par les moyens de télécommunications indiqués. En cas de non-réponse, l'appel est renouvelé et si cette nouvelle tentative s'avère infructueuse, le télégramme est remis par les moyens de la Poste.Dans tous les cas, le destinataire, reçoit une confirmation écrite immédiatement expédiée.Vous pouvez demander une copie du télégramme au moment du dépôt ou dans le délai d'un an après son émission. (Pas d'abonnement au service).

6 Ventes, locations, et dépannages.

A. Find the French for the following:-
1. sale
2. hire
3. repairs
4. heating
5. dry-cleaning
6. laundry
7. laundrette
8. locksmith's
9. household electrical goods
10. cobbler

B. Which shop/s would you go to:-
1. For car repairs?
2. Get some clothes cleaned?
3. Hire a bike?
4. Get a bag mended?
5. Take in some laundry?
6. Unblock a sink?
7. Mend an electric kettle?
8. Hire a video machine?
9. Do your own laundry?
10. Hire a country cottage?

7 Pas de vacances pour le Syndicat d'Initiative

PAS DE VACANCES POUR LE SYNDICAT D'INITIATIVE !

« Qu'est-ce qu'on peut visiter à Bourg ? ». Ce n'est pas une question pour jeu de l'été, mais celle la plus fréquemment posée par les visiteurs au Syndicat d'Initiative. Seconde au hit-parade : *« Où se loger dans la région ? »*. Avec des préférences pour les gîtes, la chambre d'hôte. Viennent ensuite les distractions, les plaisirs de la baignade ou de la table.

Il y a aussi ceux qui s'arrêtent pour signaler qu'on leur a volé leur argent ou demander où sont les fleurs de Bourg. Bref, tandis que les aoûtiens se bronzent, au Syndicat d'Initiative, on n'a pas le temps de penser aux vacances. Sinon à celle des autres...

Cent par jour

A mi-saison, c'est la satisfaction. *« Nos statistiques de juillet sont meilleures qu'en 87 »*, indi-que Martine Bannand, responsable. *« Il y a beaucoup d'étrangers, dont de nombreux Italiens et des Canadiens »*.

Durant ce mois-là quelque 2 960 personnes sont venues se renseigner au Syndicat d'Initiative, soit plus de cent par jour d'ouverture et 400 de plus qu'en 1987. Les Français sont très largement majoritaires (2 400). En tête des étrangers, les Anglais (159) qui ont doublé les Allemands (une centaine) et quelque 200 sujets de différentes nationalités parmi lesquelles de plus en plus d'Italiens et de Canadiens.

Difficile d'évaluer pour l'instant l'impact économique de ces visiteurs. Après une première quinzaine « calme », il semble que les hébergements traditionnels affichent complet. Seule certitude : les hôteliers ne sont pas plaints du manque de clientèle auprès du Syndicat d'Initiative qui regrette parfois de n'être pas mieux informé.

Un nouveau son et lumière

Autre motif de satisfaction pour le Syndicat d'Initiative : le succès des visites du Vieux Bourg et des « Son et Lumière » à Brou. *« On pensait que cela allait s'essouffler, mais pas du tout »*, constate Martine Bannand. Un exemple : le dernier « Son et Lumière » plafonnait à 233 personnes, ce qui oblige à dédoubler le spectacle. La visite du Vieux Bourg a été suivie par 170 auditeurs et une masse de promeneurs qui se sont joints au cortège...

Touristes français et étrangers sont les principaux clients de ces animations. *« Il y a aussi beaucoup de Burgiens qui y participent lorsqu'ils reçoivent des amis »*. Une manière originale de découvrir sa ville... *« Certains viennent de loin exprès »*.

Quant au nouveau rojet de « Son et Lumière » proposé par la ville de Bourg, il n'est pas certain qu'on puisse y assister cette année. Concocté par Gérard Authelain, il aura pour support trois écrans géants disposés à l'entrée de l'église de Brou et sur lesquels seront projetés des diapositives en fondu enchaîné. Il devrait permettre d'accueillir 200 à 300 personnes alors que celui du S.I. oblige à limiter chaque intervention à une centaine de visiteurs...

1. What are the first two things people ask at the SI. at Bourg?
2. What do the next three requests concern?
3. What kind of problem do they come to report?
4. From which two countries are visitors on the increase?
5. Which part of August was the busiest?
6. What are the two special attractions put on for visitors?
7. Who, apart from foreign and French tourists, have attended these attractions?
8. How does the town propose to increase the capacity for the attraction at the Eglise de Brou?

SPEAKING PRACTICE

1 Higher level role-play.

At this level you need to go beyond the informational-transactional items of language, as set out in the key speaking tasks. In addition to a thorough knowledge of basic vocabulary, you will need to be able to negotiate situations and inter-act with information given or new information. Situations at this level include:-

*   dealing with lost property: describing items lost, when & where
*   getting things repaired or cleaned: negotiating time needed and cost
*   using the Tourist Office more extensively: making travel arrangements & advance booking to other parts of France, using their computerized services; discussing your wants, their availability; making a choice on information given.
*   using the services of the PTT more extensively: sending parcels, greetings, telegrams, using the MINITEL (computerized services); making phone calls; changing (foreign) money.

However complicated the situations/role-play may appear, remember that the content (notions) of what you need to say, and the functions (the way you need to say it) remain essentially basic: such as numbers - for cost, time; descriptions - colour, material, size, likes and preferences, and so on.

Here are some questions/statements to make.

Je voudrais savoir s'il est possible de visiter/aller à/voir/réserver/prendre/ avoir/changer de	would like to know if I can...
J'ai perdu/égaré; je me suis trompé de	have lost/mislaid/made mistake
Vous pouvez me dire/m'indiquer s'il est possible de	can you tell me: possibility
combien de temps faudra-t-il	time needed
si ce sera plus cher/rapide/ pratique	more expensive/quicker/more useful
moins cher/rapide/pratique	less expensive/slower/less useful

ROLE-PLAYS (higher level).

At the end of a stay in Paris you have gone to the tourist office to enquire about other areas of France. The examiner will play the part of the receptionist.

1/2. Ask if they have information about other areas of France and answer the next question.

3. Tell the receptionist what you enjoy visiting.

4/5. When he/she suggests an area, say that you have never been there and ask what there is to see.

6. Ask him/her to recommend a place to stay.

7. Ask if you can get there by train.

(LEAG C 1988)

Situation	You are in a French Post Office. You want to send a parcel to England. It contains a birthday present for a friend. Your teacher will play the part of the counter assistant and will start the conversation.
Essential Information	Your friend's birthday is on May 24th and you want the present to arrive on time.
You must	- Say you want to send a parcel to England. - Ask how long it will take to get there. - Respond appropriately to what the counter assistant says. - Ask if it will cost much more.

(NEA Higher 1988)

You have lost your bag. You are now at the lost property office. The examiner will play the part of the employee.

1. Say that you have lost your bag this morning.
2. State the colour and what it's made of.
3. Reply that you think it was after your visit to the cathedral.
4. Explain that you didn't notice the time.
5. Say that you're worried and explain why.
6. Answer the employee's questions.
7. Ask what you should do to find it.

(LEAG C 1988)

At the Garage

When travelling in France the family car breaks down. You go to a garage to get help. Your teacher will play the part of the garage employee.

1. Say the car has broken down and ask if they do repairs.
2. Say where your car is.
3. Describe your car and give its registration number.

(Northern Ireland, higher 1988)

WRITING PRACTICE

1   Objets trouvés/perdus (basic level)

Note down the details of the following lost property:
WATCH BRIEFCASE JACKET SUITCASE CAMERA WALLET TRANSISTOR RING

One example is shown   - marks details not applicable.

désignation de l'article	bracelet
couleur	-
taille	moyenne
marque	-
particularités	en or
autres remarques	dessins fleurs
	inscription: DV
perdu le:	samedi 12 août
à/dans	bus No.37

2 Je pense avoir laissé (basic level)

Whilst staying at the **Hotel Les Pins** you lost:

a watch/toilet bag (trousse de toilette)/pair of shorts/ring/bracelet

Write a letter to the hotel describing the item, and giving other appropriate details - in the numbered blanks.

.... 1 .... 2 ....

           .... 3 ....
           Lors de mon séjour à l'hôtel Les Pins je pense y avoir laissé
.... 4 ...., **soit dans** .... 5 ...., **soit dans** .... 6 ....
Il s'agit de .... 7 ....; .... 8 ....
Vous pouvez me joindre à la Poste Restante de Rouen .... 9 ....
.... 10 ....

1.   Address the Management.
2.   Date of letter.
3.   Formal beginning.
4.   Name article.
5. and 6. Places where you think you might have lost article in the hotel.
7. and 8. Article + make/colour/material/special features.
9.   Until and give date.
10.   Thank them formally.

Finally; write the letter out from memory and in full.

LISTENING PRACTICE

1   Musée Claude Monet à Giverny (basic level)

1. Days open _____ to _____ .
2. Day shut _____
3. During months of _____ to _____ .
4. Open in morning from _____ to _____ .
5. In afternoon from _____ to _____ .
6. Garden open _____ .
7. Distance from Paris _____ .

2   Allo - SVP! (basic level)

Note down the phone numbers you are given for these places:

A. **Maison du tourisme**
B. **Piscine Olympique**
C. **Camping Municipal**
D. **Centre de Loisirs**
E. **Gare Routière**
F. **Casino**

3   Pour connaître la ville... (higher level)

Note down the details you are given:

1. What is held on Sunday mornings?
2. The guided tour is aboard what?
3. Which day is Market Day?
4. Where does it take place?
5. What kind of fair is there on Saturday?

VOCABULARIES

Basic vocabulary

KEY VERBS

appeler to call
chercher to look for
composer le numéro to dial the number
savoir to know
contacter to contact

décrocher le combiné to lift the receiver
devoir to have to
distribuer le courrier to deliver mail
écouter to listen to
entendre to hear

envoyer to send

mettre à la poste to post

payer au mot to pay by the word
poster to post
raccrocher to hang up
rappeler to call back
remplacer to replace

remplir to fill in
se rendre compte to realise
sonner to ring
téléphoner to telephone
toucher un mandat
  to cash a money order
vérifier to check

At the Post Office; using the telephone.

f   **adresse** address
m   **affranchissement** franking
m   **annuaire** telephone directory
f   **boîte aux lettres** letterbox
m   **bureau de poste** post office

f   **cabine téléphonique**
  telephone booth
f   **carte postale** postcard
m   **change** exchange
m   **colis** parcel
m   **coup de téléphone** telephone call

m   **courrier** mail
    de la part de on behalf of; from
    en PCV reverse charge
    étranger foreign
m   **facteur** postman

f   **fente** slot
m   **formulaire** form
m   **guichet** counter

m   **horaire des levées** collection times
m   **imprimés** printed matter
f   **lettre** letter
f   **lettre recommandée** registered letter
m   **mandat postal** postal order

    Minitel Minitel (computerised
      information service)
m   **numéro** number
    occupé engaged
f   **opératrice** operator
m   **paquet** parcel

    par avion by airmail
f   **pièce** coin
f   **poste** post office
m   **tarif** rate
f   **télécarte** phone card

f   **télégramme** telegram
m   **timbre poste** postage stamp
f   **tonalité** (dialling) tone

Additional higher vocabulary

KEY VERBS

appartenir	to belong	**oublier**	to forget
cambrioler	to burgle	**perdre**	to lose
casser	to break	**promettre**	to promise
compter	to want	**proposer**	to propose;suggest
déchirer	to tear	**prouver**	to prove
découvrir	to discover	**raccommoder**	to mend, repair
décrire	to describe	**réclamer**	to complain
disparaître	to disappear	**reconnaître**	to recognise
douter	to doubt	**refuser**	to refuse
échanger	to exchange	**rembourser**	to reimburse
emprunter	to borrow	**rendre**	to give back
faire nettoyer/ réparer to have cleaned/ repaired		**réparer**	to repair
fixer	to fix	**revenir**	to come back
garantir	to guarantee	**s'adresser**	to apply
laisser	to leave	**se plaindre**	to complain
laisser tomber	to drop	**se souvenir**	to remember
laver	to wash	**suggérer**	to suggest
marcher	to walk	**tomber en panne**	to break down
marquer	to mark	**voler**	to steal
nettoyer	to clean		

Getting things repaired and cleaned

f	**batterie**	battery		**malgré**	in spite of
m	**bouton**	button	*m*	**mécanicien**	mechanic
m	**bruit**	noise	*m*	**nettoyage à sec**	dry-cleaning
	capable	capable	*f*	**pièce de rechange**	spare part
f	**cordonnerie**	shoemaker's shop	*f*	**pile**	battery
	crevé	flat (tyre)	*m*	**plombier**	plumber
m	**dépannage**	breakdown service	*m*	**pneu**	tyre
m	**électricien**	electrician	*m*	**radiateur**	radiator
m	**embrayage**	clutch	*f*	**réclamation**	complaint
m	**état**	state, condition	*m*	**reçu**	receipt
m	**frein**	brake	*f*	**roue de secours**	spare tyre/wheel
f	**fuite**	leak		**satisfait**	satisfied
f	**lampe de poche**	torch	*f*	**sécurité**	safety
f	**laverie automatique**	launderette	*m*	**trou**	hole
f	**machine à laver**	washing machine	*f*	**vitesse**	speed; gear (of car)

Lost Property Office

f	**(mes) affaires** (my) things/ belongings		**(tout) neuf** (brand) new
m	**appareil** camera		**nulle part** nowhere
f	**bicyclette** bicycle	*m*	**parapluie** umbrella
m	**bureau des objets trouvés** lost property office		**partout** everywhere
m	**cambrioleur** burglar	*m*	**passeport** passport
m	**carnet de chèques** cheque book	*f*	**pièce d'identité** identity card
f	**ceinture** belt		**plein** full
f	**clé** key	*f*	**poche** pocket
	(mé)content (dis)pleased	*m*	**porte-feuille** wallet
f	**couleur** colour	*m*	**porte-monnaie** purse
	déçu disappointed	*f*	**récompense** reward
	étroit narrow		**rond** round
f	**fiche** form	*m*	**sac à dos** rucksack
f	**forme** shape	*m*	**sac à main** handbag
	furieux angry		**solide** solid; sound
	(mal)heureux (un)happy	*f*	**taille** size
	hier yesterday		**une sorte de** a sort of
	il s'agit de it's about	*f*	**valise** suitcase
m	**machin** gadget	*m*	**vélomoteur** moped
f	**malchance** bad luck		**vide** empty
f	**marque** make		**vieux** old
f	**montre** watch	*m*	**vol** theft
m	**mouchoir** handkerchief	*m*	**voleur** thief
	moyen medium;average		

TOPIC AREA 6　FOOD AND DRINK

SETTINGS

Eating out in France; understanding menus; choosing what and where to eat.

KEY NOTIONS AND
FUNCTIONS
(refer to Starter Kit)

Attracting attention. Availability and non-availability; expressing wants, preferences, likes and dislikes. Number, cost.

KEY STRUCTURES
(refer to Grammar Section)

Key verbs; commands. Negatives; partitives.

CONTENTS

KEY SPEAKING TASKS

1   Menu cafetaria

This is the menu on a French boat between Newhaven and Dieppe; not all the items are displayed, and some are not available. The crew speak French only!

1.   Check that you know what to say in French.
2.   Ask if they've got what you want.
3.   Be ready to order something else if it's not available.
4.   Ask how much each item costs.
5.   Order several things to eat and drink (for friends as well as yourself).

Look back to the *Starter Kit* on availability, cost.

MENU CAFETARIA

ITEM
All day breakfast
Sausages, beans + chips
Fish, chips, peas + lemon
Scampi, chips + lemon (basket)
Dish of the day
Nicoise salade
Melon
Raw vegetables
Ham salad
Chicken salad
Fruit yoghurts
Chocolate fudge cake
Blackcurrant gateau
Cheese and biscuits
Bread roll
Butter
Sauces
Jam/Marmelade
Jaffa cakes
Fruit (orange - apple)
Cereals (inc.milk)
Coca Cola, Diet Coke, Fanta, Lilt
Mineral water
"Long Life" Beer
Lager beer
Flavoured milks
Red/white wine (—)
Apple/orange juice
Fresh milk
Coffee + cream
Tea & milk

---

2 Quel parfum?

Order a double-cornet; two different flavours.

What should you say (...)?

- **Qu'est-ce que vous prenez?**
- **(...)**
- **Quel parfum?**
- **(... et ....)**
- **Ah ! je regrette, il ne reste plus de ce parfum-là!**
- **(....)**

Ask the price!
Repeat the order, ask for different flavours.

3 Qu'est-ce que vous avez comme..?

Find out if they've got any other sandwiches and fruit-juices other than the ones marked.

Order something to eat; and a soft drink.

GLACIER
SALON DE THE

GLACES
parfums du jour

PRIX CORNETS
Simple F,05 Double 49,05 Triple 16,05

VANILLE
CAFE
CHOCOLAT
PRALINE
FRAMBOISE
CASSIS
FRUITS DE LA PASSION
NOIX DE COCO
BANANE
POIRE
CITRON

SYNDICAT GENERAL DE L'INDUSTRIE HOTELIERE DE LA GIRONDE

- TARIF -

DES BOISSONS ET DENREES LES PLUS COURAMMENT SERVIES

Dénomination Des Boissons et Denrées	Prix Comptoir Prix Net	Prix TERASSE S. Compris
	PRIX	PRIX
LA TASSE DE CAFÉ NOIR	3,50 F	3,50 F
Un Demi de Bière à la pression	6 F	7 F
UN FLACON DE BIERE KR ORD	7 F	8 F
UN JUS DE FRUIT ANANAS	7 F	8 F
UN SODA ORANGINA	7 F	8 F
UNE EAU MINERALE VL PERRIER Plate ou Gazeuse	6,50 F	7,50 F
UN APERITIF ANISE PASTIS 51	7 F	8 F
UN PLAT DU JOUR		
UN SANDWICH SAUCISSON	7 F	7 F

READING PRACTICE

1 Faites le tour du monde

Faites le tour du monde des petits déjeuners

Russe
thé fort, dilué avec beaucoup de lait
petits pains de seigle
poisson fumé
blinis : (petites crêpes).

Anglais
thé au lait
marmelade
oeuf au plat + bacon
toasts.

Allemand
pain de seigle ou de sarrazin
beurre,
compote
fromage en lamelles.

Pays-Bas
pain complet
jambon
entremets à base de lait
jus de fruit.

Etats-Unis
jus de fruit
café
flocons de céréales au lait
french toast: (pain perdu)

---

1. What are the countries whose breakfasts are given as examples?
2. Which countries have tea for breakfast?
3. Which countries don't have a hot drink?
4. Which countries give meat a miss?
5. What item do they all have in common?
6. Find out the meaning of **pain de seigle, pain de sarrazin, pain complet**

2 Premier plaisir de la journée

LE PETIT DÉJEUNER
PREMIER PLAISIR DE LA JOURNÉE

Un petit déjeuner complet:
- **permet de passer une bonne matinée sans fatigue, ni "creux de 11 heures"**

- **permet de prendre un repas moins lourd et copieux à midi et évite donc la somnolence de l'après-midi provoquée par une digestion difficile.**

aliments essentiels

- **Laitage: source de calcium et de protéines qui permettent de construire, entretenir et renouveler les tissus du corps**

- **Pain ou céréales: source de glucides complexes (amidon) qui fournissent de l'énergie lentement distribuée dans l'organisme.**

---

1. Give three reasons why a proper breakfast is advised here.
2. Give three reasons why protein is important to body tissue.
3. What is the function of bread or cereals?

3 Choisir un menu

MENU Nº 2

Mousse de foie de volaille
au Porto

★★★

Carré de porc vigneronne
aux deux purées

★★★

Fromage du pays

★★★

Bavaroise framboise

Prix: **65,00 f**

MENU Nº 3

Terrine campagnarde
"Maison" en gelée

★★★

Jambon braisé des gourmets

★★★

Pommes rissolées

★★★

Fromage du pays

★★★

Miroir cassis

Prix: **72,00 f**

MENU Nº 4

Salade bourguignonne

★★★

Fricassée de volaille
à la bourguignonne

★★★

Tagliatelles au beurre

★★★

Fromage du pays

★★★

Sorbet cassis

Prix: **79,00 f**

MENU Nº 5

Rosette de canard pistachée
en gelée

★★★

Bœuf bourguignon

★★★

Pommes paysannes

★★★

Fromage du pays

★★★

Framboisine

Prix: **89,00 f**

Which menu has the following as the main course?
A.   steak
B.   beef casserole
C.   chicken
D.   ham
E.   pork
F.   What fruit flavour are the desserts on each menu?
G.   What do all the menus have in common?

MENU Nº 6

Jambon persillé "Maison"

★★★

Filet mignon à la crème de ciboulette

★★★

Gratin Dauphinois

★★★

Fromage du pays

★★★

Poème orange

Prix: **105,00 f**

4 La Jonquière

1. Which part of the menu should you look at to find out what meat dishes they have?
2. And fish?
3. How many courses are there on the 59 F 50 menu? How many do you get?
4. What's on the children-only menu?
5. What will you find written on the slate (**l'ardoise**)?
6. What do you get free?

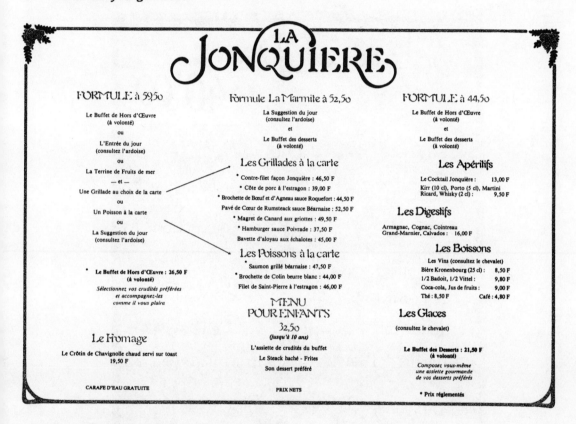

LA JONQUIÈRE

FORMULE à 59,50

Le Buffet de Hors d'Œuvre
(à volonté)
ou
L'Entrée du jour
(consultez l'ardoise)
ou
La Terrine de Fruits de mer
— et —
Une Grillade au choix de la carte
ou
Un Poisson à la carte
ou
La Suggestion du jour
(consultez l'ardoise)

* Le Buffet de Hors d'Œuvre : 26,50 F
(à volonté)
*Sélectionnez vos crudités préférées
et accompagnez-les
comme il vous plaira*

Le Fromage

Le Crotin de Chavignolle chaud servi sur toast
19,50 F

CARAFE D'EAU GRATUITE

Formule La Marmite à 52,50

La Suggestion du jour
(consultez l'ardoise)
et
Le Buffet des desserts
(à volonté)

Les Grillades à la carte

* Contre-filet façon Jonquière : 46,50 F
* Côte de porc à l'estragon : 39,00 F
* Brochette de Bœuf et d'Agneau sauce Roquefort : 44,50 F
Pavé de Cœur de Rumsteack sauce Béarnaise : 52,50 F
* Magret de Canard aux griottes : 49,50 F
* Hamburger sauce Poivrade : 37,50 F
Bavette d'aloyau aux échalotes : 45,00 F

Les Poissons à la carte

* Saumon grillé béarnaise : 47,50 F
* Brochette de Colin beurre blanc : 44,00 F
Filet de Saint-Pierre à l'estragon : 46,00 F

MENU POUR ENFANTS
32,50
(Jusqu'à 10 ans)

L'assiette de crudités du buffet
Le Steack haché - Frites
Son dessert préféré

PRIX NETS

FORMULE à 44,50

Le Buffet de Hors d'Œuvre
(à volonté)
et
Le Buffet des desserts
(à volonté)

Les Apéritifs

Le Cocktail Jonquière :   13,00 F
Kirr (10 cl), Porto (5 cl), Martini
Ricard, Whisky (2 cl) :   9,50 F

Les Digestifs

Armagnac, Cognac, Cointreau
Grand-Marnier, Calvados :   16,00 F

Les Boissons

Les Vins (consultez le chevalet)
Bière Kronenbourg (25 cl) :   8,50 F
1/2 Badoit, 1/2 Vittel :   9,80 F
Coca-cola, Jus de fruits :   9,00 F
Thé : 8,50 F   Café : 4,80 F

Les Glaces

(consultez le chevalet)

Le Buffet des Desserts : 21,50 F
(à volonté)
*Composez vous-même
une assiette gourmande
de vos desserts préférés*

* Prix réglementés

SPEAKING PRACTICE

1 Je vais prendre

1. What will you ask for if you wanted only starters and dessert?
2. Steak?
3. Kebabs?
4. Cheese on toast?
5. Ask for some mineral water.
6. Ask for the bill!

READING PRACTICE

5 Salade et dessert

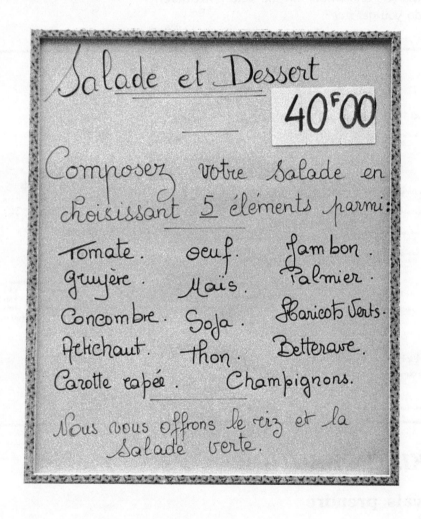

1.   Check that you know what all the items are.
2.   What do you get for 40 francs?
3.   How many items are you allowed?
4,   What - if anything - do you get free?
5.   Which items should you avoid if you don't like fish or meat?

6 Cadre et spécialités

RESTAURANTS.

Réf. Plan	Nom - Adresse - Téléphone	Fermeture		Heure limite service	Nb de couverts	Spécialités	Cadre
		hebdo.	annuelle				
P 17	RÉSERVE RIMBAUD - 820, avenue de St-Maur Quartier des Aubes - 67.72.52.53 ★★★★	Dim. soir Lundi	2 / 15 Janvier	14 h 22 h	55	Croquettes du Lez Gigot de mer aux herbes de garrigue	Terrasse en bord de rivière
J 11	LA CLOSERIE - HÔTEL MÉTROPOLE 3, rue Clos René - 67.58.11.22 ★★★	Non	Non	14 h 15 22 h 15	80	En fonction des saisons	Salle de style fin XIXᵉ
G 13	ISADORA - 6, rue du Petit Scel 67.66.25.23	Sam. midi Dim.	Non	14 h 21 h 30	47	Cuisine traditionnelle et moderne - Poissons	Voutes XIIIᵉ Style 1900 Fleurs naturelles
HP Y 10	LE MAS - MICHEL LOUSTAU - Route de Vauguières (Rond point Richter - Route de Mauguio) - 67.65.52.27	Dim. soir Lundi	15 / 01 15 / 02	14 h 22 h	60	Cuisine selon saison	Mas languedocien Terrasse d'été
G 13	LE MENESTREL - Impasse Perrier (Place de la Préfecture) - 67.60.62.51	Dim. Lundi	1-15/06 25/12 au 10/01	13 h 30 21 h 45	90	Formule à 95 F	Halle aux grains XIIIᵉ
L 13	LOU PAIROL - Hôtel Altea Antigone Le polygone - 67.64.65.66	Sam. Midi Dim.	20/12 05/01	14 h 22 h	50	Aumônière de ris de veau et langouste	Moderne
F 12	LE ROLLIN - 11, bd Ledru-Rollin (5mn de la Comédie) - 67.60.47.50 ★	Non	Non	13 h 45 22 h 30	80	Nombreuses spécialités et cuisine traditionnelle	Rustique
I 16	LE VIEIL ECU - 1, rue des Ecoles Laïques 67.66.39.44	Dim.	Fév.	14 h 30 23 h 30	70	Cochon de lait Spécialités du Gers	Ancienne chapelle du XVIᵉ

Which restaurant/s can you choose from if you wanted:-

1. Classic French cooking?
2. A variety of specialities to choose from?
3. A fixed-price menu?
4. A choice of fish specialities?
5. Sit out in the open on a warm summer evening?
6. Be in an historic, old, setting?
7. Which restaurants are closed over Christmas?
8. Which restaurants are open all year round?

7 Les fruits de la Vallée du Rhône

myrtilles = bilberries

> **Le site favorable de la Vallée du Rhône est certainement un facteur primordial pour la production importante de fruits de qualité exceptionnelle. L'ensemble de ces fruits, à noyau (abricots, pêches), à pépins (pommes, poires), ou fruits rouges (cerises, fraises) a acquis une réputation mondiale.**
>
> **Le printemps dans la Vallée du Rhône, la floraison des cerisiers du Jarez dans la Loire, des pêchers de la Vallée de l'Eyrieux en Ardèche, site de Mirmande dans la Drôme sont des spectacles inoubliables.**
>
> **Les myrtilles, fameuses baies sauvages poussent en altitude dans les bois du massif du Pilat et les monts du Forez. Elles se récoltent de fin juillet au 15 août.**

Why have these been paired?
1. Apricots and peaches.
2. Apples and pears.
3. Cherries and strawberries.
4. What breath-taking sight takes place, and when, in the valleys of the Loire and the Ardèche?
5. In what kind of country should you go to pick bilberries?
6. When?

8 Lentilles: conseils et informations

What are the suggestions for:-
1. Rinsing?
2. Soaking?
3. Cooking?
4. Portions?
5. Serving?

What are:-
6. The advantages of using a pressure cooker?
7. The nutritional ingredients in lentils?

WRITING PRACTICE

1   Les menus de la semaine (basic level)

1.   Write out what you had for supper yesterday, as a menu ...
2.   And for lunch - in school/canteen ...
3.   Sunday lunch, supper.

2   Menu de fête (basic level)

Make a menu for a 'typical' English Christmas dinner (or any other celebration).

3   Liste - courses à faire (basic level)

Write out your shopping lists in French.

LISTENING PRACTICE

1   Râpées de pommes de terre (basic level)

 Here is a simple, filling dish. What are the instructions?
Fill in the blanks.

1.   Peel and grate ....
2.   Drain them .... (how long?)
3.   Put into ....
4.   Break eggs and ....
5.   Add .... and ....
6.   Cook with ....
7.   for ....(how long) each side.
8.   Serve ....

2 Potée bretonne (basic level)

Tick the ingredients this dish contains.

cabbage	
cauliflower	
carrots	
leeks	
potatoes	
sausage	
meat	

VOCABULARIES

Basic vocabulary

KEY VERBS

adorer   to love
manger   to eat
aimer   to like
nettoyer   to clean
avoir faim/soif   to be hungry/thirsty

passer   to pass
préférer   to prefer
boire   to drink
prendre   to take; have (a meal)
choisir   to choose
commander   to order

préparer   to prepare
coûter   to cost
recommander   to recommend
désirer   to want
servir   to serve

détester   to hate
trouver   to find
donner   to give
vouloir   to want
goûter   to taste

Food and drink

m   **abricot**   apricot
m   **agneau**   lamb
m   **ananas**   pineapple
m   **artichaut**   artichoke
m   **assiette anglaise**   plate of cold meats

f   **banane**   banana
m   **beurre**   butter
f   **bière**   beer
m   **biftek**   steak
m   **boeuf**   beef

f   **boisson**   drink
m   **café crème**   white coffee
m   **canard**   duck
f   **carotte**   carrot
f   **cerise**   cherry

m   **champignon**   mushroom
     chaud   hot
m   **chocolat**   chocolate
m   **chou**   cabbage
m   **chou-fleur**   cauliflower

m   **cidre**   cider
m   **citron pressé**   fresh lemon drink
m   **concombre**   cucumber
f   **confiture**   jam
m   **côte de porc**   rib of pork

m   **jambon**   ham
m   **jus de fruit**   fruit juice
m   **lait**   milk
m   **lapin**   rabbit
f   **légume**   vegetable

f   **limonade**   lemonade
m   **maquereau**   mackerel
m   **morceau**   piece
f   **moules**   mussels
f   **noix**   walnut

m   **oeuf**   egg
m   **oignon**   onion
m   **pain**   bread
f   **pâtisserie**   cakes, pastries
f   **pêche**   peach

m   **petit déjeuner**   breakfast
m   **petit pois**   peas
m   **pique-nique**   picnic
m   **plat du jour**   dish of the day
f   **poire**   pear

m   **poireau**   leak
m   **poisson**   fish
f   **pomme de terre**   potato
f   **pomme**   apple
m   **porc**   pork

m	**crabe** crab	m	**potage** soup
f	**crêpe** pancake	m	**poulet** chicken
f	**crevettes** shrimps	f	**prune** plum
m	**croque- monsieur**	f	**quiche lorraine**
	toasted ham & cheese sandwich		egg,bacon (& cheese) flan
f	**crudités** raw vegetables	m	**raisin** grape
m	**déjeuner** lunch	m	**riz** rice
m	**dîner** dinner	m	**rôti** roast
f	**eau minérale** mineral water	m	**saucisson** salami
m	**épinard** spinach	m	**sel** salt
m	**filet de sole** fillet of sole	f	**soupe** soup
f	**fraise** strawberry	m	**sucre** sugar
f	**framboise** raspberry	f	**tarte** tart
f	**frites** chips	f	**terrine** (chef's) paté
	froid cold	m	**thé** tea
m	**fromage** cheese	f	**tomate** tomato
m	**fruits de mer** sea food	f	**tranche** slice
m	**gâteau** cake	f	**truite** trout
f	**glace** ice cream	f	**vanille** vanilla
m	**goût** taste	m	**veau** veal
f	**groseille** gooseberry	f	**viande** meat
m	**haricot vert** green bean	m	**vin** wine
f	**huile** oil	m	**vinaigre** vinegar
f	**huîtres** oysters	m	**yaourt** yoghurt

Note   for adjectives describing food, refer to the Starter Kit

Eating out: at the café, restaurant, bar, brasserie, bistro, buffet

f	**à point** medium (meat)		**(de la) maison** house-special
	addition bill	f	**note** bill
	assez quite; enough	f	**odeur** smell
	bien cuit well done(meat)	m	**patron** boss
	bon good	m	**plat** dish
	bon appétit! enjoy your meal!	f	**pourboire** tip
f	**bouteille** bottle	m	**quart** quarter
f	**carte** menu list	m	**repas** meal
	compris included	m	**restaurant** restaurant
m	**demi** half		**saignant** rare (meat)
	en sus extra		**sans** without
	encore more; again		**seul** alone
f	**entrée** entree	f	**spécialité** speciality
m	**garçon** waiter	f	**tasse** cup
m	**hors-d'oeuvre** hors-d'oeuvre	f	**toilette** toilet
	menu (à 65 francs etc.)	m	**verre** glass
	(fixed price) menu		

Additional higher vocabulary

KEY VERBS

apporter	to bring	**inviter**	to invite
apprécier	to appreciate	**offrir**	to offer
approuver	to approve	**plaire**	to please
avoir envie de	to feel like	**protester**	to protest
désapprouver	to disapprove	**régler l'addition**	to settle the bill
féliciter	to congratulate	**se mettre en colère**	to get angry
		se plaindre	to complain

All settings

m	**apéritif**	aperitif		f	**moitié**	half
	appétissant	appetising		f	**moutarde**	mustard
f	**bière pression**	draught beer		m	**mouton**	mutton
	ça suffit	that's enough		m	**pichet**	jug, pitcher
f	**carte de crédit**	credit card			**piquant**	spicy, strong
f	**carte des vins**	wine list		m	**poivre**	pepper
m	**choix**	choice		m	**prix net**	all inclusive price
	complètement	completely			**salé**	salty
m	**couvert**	cover charge			**satisfait**	satisfied
	égal	equal		m	**serveur**	waiter
	entièrement	entirely		f	**serveuse**	waitress
f	**erreur**	mistake			**sorte**	sort, kind
f	**félicitations**	congratulations			**varié**	various
	inadmissible	unacceptable		f	**vinaigrette**	french dressing

TOPIC AREA 7　　HEALTH, WELFARE AND EMERGENCY SERVICES

SETTINGS	Identifying and talking about minor ailments, aches, pains and injuries. Using the pharmacist, doctor. Recognising emergency services in France.
KEY NOTIONS AND FUNCTIONS *(refer to Starter Kit)*	Identifying aches, pains, hurt, cuts. Finding advice, availability. Describing time, duration, frequency. Expressing wants and needs.
KEY STRUCTURES *(refer to Grammar Section)*	Perfect tense of reflexive verbs. Direct object pronouns. Use of **depuis**.

CONTENTS

169

KEY SPEAKING TASKS

For this topic, at basic & higher level, you need to be completely familiar with the **avoir mal à** expressions in French, where English uses a variety of different expressions for pain, hurt, discomfort, sick, ache etc.

1 Identifying aches and pains

Refer to the *Vocabulary List* - as needed - and pick out the expressions you need to identify:

a headache

earache

something wrong with an eye

stomachache

toothache.

sore throat

feeling sick

a painful knee

backache

2 Identifying cuts, burns, stings, accidents

Complete the following:

Je me suis coupé le/la.................................... (finger; knee; hand; leg....)

Je me suis brûlé le/la.................................... (hand; foot, back; neck....)

Je me suis fait piqué par un/une................... (wasp; bee; ant; insect....)

Je me suis fait mal à la/au............................ (elbow; knee; back; ankle....)

3 Expressing want/need

Complete the following:

Je voudrais, je cherche............................ (sticking plaster; aspirin; tablets; cough

Il me faut... mixture; drops; cream; capsules)

4 Asking about availability of medicines/for advice

Complete the following:-

Qu'est-ce que vous avez pour.......................? (a cough; a fever; a pain;'flu;

Qu'est-ce que vous conseillez pour.............? a cold; sun-burn; a sting)

5 Finding out application, and dosage, of medicine.

Learn these expressions:

Comment est-ce que je le/la * prends?	How do I take it?
Comment est-ce que je le/la * mets?	How do I put/use it?
Combien de fois par jour je le/la * prends? je le/la * mets?	How often do I take/use it a day?

* le: le sirop
  la: la crème

6 Identifying time: when, how long ago; duration; of ailment

Learn these phrases:.

WHEN
(C'était) ce matin/hier/la semaine dernière...

HOW LONG AGO
Il y a 2,3 jours,/quelques jours/une semaine/longtemps...

DURATION
J'ai mal/je suis enrhumé/j'ai une température:-
depuis hier/depuis quelque temps/depuis quelques jours/depuis une semaine/depuis toujours/depuis je ne sais pas...

READING PRACTICE

1 Posologie, présentation

This is a COMPOSITE OF VARIOUS MEDICATIONS: how to take, what to avoid, and so on.

INDICATIONS	POSOLOGIE	PRESENTATION	PRECAUTIONS
1 douleurs musculaires	avaler	boîte	NE PAS LAISSER A LA PORTEE D'ENFANTS
2 névralgies dentaires	ne pas avaler	crème	EVITER LES EXPOSITIONS AU SOLEIL
3 états infectieux de l'oreille	usage externe	flacon	NE PAS DEPASSER LES POSOLOGIES INDIQUEES
4 brûlures	prendre après les repas	sachet	NE PAS UTILISER DE FACON PROLONGEE
5 piqûres d'insectes	étendre la crème	gouttes	NE PAS ABUSER DES BOISSONS ALCOOLISEES
6 diarrhées	masser légèrement	pansements	NE PAS UTILISER SUR LES LESIONS INFECTEES
7 règles douloureuses	dissoudre dans le l'eau	comprimés	
8 toux sèches	réchauffer	gélules	
9 maux de gorge		comprimés dragéifiés/ dragées	
10		suppositoires	
11		sirop	

Which of these headings should you look at to find out:-

1. What *FORM* the medication takes?
2. How to *TAKE/USE* the medication?
3. What to *AVOID* during the medication?
4. The *SYMPTOMS* for which it is prescribed.
5. What are *ALL THE SYMPTOMS* listed?
6. What are the *INSTRUCTIONS* for taking/using a medication?
7. What *CONTAINER* or *FORM* do the various medications come in?
8. What are all the *WARNINGS* listed when taking a medication?

2 Premiers soins

SACHEZ QUOI FAIRE

VOUS DEVEZ QUELQUEFOIS PORTER ASSISTANCE A VOTRE ENTOURAGE.

PIQURES

OTER si possible le dard. **DESINFECTER** soigneusement le point de la   piqûre **SURVEILLER** pendant quelques heures la personne pour   intervenir en cas de réaction allergique

COUPS - HEMATOMES

DECONGESTIONNER rapidement avec un spray réfrigérant local pour limiter l'apparition de l'oedème ou de l'hématome

FAIRE PRENDRE un produit contre la douleur

ENTORSES

APPLIQUER localement un liquide froid

RECOUVRIR par une pommade sans masser

IMMOBILISER par une contention adhésive (bandage)

What advice does this first-aid leaflet give for dealing with:-

1. Insect bites?
2. Bruises?
3. Sprains?

3 Allo-secours

Which of the following emergency services would you contact in the following situations

1.	Need for an all-night chemists?
2.	A serious burns case?
3.	To call a doctor?
4.	The fire brigade?
5.	To find the lost property office?
6.	Suspected explosives?
7.	Children's specialists?
8.	Old peoples' specialists?
9.	Police matter?
10.	Toxic substances?
11.	Loss of cheque book?
12.	To call an ambulance?

ALLO-SECOURS

Police Secours

Pompiers
Ambulances
Brûlures graves
Centre anti-poison
Objets trouvés
Perte chéquiers
Pharmacies ouvertes
S.O.S. Explosifs
S.O.S. Médecins
S.O.S. Petite enfance
S.O.S. 3 âge

4 Offrez votre sang (higher level)

This is a leaflet you might find on your car windscreen!

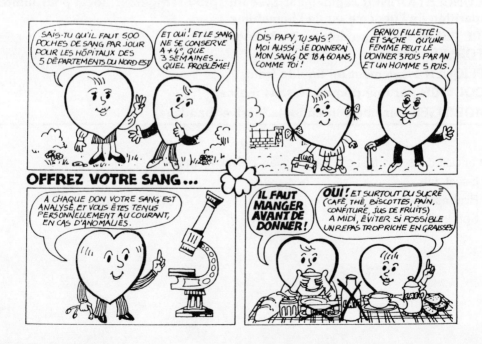

1. According to the leaflet, how often can you be a blood-donor if you are a man? a woman?
2. What three pieces of advice does the leaflet give about food and drink before you volunteer to give blood?
3. What do you think is the significance of 'Grandfather Heart'?
4. What is the purpose of including a microscope in the cartoon?
5. What sort of attitudes do the children display in the cartoon?
6. Why do you think that very young children are being targeted in this leaflet?

5 Vivez mieux la ... (higher level)

The Government leaflet on the following page gives some practical advice on how to enjoy your holiday in France, without coming to grief.

Read it, and pick out the main points under 4 headings:-

A. Advice common to both types of holiday (5 items).
B. Advice specific to seaside holidays (3 items).
C. Advice specific to mountain holidays (2 items).
D. What to do if in distress (1 item each holiday area).

VIVEZ MIEUX LA MER!

Le sport en vacances, c'est important. Autant le pratiquer dans d'excellentes conditions. La meilleure manière de mieux vivre la mer, c'est de bien la connaître. Voici quelques conseils. Suivez-les bien. Vous profiterez pleinement de vos vacances :

● Avant vos premières activités nautiques, mettez votre corps "au point" par une remise en forme.

● Après un bain de soleil, entrez progressivement dans l'eau, aspergez-vous la nuque et la poitrine.

● Un repas léger autorise la baignade si la température de l'eau dépasse 20°C.

● A la mer, en rivière ou sur un lac, restez dans les zones surveillées ou spécialement aménagées.

● Méfiez-vous des "hauts fonds" et des courants dangereux.

● Vérifiez le bon état de votre bateau, de votre planche ou engin nautique. Vos équipements de secours et de sécurité doivent être opérationnels.

● Renseignez-vous sur les conditions météo. Consultez les répondeurs automatiques des stations météo.

● Evitez de partir seul.

● Ne surestimez pas vos forces.

● Sur un matelas pneumatique ou avec une planche à voile, attention au vent de terre qui vous éloigne du rivage; en cas de fatigue restez sur votre planche à voile, ne rentrez jamais à la nage.

VIVEZ MIEUX LA MONTAGNE!

Le sport en vacances, c'est important. Autant le pratiquer dans d'excellentes conditions. La meilleure manière de mieux vivre la montagne, c'est de bien la connaître. Voici quelques conseils. Suivez-les bien. Vous profiterez pleinement de vos vacances :

● Mettez votre corps "au point" par une remise en forme avant d'attaquer vos premiers parcours en montagne.

● Prenez connaissance du trajet et de ses difficultés.

● Ne surestimez pas vos forces.

● Renseignez-vous sur l'évolution des conditions météo. Consultez les répondeurs automatiques à votre disposition dans toutes les stations.

● Evitez de partir seul ; indiquez votre itinéraire et votre heure de retour à un proche.

● Prévoyez un petit ravitaillement (eau et fruits secs) et des vêtements chauds et imperméables.

● Vérifiez le bon état de votre équipement. Choisissez des chaussures bien adaptées.

● Respectez le milieu naturel. Attention aux incendies de forêt.

● Souvenez-vous du signal de détresse (les bras levés formant un Y avec le corps).

SPEAKING PRACTICE

1   Role play: past papers (higher level)

During a holiday in France you fall from a bicycle and badly graze your knee. You go to a chemist's shop for some ointment and advice.
The role of the chemist will be played by the examiner.

1.   Say that you have hurt your knee. 2.   Explain how it happened. 3,   Ask for some antiseptic cream. 4.   Say which one you want. 5.   Ask if you should put on a plaster.

(MEG Higher 1. 1988)

SITUATION	You are in a hospital in France. You are talking to a doctor and explaining what your symptons are. Your teacher will play the part of the doctor and will start the conversation.
ESSENTIAL INFORMATION	You hurt your head when you fell at the swimming pool this morning.
YOU MUST	Tell the doctor you are not feeling well. Explain that you have hurt your head. Respond appropriately to what the doctor says. Ask if you have to stay in hospital.

(NEA Higher 1988)

You feel ill whilst on holiday and have gone to the local doctor's surgery. The examiner will play the part of the doctor.

1.   Apologise for not having an appointment. 2.   Tell the doctor that you are on holiday in the town. 3.   When asked about symptoms, say what is wrong. 4.   Answer the doctor's question about the previous day. 5.   Ask if he/she can give you a prescription. 6.   Find out where the nearest chemist is. 7.   Ask if you have to come back.

(LEAG C 1988)

WRITING PRACTICE

1. Je me porte bien/mal (higher level)

There is no genuinely authentic situation where you would need to write anything in French in this Topic Area purely for its own sake. There are however many occasions - in other situations, Topic areas - where you might well include a sentence or two on your state of health, well being, illness or accident; or ask the same - in writing - of your correspondent.

The following expressions are useful in writing; learn them, adapt them to your particular circumstances.

1.	Je me porte bien - et toi?	1.	I'm well, how about you?
2.	J'espère que tu vas bien.	2.	I hope you are well.
3.	Je vais bien, et ma famille aussi.	3.	I'm fine, family too.
4.	Comment vas-tu?	4.	How are you?
5.	Je suis malade.	5.	I'm ill.
6.	J'ai de la température/fièvre.	6.	I've got a temperature.
7.	Ce n'est pas grave.	7.	It's not serious.
8.	J'ai la grippe depuis samedi.	8.	I've had flu since Saturday.
9.	Je ne peux pas sortir.	9.	I can't go out.
10.	Je suis enrhumé - j'ai un rhume.	10.	I've got a cold.
11.	Je me sens tout le temps fatigué.	11.	I feel tired all the time.
12.	Je ne suis pas en forme.	12.	I'm feeling below par/ under the weather.
13.	Le médecin m'a dit de rester au lit - je dois rester au lit/ garder mon lit.	13.	Doctor's told me to stay in bed.
14.	Je me suis cassé le bras/la jambe.	14.	I've broken my arm/my leg.
15.	Mon frère s'est foulé la cheville.	15.	My brother twisted his ankle.
16.	Ma soeur a eu un accident - elle s'est fait mal au dos.	16.	My sister had an accident she hurt her back.
17.	Je me suis brûlé la main.	17.	I've burnt my hand.
18.	Je me suis coupé le doigt.	18.	I cut my finger.
19.	J'ai dû aller à l'hôpital.	19.	I had to go to hospital.
20.	J'ai mal au coeur depuis deux jours.	20.	I've been feeling sick for two days.
21.	Ça va mieux maintenant.	21.	It's better now.

LISTENING PRACTICE

1 A la pharmacie (higher level)

1. The customer is asking for a medication for: - earache? toothache? cough?
2. It's needed for: - an adult? a child? the customer?
3. The pharmacist suggests one or more of the following: - tablets? cough mixture? drops?
4. Which medication does the customer choose?
5. How much does it cost?
6. What should be avoided during the course of medication?
7. When is the medication to be taken?
8. What should the customer do if the symptoms continue?

2 Chez le médecin (higher level)

1. What mishap is the client reporting?
2. What particularly can the client *not* do, as a result?
3. What two items does the doctor prescribe?
4. Where is the nearest pharmacist?

179

VOCABULARIES

Basic vocabulary

Aches and pains

KEY VERBS

avoir mal à la:- to have a sore
  bouche mouth
  gorge throat
  jambe leg
  main hand
  tête head

avoir mal à l' :- to have a sore
  épaule shoulder
  oeil eye
  oreille ear
  estomac stomach

aller bien/mal/mieux
to be well/unwell/better
avoir chaud to be hot
  froid to be cold
  peur to be afraid
  un rhume to have a cold

  de la fièvre/température
to have a temperature
dormir to sleep
être en forme to be fit
être enrhumé to have a cold
piquer to sting

avoir mal au:- to have a sore:
  bras arm
  coeur (to feel sick)
  cou neck
  doigt finger
  dos back
  genou knee
  nez nose
  pied foot
  ventre tummy

avoir mal aux: to have sore:
  yeux eyes
prendre un bain/une douche
to have a bath/a shower
se brûler la main to burn one's hand
se casser le bras to break one's arm
se coucher to go to bed
se couper le doigt to cut one's finger

(se) faire mal to hurt (oneself)

se reposer to rest
soulager to comfort
tomber to fall
vouloir to want

All settings

	attention! be careful!	
	au secours! help!	
	chaud hot	
m	**cheveux** hair	
	depuis since	
	désolé very sorry	
f	**diarrhée** diarrhoea	
m	**dommage** damage	
	fatigué tired	
f	**fièvre** fever	
	fragile fragile	
	froid cold	
f	**grippe** flu	
f	**indigestion** indigestion	

m	**mal de mer** sea-sickness	
	malade ill	
	mort dead	
	normal normal	
f	**pâte dentifrice** toothpaste	
	propre clean	
	sale dirty	
m	**sang** blood	
f	**santé** health	
m	**savon** soap	
f	**serviette** towel	
m	**shampooing** shampoo	
m	**visage** face	

Additional higher vocabulary

KEY VERBS

attraper to catch
avaler to swallow
avoir l'air to look; seem
chauffer to heat
dissoudre to dissolve

étendre to spread
être admis to be admitted
exagérer to exaggerate
garder son lit to stay in bed
mordre to bite
pleurer to cry

s'inquiéter to worry
saigner du nez to have a nose bleed
se blesser to injure oneself
se cogner to bump; knock
se fouler to twist (ankle)

se noyer to drown
se sentir to feel
souffrir to suffer
tousser to cough
vomir to be sick; vomit

All settings

f **angine** tonsillitis
f **antiseptique** antiseptic
f **aspirine** aspirin
f **assurance** insurance
blessé hurt, injured

cardiaque heart
f **cheville** ankle
f **clinique** clinic
m **comprimé** tablet
constipé constipated

m **corps** body
m **coton hydrophile** cotton wool
m **cou** neck
m **coup de soleil** sun stroke/burn
f **crème** cream

f **crise** crisis
f **cuillerée** spoonful
d'habitude usually
m **dentiste** dentist
m **docteur** doctor

f **insolation** sun stroke
f **langue** tongue
f **lunettes** glasses
f **maladie** illness
m **médecin** doctor

m **médicament** medecine
f **naissance** birth
m **opticien** optician
f **ordonnance** prescription
m **pansement** dressing, bandaging

f **pastille** lozenge
f **peau** skin
f **pharmacie** chemists
m **pharmacien** pharmacist
f **pilule** pill

f **piqûre** sting
m **plâtre** plaster
f **poitrine** chest
f **posologie** dosage
f **précaution** precaution

f	**douleur** pain		*m*	**problème** problem
	endormi asleep			**quelque chose** something
	faible weak		*m*	**remède** remedy
m	**foie** liver		*f*	**salle de consultation** consulting room
	fort strong		*m*	**sirop** (cough) mixture
	gonflé swollen		*m*	**sommeil** sleep
f	**goutte** drop			**souffrant** in pain
	grave serious		*m*	**sparadrap** sticking plaster
	gravement seriously		*m*	**suppositoire** suppository
m	**hôpital** hospital		*m*	**traitement** treatment
	immobile motionless			**vivant** alive
	inquiet worried		*f*	**voix** voice

TOPIC AREA 8　　SELF, HOUSE, HOME AND FAMILY

SETTINGS

At home; in a French friend's home.

KEY NOTIONS AND
FUNCTIONS
(refer to Starter Kit)

Appearance, size, colour, number,
nationality, personal characteristics,
ownership, number, calendar, location.
Describing; expressing likes, dislikes and
preferences; comparing.

KEY STRUCTURES
(refer to Grammar Section)

Present tense, adjectives, possessive
adjectives, reflexive verbs.

CONTENTS

KEY SPEAKING TASKS

1 IDENTIFYING: **names, members of the family**

   NUMBER :   **age, date of birth, calendar**

   ORIGIN :   **place of birth**

QUESTIONS	SAMPLE ANSWERS
Comment t'appelles-tu?	**Je m'appelle..............**
Quel est ton nom de famille?	**C'est............... C'est un nom d'origine italienne/nigérienne/indienne/chinoise.**
Quel âge as-tu?	**J'ai 16 ans.**
En quelle année es-tu né?	**Je suis né/e en 1974/1975.**
Quelle est la date de ton anniversaire?	**C'est le 25 juin/3 février.**
Où es-tu né?	**Je suis né - en Irlande/Ecosse/ Angleterre/au Pays de Galles.** **- à Derby/Perth/Belfast/Bangor**
Tu viens d'où?	**Je viens de Yorkshire/Devon/Glasgow/ Cardiff.**
Tu es de quelle nationalité?	**Je suis/Britannique/Portugais(e).**
Combien de personnes y a-t-il dans ta famille?	**Il y en a quatre, mes parents, ma soeur et moi.**
Tu as combien de frères et de soeurs?	**Je n'ai pas de frères ou de soeurs. Je suis enfant unique.**
Qui est l'aîné/e?	**Moi. J'ai deux soeurs et trois frères.**
Qui est le cadet/la cadette?	**Mon frère Ben. Il a 21 ans.**

2 Describing self, family, friends; appearance and characteristics

(Refer back to Describing People in the Starter Kit).

QUESTIONS	SAMPLE ANSWERS
Fais-moi une description de ton père/ta mère.	**Il /elle est assez grand(e)/de taille moyenne. Il/elle mesure 1m.60.**
	Il/elle a les yeux bleus/bruns/verts et les cheveux châtains/noirs/blonds.

Décris tes parents/tes grandparents.

Ma mère a 41 ans. Elle travaille dans un bureau au centre-ville. Elle est très gentille. Je m'entends bien avec elle. Mon père ne travaille pas en ce moment. Il est au chômage. Il aime faire du jardinage et jouer au golf.

Comment est ta soeur/ton frère?

Elle m'embête tout le temps. Elle a 13 ans et elle est très méchante.

Il est sympa. Nous faisons beaucoup de choses ensemble.

Est-ce que tu as des tantes/des oncles/des cousins/cousines?

J'ai deux oncles et une tante. J'ai deux cousines et un cousin. Ils habitent tous en Ecosse, près d'Edimbourg.

Décris-moi un de tes copains/tes copines.

Ma copine Jeanne a 17 ans, comme moi. Je la vois tous les jours au collège. Nous avons les mêmes goûts et les mêmes interêts.

Mon copain Andrew aime jouer au cricket et il joue bien. Il est sportif, mais en classe il est paresseux. On s'entend bien.

SPEAKING PRACTICE

1   Je vous présente ma famille

Talk about these people as if they were your family.

Use these expressions to help you.

Mon grandpère/père/oncle.................. âge?
Ma mère/tante...................... **couleur des yeux/cheveux?**
Mon petit frère.......................... **défauts/qualités?**
Mes cousines.......................... **ce qu'ils/elles aiment/n'aiment pas?**

2 Je vous décris ma maison.

QUESTIONS	SAMPLE ANSWERS
Où est-ce que tu habites?	J'habite à Manchester
Tu habites là depuis longtemps?	Depuis 1980/six mois/quatre ans.
C'est loin du collège?	A dix kilomètres/vingt minutes à pied. Non, c'est tout près.
Comment est ta maison/ton appartement?	Elle est située dans une petite rue calme/une rue principale avec beaucoup de circulation.
	Nous avons trois chambres, une salle de séjour, une cuisine et une salle à manger. C'est une maison moderne, à deux étages. C'est agréable, mais trop petit pour nous.
Y a-t-il un jardin?	Oui, avec une pelouse, des légumes et des fleurs. Non, mais nous avons un balcon avec des plantes.
Décris-moi ta chambre	C'est assez petit. Il y a mon lit, un placard, une table et un tapis bleu. Les murs sont bleus aussi.
Est-ce que tu partages ta chambre avec ta soeur/ton frère?	Non, j'ai une chambre à moi.
	Oui, avec ma soeur ainée/mon frère cadet.
Qu'est-ce que tu fais dans ta chambre?	J'écoute de la musique/la radio/mes disques.
	Je joue de la guitare.
	Je fais mes devoirs le soir.
	Je ne passe pas beaucoup de temps dans ma chambre - je préfère sortir avec des copains.
Raconte-moi ce que tu fais normalement le matin. Tu te lèves à quelle heure, par exemple?	D'habitude je me réveille à 7h30 et je me lève tout de suite. Je m'habille et puis je descends pour prendre le petit-déjeuner avec ma famille.
	Je fais mon lit, avant de partir pour le collège.
	J'aide mon père à faire la vaisselle.
	Je prépare un sandwich pour midi.
	Je prends le bus/train/métro à 8h10.
	J'arrive au collège 25 minutes plus tard.

Quels sont tes passetemps favoris?

J'aime danser/faire du sport/aller au cinéma.

Je collectionne des timbres. Je lis tout le temps.

Je préfère ne pas regarder trop de télé.

Est-ce que tu as des animaux à la maison?

Oui, un chien/chat/hamster. C'est moi qui s'occupe de lui.

Non, parce que mon père n'aime pas les animaux.

3 Normalement, le matin...

Re-arrange these sentences into a logical order. They describe Anne-Marie's daily morning routine.

1. **Je fais mon lit.**
2. **Je prends le bus pour aller en ville.**
3. **Je me lève vers 7h15.**
4. **Je me lave, avant de prendre le petit-déjeuner avec ma famille.**
5. **Le trajet dure quinze minutes.**
6. **En y arrivant, je vais directement à ma salle de classe.**
7. **Je retrouve mes copines et nous causons dans la cour.**
8. **Je pars pour le collège vers huit heures et demie.**

Now describe what you usually do in the morning.

Try to use some of these conjunctions and adverbs to improve the flow of what you say :

- **d'abord, premièrement**
- **ensuite, puis, après cela**
- **normalement, d'habitude, généralement**
- **quelquefois**

4 D'habitude le soir...

ASKING QUESTIONS	SAMPLE ANSWERS
A quelle heure est-ce que tu quittes le collège?	**Vers 15h30.** **A 16h00, sauf le lundi.**
Comment est-ce que tu rentres chez toi?	**Je rentre à pied.** **Je prends le métro.** **Mon frère vient me chercher avec la voiture.**
Qu'est-ce que tu fais quand tu arrives a la maison?	**Je me repose un peu. Je prends une tasse de thé avec mon frère.** **Je change de vêtements.**
Qui prépare les repas chez toi? Et le soir, que fais-tu après avoir dîné?	**C'est moi qui prépare le repas du soir. Je fais mes devoirs.** **J'aide mon père dans la cuisine.** **J'écoute des disques.** **Je sors au club.**
Tu te couches à quelle heure?	**Ça dépend. D'habitude vers onze heures.**

5 En famille (higher level)

You have just arrived at your French pen-friend's house and have met his/her parents. You have just been shown your room and are discussing where to put your things. The examiner will play the part of the mother/father.

1. Say you like your room very much.
2. Say that, at home, you sleep in the same room as your brother/sister.
3. Enquire where you can put your case.
4. Say you haven't brought any towels.
5. Ask at what time he/she gets up in the morning.

(LEAG B 1988)

You are spending some time in a French family and offer to help in the kitchen. The examiner will play the part of the father/mother.

1. Offer to help him/her do the washing up.
2. Say what you thought of the meal.
3/4. Reply by saying that you do not help a lot in the kitchen. Give an example of a job you sometimes do at home.
5. When asked about your family say your sister no longer lives at home.
6. Ask where you can put the large plate.
7. Say that you don't drink what is suggested before going to bed.

(LEAG C 1988)

6 Nouvelles Rencontres (higher level)

The photographs and notes below give details of some people you met during a recent touring holiday in S.W. France.

You have met the new French **Assistant(e)** your school and you tell him/her about these people, where you met and what you did.

The role of the **Assistant(e)** will be played by the examiner.

You need not mention every detail contained in the notes, but you should try to include at least one of the items in each group.

(MEG 1988 Higher Level)

Royan
le 16 août

Marc
16 ans
Parisien

– sports nautiques
– disco
– invitation chez lui

Arcachon
le 19 août

Annick
15 ans
Bordelaise

– restaurant chinois
– partie de tennis
– concert

Cognac
le 23 août

Sylvie
17 ans
Canadienne

– travaille au camping
– cinéma, le soir
– visite aux caves (jour de congé)

Saintes
le 29 août

Bruno
18 ans
Grenoblois

– visite à la forêt
– photos d'animaux
– promenades à vélo

READING PRACTICE

1 Échange scolaire

You have received this form from a French school. Your teacher has suggested Bernard as your exchange partner. What are the details he has given?

ECHANGE SCOLAIRE: FRANCE - GB

Nom de famille : Durand	**Classe :** 5ème
Prénoms : Bernard Maurice	**Date de naissance:** 10/03/72

Adresse: Quartier les Pins, Mercurol, 26600 TAIN L'HERMITAGE

No de téléphone: 99.08.45.99

No de téléphone à utiliser pendant la journée ouvrable: 99.16.34.33

Nom et profession des parents: Jean-Paul - directeur de banque
Annie - professeur

Frère(s): Patrice, 11 ans et Gilbert, 14 ans

Soeur(s): Jaqueline, 8 ans

Matières préférées: maths, dessin

Passetemps: vélo, marche, musique, bricolage

Autres langues parlées: italien

Si votre enfant suit un régime alimentaire spécial, veuillez l'indiquer: n'aime pas le poisson

Autres remarques jugées utiles: animaux domestiques, un chat, deux chiens

enfant allergique à la penicilline

NOTA : Veuillez remplir cette fiche à trois exemplaires.

Bernard is a .... (1).....year old French student who lives in .....(2)..... He has two .....(3)..... and .....(4).....sister. His hobbies are .....(5)..... His favourite subjects are .....(6)..... Apart from French he speaks .....(7)..... His father works in a .....(8)..... and his mother is a .....(9)..... He doesn't like eating .....(10)..... and he is allergic to.....(11).....

WRITING PRACTICE

1   Fiche personnelle

Using Bernard's application, design a form and fill in details about yourself, in the same - note-form -manner.

2   Premiers contacts

Write a letter - in which you are making contact with a pen-friend in France for the first time - to tell him/her about yourself: say where you live & which part of the country it's in; describe what you look like; say what your hobbies are; what you like and dislike particularly.Remember to start and end your letter correctly.

READING PRACTICE

2   Maisons/appartements à louer

1. **A louer, centre ville Bourg appartement rénové gd confort Tel 16.37.92.66**

2. **Loue gîte rural état neuf, 3/4 personnes, 2e quinzaine août, sept., oct., mer à proximité Tel 45.76.88.34 h repas**

3. **A louer Bourg studio neuf gd confort, cuis. équipée, SdB 1800f charges compr. Tel 16.34.63.78**

4. **A louer Dinard quartier calme plein sud 78 m, balcon, parking couvert, cave, cuisine, lave-vaisselle.** **Tel 18.33.22.**

5. **Loue appartement libre de suite, stationnement, balcon, 200 m plage. Tel 73.38,28.39**

6. **A louer Pleboulle, rez de chaussée, meublé, 1, 100f mensuel, golf à proximité. Tel 54.33.74.28**

7. **A louer début août 3 semaines 3 ch. office, s. de b., séjour, cuis., WC, 5e étage asc.. Tel 34.51.13.12**

8. **A louer maison avec jardin clos, arboré, garage, tout confort Tel 45.27.49.81**

Which ads would you answer if you wanted.

a) A flat to move into immediately?

b) A holiday in the countryside?

c) To be near the sea?

d) A small modern flat?

e) Somewhere quiet?

f) A flat in the town centre?

g) A fully equipped kitchen?

h) A house with a garden?

i) A golfing holiday?

j) A holiday during the last fortnight in August?

WRITING PRACTICE

3 Je loue maison/appartement (higher level)

Now write your own advertisement for these houses/flats. Include rooms, facilities (e.g. lift for flats); area (countryside, town); availability.

READING PRACTICE

3   Petits conseils

Having arranged to swop houses for the summer holidays with your French friends, you arrive at their villa in the Ardèche and find this note pinned to their message-board.

WELCOME!

LES CLES :   pour fermer, mettre la poignée à la verticale, ensuite faire un tour de clé.

LA CUISINIERE A GAZ :   couper le gaz pour la nuit, en tournant le bouton dans le sens des aiguilles d'une montre. : pour ouvrir, tourner dans le sens contraire. le four : il est très rapide! mettre sur 2 ou 3 pour rôtir un poulet., par exemple.

L'EAU CHAUDE :   Attention! elle est très chaude.

POUR LA LESSIVE :   il y a un séchoir dans le garage.

FER/TABLE A REPASSER: : les demander à Madame Moreteau qui habite en face.

ORDURES MENAGERES: : les mettre dans un sac en plastique.

mettre les sacs en plastique dans les grosses poubelles au garage.

Le ramassage des ordures se fait les vendredi matin.

LA PISCINE :   elle est habituellement utilisée par la famille, ainsi que 2 amies qui viennent tard dans la matinée, et en début de l'après-midi.

---

1. How, and when, should you turn off the gas?
2. What advice are you given about the oven?
3. What are you warned about and why?
4. Where will you dry your washing?
5. Where will you find an iron?
6. What should you do with rubbish?
7. When are the dustbins emptied?
8. What time of day do friends use the pool?

WRITING PRACTICE

4   Soyez les bienvenus! (higher level)

Before you left, you left a similar note for your French friends to find on their arrival at your house. Tell a French person how to use your house. Write them a note in French telling them what to look out for.

READING PRACTICE

4   Cherche/vends animaux

---

1. **Recherche cheval à l'herbage**

   Tel: 42.53.65.75

2. **A vendre cabriolet pour poneys**

3. **Chenil prend chiens en pension, juillet, 3 août. S'adresser au magasin.**

4. **Cherche chiot boxer femelle**

5. **Vds souris Toutes offres considérées. Tel: 55.46.87.66 après 8h**

6. **Donne chat - 2 ans. 6 si bons soins assurés. S'adresser au magasin.**

7. **Vends chiots berger allemand. 1 an 250f. Très beaux parents Hulot, 15 Rue de la Paix. Tours**

8. **Donne poissons tropicaux. Aquarium avec pompe et éclairage. Tel: 77.66.56.21 (le matin seulement)**

9. **Recherche perruche et cage. Prix sans imp.**

   Tel: 49.92.64.81.

You are looking in a pet-food shop window in France.

1. Which advert would you answer if you were looking for, or selling.

   a)   a pet fish?

   b)   a cat?

   c)   a mouse?

   d)   a budgie?

2.   How can you find out more about the cat advertised?

3.   How much are

   a)   the mice?

   b)   the Alsatian puppies?

   c)   the fish?

4.   Three of the ads are from people looking for animals or pets. Name the animals/pets they are looking for?

5.   What additional information is given about the Alsatian puppies?

LISTENING PRACTICE

1 Maisons en Écosse (higher level)

Listen to this French couple discussing three houses they might rent for a summer holiday in Scotland. Fill in the details about the houses.

Which house did they eventually choose?

A

Bedrooms..........(1) ..... sleeps....(2)
Available ....(3) ....
Monthly rent.....(4) ....
Situated.............(5) ....
Local amenities..(6)

B

Bedrooms..........(1) ..... sleeps....(2)
Available ....(3) ....
Monthly rent.....(4) ....
Situated.............(5) ....
Local amenities..(6) ....

C

Bedrooms..........(1) ......sleeps ...(2)
Available ....(3) ....
Monthly rent.....(4) ....
Situated.............(5) ....
Local amenities..(6) ....

VOCABULARIES

Basic vocabulary

KEY VERBS

accrocher to hang up (clothes)	**mettre** to put
acheter to buy	**mettre le couvert** to set the table
adorer to love	**naître** to be born
aider to help	**nettoyer** to clean
aimer to like	**ouvrir** to open
allumer to light	**partager** to share
appeler to call	**passer l'aspirateur** to hoover
apporter to bring	**payer** to pay
appuyer to support; press	**penser** to think
avoir to have	**pleurer** to cry
avoir l'air to look (ill etc.)	**porter** to wear; carry
avoir x ans to be x years old	**préférer** to prefer
commencer to begin	**prendre le déjeuner** to have lunch
construire to build	**prendre un bain** to have a bath
coudre to sew	**prendre une douche** to have a shower
couper to cut	**préparer le repas** to prepare the meal
croire to believe	**quitter** to leave
débarrasser to clear (table etc.)	**ranger** to tidy
déménager to move house	**regarder** to watch; look at
détester to hate	**rentrer** to go home
devoir to have to	**repasser** to iron (clothes)
donner to give	**ressembler** to look like
dormir to sleep	**rire** to laugh
écouter to listen to	**s'amuser** to enjoy oneself
écrire to write	**s'appeler** to be called
entrer to go in	**s'asseoir** to sit down
épeler to spell	**s'endormir** to go to sleep
être to be	**s'habiller** to dress
faire des économies to save	**se coucher** to go to bed
faire le lit to make the bed	**se déshabiller** to undress
faire la cuisine to do the cooking	**se fâcher** to get angry
faire la vaisselle to do the washing up	**se laver** to wash
faire le linge to do the washing	**se lever** to get up
faire le ménage to do the housework	**se reposer** to rest
faire les courses to do the shopping	**se réveiller** to wake up
fermer to close	**servir** to serve
finir to finish	**signer** to sign
gagner to earn	**sortir** to go out
habiter to live	**travailler** to work
jouer to play	**tricoter** to knit
louer to hire, rent	**trouver** to find
manger to eat	**venir** to come
marcher to walk	**vouloir** to want

Self and family

f	**adresse** address		f	**jeune fille** young girl
	âgé aged		f	**maman** mummy
m	**âge** age		m	**mari** husband
	aîné elder, eldest			**marié** married
m	**an** year		f	**mère** mother
f	**année** year		m	**mois** month
m	**anniversaire** birthday		m	**neveu** nephew
m	**bébé** baby		m	**nom** name
	cadet younger, youngest		m	**numéro** number
m	**code postal** postcode		m	**oncle** uncle
m/f	**cousin/e** cousin		m	**papa** daddy
f	**dame** lady		m	**pays** country
m	**département** department		m	**père** father
	divorcé divorced		m	**petit-fils** grandson
m	**enfant** child		f	**petite-fille** grandaughter
f	**famille** family		f	**place** square
f	**femme** woman		m	**prénom** first name
	fiancé engaged		f	**route** road
f	**fille** girl		f	**rue** street
m	**fils** son			**séparé** separated
m	**frère** brother		f	**signature** signature
m	**garçon** boy		f	**soeur** sister
f	**grand-mère** grandmother		f	**tante** aunt
m	**grand-parent** grandparent			**unique** only (child etc.)
m	**grand-père** grandfather			**vieux** old
m	**homme** man		m	**village** village
m	**jeune homme** young man, youth		f	**ville** town

House and home

	affreux awful			**grand** big
	agréable pleasant			**HLM** council flat
	ancien old		m	**immeuble** block of flats
m	**appartement** flat		m	**intérieur** inside
m	**bâtiment** building		m	**jardin** garden
	beau lovely			**joli** pretty
m	**bois** wood			**laid** ugly
m	**bruit** noise			**loin de** far from
	calme quiet		f	**maison** house
	cher expensive			**neuf** (brand) new

chez moi at my house, at home
chic smart
m **confort** comfort
confortable comfortable
m **étage** floor

étroit narrow
extérieur outside
f **ferme** farm

nouveau new
parfait perfect
petit small
propre clean
m **rez-de-chaussée** ground floor

sale dirty
vieux old
f **vue** view

Rooms and services

m **ascenseur** lift
m **balcon** balcony
f **cave** cellar
f **chambre** bedroom
m **chauffage central** central heating

m **couloir** corridor
f **cuisine** kitchen
f **électricité** electricity
électrique electric
f **entrée** entrance

m **escalier** stairs
f **fenêtre** window
m **gaz** gas
m **grenier** attic; loft

m **mur** wall
m **parking** car park
f **pièce** room
f **porte** door
m **radiateur** radiator

f **salle à manger** dining room
f **salle de bains** bathroom
f **salle de séjour** living room
m **salon** lounge
m **sous-sol** basement

f **toilettes** toilets
m **toit** roof
m **vestibule** hall
m **W.C.** toilet

Furniture and appliances

f **armoire** cupboard, wardrobe
m **aspirateur** vacuum cleaner
f **assiette** plate
f **baignoire** bath
m **bol** bowl

f **bouteille** bottle
f **brosse à dents** toothbrush
m **buffet** sideboard
f **casserole** saucepan
f **chaîne-stéréo** stereo system

f **chaise** chair
f **cheminée** fireplace
f **clé** key
m **congélateur** freezer
m **couteau** knife

f **couverture** blanket
f **cuiller** spoon
f **cuisinière à gaz/électrique**
  gas/electric cooker

f **fourchette** fork
m **(frigidaire)** (refrigerator)
frigo fridge
f **horloge** clock
f **lampe** light

m **lavabo** washhand basin
f **machine à laver** washing machine
m **lit** bed
m **magnétophone (à cassettes)**
  (cassette recorder)

m **magnétoscope** video recorder
m **meuble** furnished
m **oreiller** pillow
f **paire** pair
m **placard** wall-cupboard

m **plat** dish
f **poubelle** dustbin
m **rasoir** razor
m **rideau** curtain

m	**disque** record		m	**savon** soap
m	**divan** couch		f	**serviette** towel
f	**douche** shower		m	**tableau** picture
m	**drap** sheet		m	**tapis** carpet
f	**eau (chaude)** (hot) water		f	**tasse** cup
m	**électrophone** record player		f	**vaisselle** dishes
	en panne broken down;out of order		m	**vase** vase
m	**évier** sink		m	**verre** glass
m	**fauteuil** armchair			

Daily routine

m/f	**ami/e** friend		f	**généralement** generally
	chaque each		f	**heure** hour; time
m	**courrier** mail			**libre** free
	d'abord firstly		m	**livre** book
	d'habitude usually		m	**passe-temps** pastime
m	**devoirs** homework			**plus tard** later
m	**dîner** dinner			**puis** then
	enfin finally; at last		m	**repas** meal
	ensuite next, then			

Pocket money

m	**argent de poche** pocket money		f	**livre sterling** pound(sterling)
	assez enough			**par semaine/mois** per week/month
f	**banque** bank		m	**porte-feuille** wallet
	beaucoup a lot		m	**porte-monnaie** purse
	combien? how much?		m	**week-end** weekend
m	**franc** franc			

Garden and family pets

m	**animal domestique** pet		m	**hamster** hamster
m	**arbre** tree		m	**lapin** rabbit
m	**chat** cat		m	**oiseau** bird
m	**chien** dog		f	**perruche** parrot
m	**cochon d'Inde** guinea pig		f	**plante** plant
f	**fleur** flower		m	**poisson rouge** gold fish
m	**fruit** fruit		f	**souris** mouse
f	**grenouille** frog		f	**tortue** tortoise

Additional higher vocabulary

KEY VERBS

aller chercher to fetch
arrêter to stop
arroser to water
avoir envie de to feel like
avoir tort to be wrong

balayer to sweep
brancher to plug in
couler to flow
critiquer to criticise
cultiver to grow; cultivate

demeurer to live; reside
dépenser to spend

déranger to disturb
discuter to discuss
éplucher to peal

épouser to marry
essuyer to wipe
faire cuire to cook
faire du bricolage to do d.i.y.
faire pousser to grow

interdire to forbid
laver to wash
offrir to offer

oser to dare
paraître to appear
plaire to please
prouver to prove
recommencer to start again

s'allonger to stretch out
s'en aller to go away (with people)
s'entendre to get on
s'occuper de to look after
se brosser to brush

se disputer to argue
se faire couper les cheveux
    to have a haircut
se marier avec to marry
se mettre en colère to get angry
se présenter to introduce oneself

se promener to go for a walk
sembler to seem
tapisser to carpet
tondre la pelouse to cut the grass
utiliser to use

vendre to sell
vivre to live

Self and family

	à proximite near	
	adolescent teenage	
f	**allocation** allowance	
m	**beau-père** father-in-law	
f	**belle-mère** mother-in-law	
	célibataire single; unmarried	
m	**domicile** residence	
m/f	**époux/se** husband/wife	
	familial family	
f	**fiançailles** engagement	
m	**lieu** place	
	majeur of age	

m	**métier** profession
m	**mineur** under age
f	**naissance** birth
	permanent permanent
m	**petits-enfants** grand children
	presque almost
m	**salaire** salary
m/f	**salarié/e** wage-earner
	temporaire temporary
m	**veuf** widower
f	**veuve** widow

House and home

	au dessus above		m	**location** rent, hire
	au-dessous below		m	**logement** accommodation
f	**différence** difference		m	**loyer** rent
	en bas downstairs		m	**mètre carré** square metre
	en bon/mauvais état			**pratique** practical
	in good/bad condition			
	en haut upstairs		m	**propriétaire** owner
	essentiel essential		m	**siècle** century
m	**gratte-ciel** skyscraper			**triste** sad
	large wide, broad			

Rooms and service

	aménagé equipped		m	**plafond** ceiling
m	**aménagements** fixtures & fittings		m	**plancher** floor
f	**cour** courtyard		f	**plomberie** plumbing
m	**entretien** upkeep, maintenance		f	**prise de courant** plug
f	**lumière** light		f	**serrure** lock
m	**palier** landing		m	**volet** shutter

Furniture and appliances

m	**ameublement** furnishing		m	**machin** gadget
f	**ampoule électrique** light bulb		f	**nappe** tablecloth
m	**appareil** appliance		m	**matelas** mattress
f	**bougie** candle			**ménager** household
m	**canapé** sofa			**meublé** furnished
m	**coussin** cushion		m	**micro-ordinateur** micro computer
f	**étagère** bookshelves		f	**poêle** frying pan
m	**fer à repasser** iron		f	**prise-rasoir** shaving socket
m	**four** oven		m	**réveil** alarm clock
m	**gant de toilette** face flannel		m	**vaisselier** dresser
f	**lave-vaisselle** dishwater			

Daily routine

f	**affaires**	business; things
m	**bain**	bath
m	**coup de main**	helping hand
f	**dentifrice**	toothpaste

f	**eau de toilette**	toilet water
f	**hygiène**	hygiene
f	**lessive**	washing
m	**maquillage**	make up

Garden and pets

m	**arbre fruitier**	fruit tree
m	**buisson**	bush
f	**fourrure**	fur
f	**herbe**	grass
f	**mauvaise herbe**	weed
m	**moineau**	sparrow

f	**patte**	paw
f	**plume**	feather
f	**queue**	tail
m	**renard**	fox
m	**sapin**	fir-tree
m	**serpent**	snake

TOPIC AREA 9 ENTERTAINMENT AND LEISURE INTERESTS

SETTINGS

Going out: to the cinema, theatre etc.
Staying in: reading, watching television.
Sporting activities.

KEY NOTIONS AND
FUNCTIONS
(refer to Starter Kit)

Likes and preference. Time, frequency,
duration, calendar. Expressing opinion,
evaluating.

KEY STRUCTURES
(refer to Grammar Section)

Tenses: present, future, perfect. Adverbs,
adverbial phrases; quantifiers.

CONTENTS

KEY SPEAKING TASKS

1 Describing interests and spare time activities

At the cinema, theatre, concert, sport club, youth club inviting friends

SAY

you go to the youth club on Thursday evening/ice rink on Saturday mornings

you play table tennis/tennis/golf/hockey

you listen to records/the radio

you prefer classical/pop/soul music

you watch television every day

you go shopping at the weekend

you meet your friends in the cafe in the evenings

you buy clothes/records/cassettes /magazines on Saturdays

you stay at home on Sundays

you go for walks in the park/in the country/in town

ASK YOUR FRIEND

what they do in their free time

what sports they play

what sort of music they like

what television programmes they prefer

what they do at weekends

if your friend likes reading

if they like the countryside

ASK FOR

2 tickets at 25 francs/3 seats at 22 francs/1 ticket in the circle

a programme/a coke/an ice cream

ASK WHEN

the play/film/disco begins/ends

SAY

at 21.15/22.05/23.35h

ASK HOW MUCH

it is to get in

SAY

20/24/26/30/35 francs

ASK

which film is showing this week

if it is in English or French

if it is a new film

if you can buy sweets

SAY

it's a western/horror film/cartoon/thriller

ASK A FRIEND

if they are free this evening

if they want to go to the cinema/match/ concert/disco with you

SAY

yes, what's on at the cinema/stadium/town hall/disco at 8.30

READING PRACTICE

1 Allons sortir

Which of these tickets shows entrance to:

1. An army museum?
2. Caves?
3. A tropical garden?
4. A poster exhibition?
5. Sculptures in wood?
6. A church treasury?
7. A castle?

Find the French for:-
8. Full price.
9. Half-price.
10. Entry free
11. Exhibition.
12. What are the 5 things you are not allowed to do at the **Jardin Exotique**?
13. Apart from the museum, what else do you get to see at the **Musée de l'Armée**?
14. Which days is it open?
15. When does it shut in summer? In winter?

A

Ville de CANCALE

MUSÉE DES BOIS SCULPTÉS

Adultes

N° 02557

MP. DOLOISE PICHON

B

C27786
TRÉSOR
Plein Tarif 10 F
TRÉSOR

Plein Tarif 10 F
027786
M.P.   ARGENT

C

034328
Musée de l'Affiche
Plein Tarif
U.C.A.D.
MUSÉE DE L'AFFICHE
EXPOSITION
PLEIN TARIF
034328

D

SITES ET MONUMENTS

Grottes Préhistoriques

DE VILLARS

ENTRÉE: 12 F

N° 036

Droit de timbre payé sur état
IMP. VIRMOUNBIX - THIVIERS

E

MUSÉES de la Ville de PARIS

ENTRÉE GRATUITE

704931

F

MUSÉE RODIN

ENTRÉE 4 F

609560

G

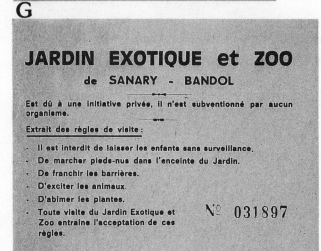

JARDIN EXOTIQUE et ZOO

de SANARY - BANDOL

Est dû à une initiative privée, il n'est subventionné par aucun organisme.

Extrait des règles de visite :

- Il est interdit de laisser les enfants sans surveillance.
- De marcher pieds-nus dans l'enceinte du Jardin.
- De franchir les barrières.
- D'exciter les animaux.
- D'abimer les plantes.
- Toute visite du Jardin Exotique et Zoo entraine l'acceptation de ces règles.

N° 031897

H

22 IV 87

MUSÉE DE L'ARMÉE

DROIT D'ENTRÉE
1/2 TARIF

CONTROLE

A PRÉSENTER A
TOUTE RÉQUISITION
MACHINE N° 2

3 1 2 1 8

I

CHATEAU DE BIRON

La plus étonnante forteresse du Périgord méridional : vigie vers l'Agenais et, au-delà, vers les Pyrénées.

2 Découverte de la randonnée ski-alpinisme

BUT: formation en ski-alpinisme des débutants

FORMATION THEORIQUE EN SALLE (3 soirées de 2 h)
- **présentation matériel**
- **sécurité; neige et avalanches; météo; secourisme**

FORMATION PRATIQUE (4 sorties à définir selon météo)
- **utilisation du matériel;**
- **application des règles de sécurité**
- **préparation d'une course; topographie**
- **perfectionnement descente toute neige avec matériel randonnée**

1. For whom is this course intended?
2. Apart from an introduction to equipment, what else is included in the theory classes?
3. What amount of time is spent on theory classes?
4. What do the practical sessions cover before the final downhill practice?
5. What do the practical sessions depend on?

3 A vos magnétoscopes!

A

🎬 20.30

𝟭𝟭 JUGE ET HORS-LA-LOI
de John Huston

Western. Expéditif ce juge hors du commun (Paul Newman), ancien hors-la-loi, qui s'est imposé comme shérif dans une ville de l'Ouest. Il rend de curieux jugements tous profitables... pour ses deniers ! Avec Anthony Perkins, Victoria Principal, Jacqueline Bisset. Un film parodique qui manie la verve et l'humour aussi bien que le pistolet. *(Durée : 2 h, p. 123.)*

B

VENDREDI

CANAL+ 21.15

𝟳 MITRAILLETTE KELLY
de Roger Corman

Policier. Un affrontement classique de bandes rivales autour d'un hold-up et d'un kidnapping d'enfant. Charles Bronson est la brute idéale et Susan Cabot, gangster au féminin, pleine de charme. L'ambiance des années 30 toujours photogénique et ici brillament évoquée à grand renfort de voitures de rêve. Un bon polar pour passer un bon moment. *(Durée : 1 h 20, p. 137.)*

C

DIMANCHE

FR3 22.30

𝟳 SABOTAGE A BERLIN
de Raoul Walsh

Guerre. Ils sont cinq à bord d'un bombardier : un Anglais, un Américain, un Australien, un Canadien, un Écossais. En mission au-dessus de l'Allemagne, leur appareil est abattu. Ils s'en sortent tous les cinq sains et saufs, mais il leur faut rejoindre l'Angleterre. Un officier SS les traque. Avec Errol Flynn, un film haletant. *(Durée : 1 h 45, noir et blanc, VO, p. 70.)*

D

DIMANCHE

CANAL+ 20.30

𝟭𝟭 SUBWAY
de Luc Besson

Policier. Film événement qui a valu à Christophe Lambert le César du meilleur acteur, voici déjà à la télévision « Subway », sorti il y a à peine un an dans les salles ; film mode sur les couloirs du métro, film branché, tourné comme un clip, avec aussi Isabelle Adjani coiffée à l'iroquoise et J.-H. Anglade en « rollers ». Bref, un film différent : on aime ou on déteste. *(Durée : 1 h 40, p. 61.)*

E

DIMANCHE

CANAL+ 9.40

𝟳 ASTÉRIX ET LA SURPRISE DE CÉSAR
de Paul et Gaëtan Bruzzi

Dessin animé. Cette adaptation de deux albums réunis laissera encore les fans de nos joyeux Gaulois insatisfaits. On retrouve un Obélix amoureux et un Astérix qui va l'aider dans sa conquête. Meilleur que les trois précédents films. *(Durée : 1 h 15, p. 73.)*

F

DIMANCHE

📼 20.35

𝟭𝟭𝟭 FENÊTRE SUR COUR
d'Alfred Hitchcock

Suspense. Un reporter-photographe (James Stewart) est cloué à son fauteuil pour cause de jambe cassée. De sa fenêtre, il observe ses voisins à la jumelle et note l'étrange disparition d'une jeune femme. On connaît la suite. Il n'empêche ! Voici un film à revoir et palpitant. *(Durée : 1 h 50, p. 25.)*

Which film is set in:
1. Wartime?
2. The Thirties?
3. An armchair?

In which film the principal actor:
4. Plays a summary, rapacious judge?
5. Has a broken leg?
6. Won the French Oscar for best actor?
7. Plays a gang-leader?

Which film is described as:
8. Worth seeing again?
9. Better than its previous three?
10. One you'll either hate or love?
11. Fast-moving?
12. Funny?

Which film is:

13. Not dubbed into French?
14. In black & white?
15. Shown in the morning?
16. What does the title **A vos magnétoscopes!** suggest you do?

4 Les enfants du rock

1. How, and where, did the Pointer Sisters begin their singing career?
2. Why is 1973 an important date for them?
3. What happened in 1977?
4. In what way has the group's music changed since then?
5. What is the connection between their song "Neutron Dance" and the film "Beverly Hills Cop"?
6. How did this affect their careers?
7. For what particular reason is this television programme devoted to them?

22.25 LES ENFANTS DU ROCK

Par Patrice Blanc-Francard
SEX MACHINE
par Jean-Pierre Dionnet et
Philippe Manœuvre
Réalisation de Jean-Louis Cap
Ce numéro spécial de « Sex Machine » est consacré aux **Pointer Sisters** et à la musique noire.
Ces quatre sœurs, Bonnie, Ruth, Anita et June ont fait leurs débuts, en chantant des gospels dans les églises d'Oakland, en leur Californie natale. Depuis 1973, elles s'imposent dans les hit-parades. En 1977, Bonnie quitte ses sœurs et poursuit une carrière solo. Ruth, Anita et June décident d'introduire davantage de rock dans leur musique funk. En 1981, elles obtiennent un des plus gros succès de l'année *Slow hand*. Suivront plusieurs titres, entre autres *I'm so excited, Jump, Neutron Dance*. Ce titre, inclus dans la bande originale du film « Le Flic de Beverly Hill », leur permet de toucher un public plus large.
Nous les voyons en concert à Paris, sur la scène du grand Rex. Avec la participation de l'Orchestre du Splendid, qui interprète « La Salsa du démon », nouvelle version.

5 Télématin

What kind of programmes do they have on early morning television in France?

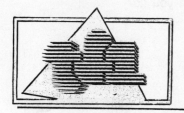

6.45 BONJOUR LA FRANCE

Magazine de Jean-Claude Narcy
Réalisation de Jacques Audoir
Toute l'actualité, par **Ladislas de Hoyos** et **Corinne Lalo** ; la météo, par **Michel Cardoze** ; le sport ; le tuyau des courses, par **Jean-François Pré** ; **Nicolas le jardinier** ; l'horoscope, par **Léon Zitrone** ; un autre regard, avec **Jacques Idier** ; les rencontres de **Viviane Blassel** ; le journal des affaires, TF1 et l'« Expansion », par **Jean Boissonnat, Jean-Michel Quatrepoint, Jean-Louis Servan-Schreiber** et **Sophie Rack** ; dessin animé ; extrait de film ; rubrique santé, par **Martine Allain-Regnault** ; vivre mieux, par **Laurence Perrier** ; trucs et astuces, par **Denis Vincenti** ; la cuisine à toute vapeur ; l'invité politique, de **Jean-Claude Narcy** et **François Lanzenberg** ; le jeu de « Bonjour la France » et Chronique d'un jour.

8.25 HÔPITAL CENTRAL

Feuilleton américain
Les amours et les multiples intrigues qui agitent les couloirs et les salles de l'hôpital central de Port-Charles.
Premier épisode
Robert Scorpio ....**Tristan Rogers**
Sean Donely ....**John Reilly**
Robert Scorpio part pour l'Australie rejoindre sa femme. Sean Donely est blessé au cours du démantèlement d'un reseau de drogue. Il est hospitalisé...

6.45 TÉLÉMATIN

Présentation de Roger Zabel
6.50 Jardins et balcons par **Michel Lis**
6.56 Le Panier de Toutoune
Les meilleurs produits du marché de Rungis et une idée de recette par **Toutoune** restauratrice à Paris
6.58 Conseils de forme
par **Marie-Christine Debourse**
7.00 JOURNAL
par **Catherine Ceylac** et **Marc Autheman**
7.08 La Diététique au quotidien
par **Agnès Mignonac**
7.14 A2 pour vous par **Hubert Schilling**
7.18 Édito politique par **Gilles Leclerc**
7.20 Sport par **Marie-Christine Debourse**
7.25 Édito économique
par **Gérard Leclerc**
7.30 JOURNAL
7.43 Les Trouvailles de **Marie-José Jouan**
7.46 Les Quatre Vérités
par **Gérard Morin**
8.00 JOURNAL
8.10 La Chronique de **Christiane Collange**
8.14 La Rubrique du jour
Votre argent
par **Jean Le Berre**
8.20 La Santé
par **Jean-Daniel Flaysakier**
ou **Catherine Singer**
8.25 Le Truc
de **Laura Fronty**
A NOTER : **flash d'information** à 6 h 48, 7 h 17, 7 h 45 et 8 h 27
Météo à 6 h45, 7 h 28 et 8 h 12

1. Compare the programmes on offer on TF 1 and A 2 by listing what they have in common, under these headings in English. Find the French which fits the headings.

eg.	TF1	A2
SHOPPING	**courses**	**produits du marché**

FOOD

HEALTH

NEWS

MONEY

SPORT

POLITICS

WEATHER

2. Which channel offers more news?

6 Apostrophes

Vendredi
22 juillet

A2
21.35

APOSTROPHES
FAITS DIVERS SANGLANTS
avec J.F. Josselin
POUR
P.D. JAMES ET RUTH RENDELL

Phyllis Dorothy James et Ruth Rendell ne seront pas sur le plateau d'« Apostrophes ». Ces deux romancières qui, avec leur roman (« Une folie meurtrière » et « L'Été de Trappelune »), sont les Agatha Christie d'aujourd'hui, ne parlent en effet qu'anglais !

Les nouvelles reines du crime passent aux aveux

Ce n'est pas l'été de Trappelune - le titre de son nouveau roman chez Calmann Lévy - mais l'été de Nusteads. Au bout d'un chemin de terre perdu au milieu de la verte campagne du Suffolk, dans une maison du XVIᵉ siècle couleur ocre rose, entourée d'un jardin qu'on croirait sorti d'un livre d'Agatha Christie. Élémentaire, mon cher lecteur ! Nous sommes chez Ruth Rendell, l'une des nouvelles stars du crime anglais, sur papier, que Bernard Pivot convie à « Apostrophes » par commentateur interposé, parce que cette bonne Anglaise ne parle qu'anglais et qu'elle se méfie des traductions simultanées.

L'inspecteur Wexford

Dommage, Ruth Rendell vaut le détour et pas seulement pour la lecture de ses romans - plus de trente déjà traduits en seize langues - qui tous révèlent une fine psychologie doublée d'une imaginative. Le jardin, la pelouse, les serres, l'étang, les quatre chats allant et venant, et un mari discret et attentionné, incitent, il est vrai, à la création d'un héros comme l'inspecteur Wexford. « Il en est, lui, à quatorze romans et l'un a été adapté en trois parties sur la chaîne ITV, le dimanche soir, avec George Baker, merveilleux dans le rôle. Les téléspectateurs anglais en raffolent. J'espère que vous le verrez bientôt à la télévision française. » Ancienne journaliste qui connaît Londres comme sa poche (ou presque) pour avoir déménagé de nombreuses fois, Ruth a créé, avec Wexford, un policier

au quotidien, proche de notre Maigret, ne nous cachant ni ses problèmes familiaux, ni ses discussions avec son assistant, Burden.

La nature aussi a une place dans les romans de Ruth Rendell. Elle sait la décrire de manière à faire monter l'angoisse par la précision qu'elle apporte dans l'évocation de chaque détail de l'histoire. Ruth Rendell est une perfectionniste. « Pour garder la forme, je fais beaucoup de gymnastique, aérobic, marche, course à pied et natation et je suis végétarienne. Grâce aux légumes du potager, je vis presque en autarcie. Nous n'allons au supermarché que lorsque les trois congélateurs sont vides. »

P.D. (prononcez Pi.Di) ou si vous préférez Phyllis Dorothy James, elle, nous ne l'avons pas rencontrée, malgré les efforts de son éditeur français Mazarine. Alors que son nouveau roman, « Une folie meurtrière », devient l'un des best-sellers de l'été.

P.D. James a des excuses. Elle est entrée « en loge » pour nous préparer un nouveau livre et se réserve pour la rentrée. Elle habite une maison verte à Londres et elle a sept ans de plus que Ruth Rendell : 67 ans. Rien qu'en Angleterre, elle vend 350 000 exemplaires de chacun de ses romans. Elle en a, il faut bien l'écrire, un peu assez d'être prise pour l'héritière d'Agatha Christie : « Les auteurs de romans policiers des années trente ne songeaient qu'à ficeler une bonne intrigue.

Regard sur la société londonienne

Aujourd'hui, des romancières, comme Ruth ou moi, utilisons un arrière-plan social qui permet d'enrichir notre récit. » Diabolique que P.D. qui, malgré l'hémoglobine et les frissons, nous oblige toujours à la lire jusqu'à la dernière page et qui, en plus, décrit dans un anglais raffiné une Angleterre qu'on aimerait en lire plus souvent. A elle, les bas-fonds et les salons bourgeois du Londres des années quatre-vingts. Nous ne sommes pas au bout de nos surprises, comme avec Ruth Rendell qui, en nous raccompagnant sur le pas de sa porte, en compagnie d'un gripon nous annonce : « Mon prochain roman paraît en septembre en Angleterre. Il s'appellera « The House of Stairs » (La Maison des escaliers). » On en frémit déjà... de plaisir.

Irène DERVIZE

Apostrophes is a prestigious, and prime-time TV programme about books. This article, in **TELE 7 JOURS** introduces the French public to P.D. James, and Ruth Rendell: English authors.

1. How are the two writers described in the title?
2. Find out why both of them will not appear in person on the programme.

Ruth Rendell

3. How many of her books have been translated?
4. Into how many languages?
5. In how many does Inspector Wexford figure?
6. In what three ways is he similar to Inspector Maigret?
7. What was Ruth Rendell's job before she started writing?
8. Give four details about her house.
9. What does she do to keep fit? (5 items)
10. How old is she?

P.D. James

11. The author of the article was unable to meet P.D. James for an interview - why? Give details of:
12. Where she lives.
13. Her book sales in Britain.
14. What, according to her, was the characteristic of thirties' thrillers?
15. In what way does her writing differ from her predecessors'?
16. In what two ways does the article characterize the settings of her books?

SPEAKING PRACTICE

1   Temps libre, loisirs: les goûts (basic level)

At basic level you will need to say what you usually or normally do; your likes/dislikes/preferences; add variety by stating frequency of activity - where it takes place; move to HIGHER LEVEL by use of tenses: i.e. what you did/saw etc. recently, or what you will do next weekend/Saturday etc.

Here are some standard questions and possible responses to start you off.

Qu'est-ce que tu aimes faire pour te distraire/pour te détendre/pour t'amuser?	
J'aime:-	**+ détails**
lire	les journaux/magazines/livres
sortir	en ville/au club/au théâtre/aux concerts
regarder	les films/la télévision/les clips
écouter	la radio/les disques
collectionner	les timbres-poste/les affiches
bricoler	à la maison/dans le jardin
jouer	du piano/de la guitare/de la batterie
	au tennis/au football/au snooker
m'occuper	du jardin/des enfants

Quel genre de films/programmes à la télévision/à la radio/lecture tu aimes/préfères?		
J'aime beaucoup/ je préfère:	(TV films)	(lecture)
les **comédies** comme	French & Saunders	les **romans historiques**
documentaires	Panorama	**policiers**
feuilletons	Eastenders	**d'aventures**
débats	Question Time	**à suspense**
dessins animés	Tom & Jerry	les **bandes dessinées**
policiers	Miami Vice	la **poésie**
variétés	Opportunity Knocks	**littérature**
jeux	The Price is Right	**classique/moderne**
séries	The Cosby Show	**science fiction**
westerns	High Chaparral	**biographie**
les **films:**		
d'épouvante	Friday the 13th	
d'aventures	Raiders of the Lost Ark	
de guerre	Platoon	
les **films classiques**	Casablanca	

Pourquoi tu aimes/tu préfères..?	
Parce que: **c'est/je trouve ça**	**Parce que:** **ça**
amusant intéressant instructif bien drôle	m'amuse m'intéresse m'instruit/m'apprend me plaît me fait rire me détend/me distrait du quotidien

2. Temps, libre, loisirs: normalement - récemment, prochainment (higher level)

1. Que fais-tu	le soir/le weekend/les dimanche	pour te distraire/comme distractions?
2. Qu'as-tu fait	hier soir/le weekend dernier	
3. Que feras-tu	samedi prochain/le weekend prochain	

1. Je vais	au cinéma/au club/au centre sportif; à la pêche; chez des copains/chez des parents; en ville
2. Je suis allé	
3. J'irai	

1. Je fais	des promenades à pied/à velo/en voiture/en bateau
2. J'ai fait	
3. Je ferai	

1. Je vais	voir ma tante/mon oncle/mes grands-parents
2. Je suis allé	
3. J'irai	

1. **Je regarde**	**la télévision**
2. **J'ai regardé**	
3. **Je regarderai**	

1. **J'écoute**	**des disques/la radio**
2. **J'ai écouté**	
3. **J'écouterai**	

1. **Je reste**	**chez moi/à la maison**	**Je ne sors pas**
2. **Je suis resté**		**Je ne suis pas sorti**
3. **Je resterai**		**Je ne sortirai pas**

3. Temps libre: les sports (basic level)

Quels sports tu aimes/aimes faire/aimes regarder?		
Je fais	**du badminton, cricket, football**	**(du/au/le** for all English names)
Je joue	**au**	
J'aime regarder	**le**	
Je fais	**de la gymnastique, natation de l'haltérophilie** (weight lifting)	

Quand? Combien de fois..?		
Très souvent	**tous les jours/soirs/weekends**	i.e. very often
Assez souvent	**deux, trois fois par semaine**	fairly frequently!
Quelquefois	**une fois par semaine**	i.e.,occasionally
De temps en temps	**deux, trois fois par mois**	now & then
Très peu	**une fois par mois**	i.e., hardly ever!
Rarement	**une deux fois par an**	

Où?
Au stade. Au collège. Au terrain de sports. Au centre sportif. Au parc municipal

WRITING PRACTICE

1 Agenda (basic level)

Keep a diary (**agenda**) regularly of the activities you do; kinds of films, TV you see; books you read etc. Write notes, not stories!

Here is an example.

vendredi	sortie voir film de guerre *(Au revoir les enfants)*. Très bien. Au café après avec copains, prendre un verre, bavarder.
samedi	Courses et ménage le matin. Partie de tennis avec Roy, copain, 1 h. au parc à côté. Soir - au théâtre: "Ice Cream" de Caryl Churchill - pas mal.
dimanche	la grasse matinée! Promenade avec chien vers midi. Après- midi: devoirs, préparation pour lundi. Lu le dernier policier de Higgins - vraiment chouette. Le soir - repos - télévision, film classique: *Casablanca*.

2 Agenda pour invités (basic level)

Make up a diary - of a week's events - as a programme of activities for some guests (French). Include a variety of things to do, to see; places to visit. Say how to get there (train, car, coach...)

3 Manifestations sportives (basic level)

Make up a list of what sporting activities there are on offer locally
- at your local leisure centre
- in your local newspaper

4 Activités sportives (higher level)

Write an informal letter to a French friend who's asked to describe what sports there are on offer in your school/college. Say how often they are available; where they are played; if in winter/summer. Express your preference and give reasons, opinions. Say also what teams you belong to; which local/national teams you support.

LISTENING PRACTICE

1 Horaires des cours (basic level)

 You've rung up to find out what time various gymnastics classes are on.
Fill in the times given.

Horaire des cours à partir du 1er octobre

Gymnastique	lundi	mardi	mercredi	jeudi	vendredi
cours de femmes					
cours mixtes					
cours hommes					
cours enfants					

2. Le Prince Randolph (higher level)

 In this review of Randolph Scott, the star of westerns who died in 1986, put
together the information and evaluation which the reviewer makes.

1. When was Randolph Scott born?
2. In what year did he begin acting?
3. How many films did he make with Ray Enright?
4. What sort of character did he play?
5. What two features characterize these films?
6. How many films did Scott make with Andre de Toth?
7. And with Bud Boetticher? Over what period of time?
8. What final touch did he add to the role of the solitary cowboy?
9. What, in the opinion of the reviewer, made these films into masterpieces?
10. How did Scott - as producer - contribute to the quality of these films?

VOCABULARIES

Basic vocabulary

KEY VERBS

accompagner to accompany	**jouer de la musique/ de la guitare/du piano etc.** to play music/guitar/piano etc.
aimer to like	**lire** to read
aller chercher to fetch	**nager** to swim
aller to go	**ouvrir** to open
assister to be present	**penser de** to think of
chanter to sing	**perdre** to lose
choisir to choose	**préférer** to prefer
collectionner to collect	**regarder** to watch;look at
commencer to begin	**réserver** to book, reserve
courir to run	**retrouver** to meet
danser to dance	**rêver** to dream
demander to ask	**rire** to laugh
détester to hate	**s'amuser** to enjoy oneself
dresser un animal to train an animal	**s'ennuyer** to get bored
échanger to exchange	**savoir** to know(how)
écouter to listen to	**se passer** to happen
être d'accord to agree	**se promener** to go for a walk
exposer to exhibit	**se rencontrer** to meet
faire des promenades to go for walks	**se reposer** to rest
faire du cyclisme to go cycling	**sortir** to go out
fermer to close	**trouver** to find
gagner to earn; win	**venir** to come
inviter to invite	**visiter** to visit
jeter to throw	**voir** to see
jouer aux cartes/au tennis/golf etc to play cards/ tennis/golf etc.	

General pastimes

m/f	**artiste** artist	m	**loisir** leisure
f	**bande dessinée** comic	m	**magnétophone** tape recorder
f	**bibliothèque** library	m	**magnétoscope** video recorder
m	**boum** party	f	**matinée** morning
	célèbre famous	m	**membre** member
f	**chaîne** channel	m	**papier** paper
f	**chaîne stéréo** stereo system	m	**passe-temps** pastime, hobby
f	**chanson** song		**presque** almost
	de temps en temps from time to time		**proche** near
m	**disque** record	f	**publicité** advertising

f	**chaîne** channel		m	**papier** paper
f	**chaîne stéréo** stereo system		m	**passe-temps** pastime, hobby
f	**chanson** song			**presque** almost
	de temps en temps from time to time			**proche** near
m	**disque** record		f	**publicité** advertising
f	**distraction** diversion, amusement		f	**réunion** meeting
m	**échange** exchange		f	**revue** magazine
m	**échecs** chess		m	**roman** novel
m	**électrophone** record player		f	**soirée** evening
f	**émission** programme		m	**temps libre** free time
f	**excursion** trip			**toujours** always
f	**exposition** exhibition			**tout le monde** everybody
m	**jeu** game (quiz)		f	**vacances** holidays
m	**journal** newspaper		m	**violon** violin
f	**lettre** letter		f	**visite** visit
m	**livre** book			

Entertainment - people and places

m	**acteur** actor			**interdit** forbidden
f	**ambiance** atmosphere		f	**maison des jeunes** youth club
m	**bal** dance		f	**pièce de théâtre** play
m	**balcon** balcony		f	**place** seat
m	**billet** ticket		f	**salle** room
m	**chanteur** singer		f	**séance** performance
	cher expensive		m	**soir** evening
m	**cirque** circus		m	**spectacle** show
f	**comédie** comedy		f	**vedette de cinéma** film stars
f	**disco(thèque)** disco(theque)			**version française/ originale** dubbed/sub-titles
f	**entrée** entrance		m	**zoo** zoo
m	**groupe** group			

Film and television - types of programmes

f	**actualités** news		m	**film d'espionnage** spy
f	**comédie musicale** musical comedy		m	**film de gangsters** gangster
m	**dessin animé** cartoon		m	**film de guerre** war
m	**documentaire** documentary		f	**informations** news
m	**feuilleton** soap opera		m	**policier** thriller
m	**film comique** comedy		m	**programme de variétés** variety show
m	**film d'amour** love story		f	**science-fiction** science-fiction
m	**film d'aventure** adventure		f	**série américaine** American series
m	**film d'épouvante** horror		m	**western** western

Sports

m	**ballon** ball		f	**pêche** fishing
m	**championnat** championship		f	**piscine** swimming pool
m	**cricket** cricket		m	**résultat** result
m	**cyclisme** cycling		m	**ski** skiing
m	**cycliste** cyclist			**sportif** sporting
f	**équipe** team		m	**sports d'hiver** winter sports
f	**gymnastique** gymnastics		m	**stade** stadium, sports' ground
m	**jeu** game		m	**terrain** pitch,court etc
m	**joueur** player		m	**Tour de France**
					Tour de France cycle race
f	**natation** swimming		m	**vélo** bike

Additional higher vocabulary

KEY VERBS

annuler to cancel
apprécier to appreciate
approuver to approve

avoir le temps to have the time
avoir horreur de to loath

battre to beat
bricoler to do odd jobs
critiquer to criticise
découvrir to discover
défendre to defend

dépenser to spend (monies)
désapprouver to disapprove
encourager to encourage
enregistrer to record
étonner to astonish

faire de l'équitation to go horseriding

faire de la peinture to paint
faire du bricolage to do odd jobs
faire une partie de tennis etc
to have a game of tennis etc.
informer to inform
marquer un but/un point
to score a goal/a point

oser to dare
participer to participate
pêcher to fish
prêter to lend
rejoindre to meet

s'intéresser à to be interested in
se réjouir to enjoy
sourire to smile
soutenir une équipe to support a team
tourner un film to make a film

General pastimes

f	**affiche**	poster
m	**environs**	surroundings
m	**faits divers**	news in brief
f	**festivités**	festivities
m/f	**gens**	people
m	**hebdomadaire**	weekly (paper)
m	**illustré**	magazine
f	**lecture**	reading

f	**location**	hire
	mensuel	monthly
f	**petite annonce**	small ad
m	**plaisir**	pleasure
	populaire	popular
m	**quotidien**	daily (paper)
m	**sommaire**	summary
m	**tricot**	knitting

Entertainment - people and places

m	**comédien**	comedian; actor
m	**entr'acte**	interval
m	**musicien**	musician
f	**ouvreuse**	usherette

m	**pourboire**	tip
f	**réduction**	reduction
	sous-titré	sub-titled

Sport

m	**arbitre**	referee
m	**aviron**	rowing
f	**balle**	ball(tennis)
m	**équipement**	equipment

m	**match nul**	draw
f	**piste**	track,ski slope
m	**spectateur**	spectator
m	**titre**	title

TOPIC AREA 10 SCHOOL, JOB, WORK, AND CAREERS

SETTINGS

The school day and routine; subjects followed, jobs and careers - at home and abroad.

KEY NOTIONS AND FUNCTIONS
(refer to Starter Kit)

Identifying; stating likes, dislikes, preferences.

KEY STRUCTURES
(refer to Grammar Section)

All tenses. Adverbs and adjectives: comparatives and superlatives. Use of quantifiers.

CONTENTS

KEY SPEAKING TASKS

This topic lends itself to role play and conversation. The key speaking tasks 1 are drawn from role-plays: and are set out in English - to encourage students to recall and practice essential vocabulary and expressions. Key speaking tasks 2 are given in French - to enable students to gain familiarity and use in this all-important topic.

1 School

1. Describing your school
2. Describing your school day
3. Stating likes, dislikes and preferences

SAY
what your school is called and where it is
whether it is mixed or not
say how many pupils there are in your class/school

ASK
your friend for this information

SAY
when you leave home and arrive at school

how you travel and with whom
when the first lesson begins
how long lessons last
what you do at lunchtime
how many lessons there are in the afternoon
when you leave school

ASK
your friend to describe his/her typical school day

SAY
what your favourite subject is and why

what subjects you dislike and why
what clubs you belong to
what sports you take part in

ASK
your friend what their favourite subject(s) is/are
what sports they take part in

2 Mon collège

Mon collège s'appelle.................

C'est assez moderne/grand/petit

Il y a trois terrains de sport/deux gymnases/une bibliothèque/une piscine...

C'est mixte/pour filles/pour garçons, situé à/au/aux dans....

Il y a.....élèves dans ma classe/environ....élèves en tout

L'ambiance est bonne/mauvaise et les profs sont/ne sont pas sympas.

Les rapports entre les profs et les élèves sont bons/ne sont pas bons.

Il n'y a pas assez de discipline/il y a trop de discipline.

Les professeurs sont assez strictes/ne sont pas assez sévères.

J'apprends beaucoup

J'ai beaucoup de devoirs, au moins deux heures par jour.

Une journée typique

D'habitude je quitte la maison à.............

Je prends le bus/le train/le métro avec mes copains/copines.

Mon père/ma mère m'amène en voiture.

Je vais au collège à pied/à velo.

J'arrive au collège à ....

Le premier cours commence à........et chaque leçon dure....minutes.

Nous avons....leçons le matin, et...l'après-midi.

A midi je mange à l'école/je rentre pour manger.

Normalement je quitte le collège vers.....de l'après-midi.

Ce que j'aime au collège

Ma matière préférée, c'est.........
C'est intéressant/drôle/facile/utile et en plus j'aime le professeur.

Je n'aime pas........parce que c'est difficile/ennuyeux/inutile.
On nous donne trop de devoirs!

Il y a plusieurs clubs à mon école - le club de guitare/d'échecs/
d'informatique.

On peut pratiquer beaucoup de sports - le tennis/le hockey/le rugby....

Work out what questions to ask in order to get the above information.

Here are some words to help you

Comment s'appelle..............?

Où se trouve..................?

Combien d'élèves..............?

A quelle heure.................?

Qu'est-ce que tu fais à midi..?

Quelle est ta/ton..............?

Pourquoi......................?

Quels sports..................?

READING PRACTICE

1 **Liste des fournitures** (basic level)

School students in France are required to buy their own consumable goods, such as exercise books, folders and so on. They are given detailed lists of what is required for each subject, for the start of each academic year.

Find out what Xavier needs!

1. Check that you know the equivalent in English of the subjects he's taking, particularly these subjects:

SC.PHYSIQUES; DESSIN; E.M.T; E.P.S.

ANGLAIS RENF = extra English

2. Make a list of the subjects which require:
   a. exercise books
   b. envelope folders
   c. ring-bind folders
   d. file paper

3. What will he need for:
   a. E.P.S.?
   b. Art

4. What must he have for all subjects?

Collège Montaigne

Rue Montaigne

- L I S T E des F O U R N I T U R E S -

MATHEMATIQUES : 2 cahiers grand format/grands carreaux (de préférence sans spirales)

BIOLOGIE : - 1 classeur petit format
- feuillets petit format grands carreaux perforés
-     "   "   "   dessin perforés.

SC. PHYSIQUES : - 1 cahier grand format Travaux Pratiques (de préférence sans spirales ou double spirales).

ANGLAIS : - 1 cahier petit format, grands carreaux, 96 pages.

ANGLAIS RENF. : - 1 cahier petit format, grands carreaux, 96 pages.

ESPAGNOL :   Idem

FRANCAIS : - 1 classeur petit format
- feuillets petit format grands carreaux perforés
- copies doubles petit format grands carreaux perforés
- intercalaires.

HIST. GEO. : - 2 cahiers grand format (travaux pratiques) grands carreaux doubles spirales
- 1 pochette 6 crayons de couleur
- 1 pochette papier calque
- 1 pochette papier millimétré

MUSIQUE : - 1 cahier de musique (1 page blanche, 1 page portées musique)

E.M.T. : - 1 cahier grand format petits carreaux (240 x 320 mm)

E.P.S. : - Tenue de sport et de natation

DESSIN : - Rien à acheter. Une cotisation sera demandée à la rentrée.

Petites fournitures valables dans toutes disciplines :

- équerre - règle plate graduée de 30 mm en plastique
- rapporteur et compas
- ciseaux à bouts ronds
- 1 boite de 6 crayons de couleur
- crayon gris + gomme

2 Madame le Proviseur (higher level)

QUE FAITES-VOUS LA JOURNÉE? - je gère, j'administre, j'anime et je conseille. A l'extérieur du lycée, je rencontre beaucoup de monde lors de commissions de travail; je fais aussi partie de la commission de contrôle des films; au lycée, tout le monde sait que le mardi soir le proviseur <<est au porno>>. je suis membre de la maison des jeunes du 6 , de l'association des langues vivantes du lycée.

VOUS PRENEZ DU TEMPS POUR VOUS PARFOIS? - Quand je suis vidée, après un conseil de classe difficile par exemple, quand je me sens bête, je fais la cuisine, j'adore la choucroute et la paëlla..., j'écoute Brahms et je lis des romancières anglaises. Ou bien je prends l'autobus. Le 63 est parfait, il roule tout le temps, même le dimanche! D'abord je vais au terminus de la gare de Lyon, je respire la gare, je regarde partir deux ou trois trains, déjà, ça va un peu mieux.

"J'aime les adolescents,

ils ont un style de langage

épatant et, surtout, .

ils acceptent l'humour."

VOUS DITES AVOIR DU MAL À COMPRENDRE LES ENFANTS, À LES CONNAITRE, À EXERCER SUR EUX L'AUTORITÉ QU'IL FAUT. AU CONTRAIRE, VOUS SERIEZ TOUT À FAIT A L'AISE AVEC LES <<GRANDS>>, LES ADOLESCENTS.
Ils m'intéressent passionnément, j'aime les voir changer, évoluer. Lorsqu'ils entrent à Fénelon, à partir de la seconde, ils ont 14, 15 ans. C'est un cap très difficile. J'ai pour eux une curiosité sans cesse renouvelée. Ils ont un style de langage épatant, et puis, surtout, ils acceptent l'humour, même s'il est difficile à manier avec eux. Je les respecte, même s'ils ne me le rendent pas toujours, mais j'aime les prendre comme ils sont souvent drôles, et totalement inédits. Pas facile, non?- L'adolescence est une crise. On ne peut pas y rester indifférent. On est mal préparé à tout cela, quand on est prof. Les adolescents ont besoin du témoignage d'adultes qui peuvent leur dire: <<C'est dur, mais on va vous aider, parce que c'est chouette, la vie.>>

A VOTRE NIVEAU, QUE POUVEZ-VOUS FAIRE? - Je suis très coincée par le statut des fonctionnaires: on ne fait pas n'importe quoi. On n'est pas un chef d'entreprise, et les parents demandent des comptes.L'inspection générale impose des contraintes, nous avons des conditions de travail peu satisfaisantes, nous manquons de crédits pour la formation continue. On ne peut pas s'arrêter pour tout repenser, par exemple fermer pour réparations. On mène un combat un peu miteux.

Propos recueillis par Marion LEVY
6 AU 12 OCTOBRE 1988 - L'EVENEMENT DU JEUDI

Mme Gentzbittel is the Head of a prestigious state school - the **Lycée Fénélon** - in Paris.

1. What commitments does she have outside school?
2. Apart from reading and cooking, what does she do to relax?
3. What are the qualities she admires in young people?
4. How does she describe adolescence?
5. What does she think adults should provide, and say?
6. How many of these puts constraints on her job?

   parents/poor pay/lack of time/lack of money/poor working conditions

7. How would you describe her attitude to young people?

3 Demandes d'emploi (basic level)

What sort of part-time work are these people looking for? What can they do? When?

1. **JEUNE FEMME cherche à faire ménage 3 ap.midi   par semaine**
   - a. 3 days a week
   - b. 3 afternoons a week
   - c. 3 mornings a week
   - d. 3 evenings a week

2. **FERAIT quelques heures de jardinage coupe gazon**
   - a. cooking
   - b. cleaning
   - c. typing
   - d. gardening

3. **JEUNE FILLE 20 ans BEP et CAP sténodactylo cherche emploi de bureau**
   - a. short hand typing
   - b. babysitting
   - c. private tuition
   - d. cleaning

4. **J. HOMME 23 ans sérieuses références, ch.heures de   ménage. Libre tous les   matins**
   - a. every day
   - b. every morning
   - c. afternoons only
   - d. some evenings

5. **DAME cherche heures de ménage garder enfants**
   - a. office work
   - b. cleaning
   - c. babysitting
   - d. private tuition

6. **PEINTRE OQ SERIEUX LIBRE DE SUITE**
   ready to start work
   - a. next week
   - b. tomorrow
   - c. immediately
   - d. soon

7. **DACTYLO EMPLOYÉE DE BUREAU CHERCHE PLACE STABLE**
is looking for

    a.   babysitting
    b.   typing
    c.   cleaning
    d.   tuition work

8. **J.F. 25 ANS CHERCHE PLACE HOTELLERIE AIDE-CUISINIERE**
wants work as

    a.   hotelier
    b.   receptionist
    c.   clerk
    d.   assistant cook

9. **JF LIBRE DE SUITE CHERCHE PLACE CHAUFFEUR**
wants work as

    a.   driver
    b.   salesperson
    c.   telephonist
    d.   hairdresser

10. **JF 27 ANS JOURNALISTE RECHERCHE TOUT TRAVAIL**
wants to do

    a.   chauffeuring
    b.   office work
    c.   accountancy
    d.   anything

11. **JH 21 ANS POSSÉDANT B.A.C. 2 ANS D'EXPÉRIENCE CHERCHE PLACE VENDEUR**
wants work as

    a.   salesperson
    b.   gardener
    c   mechanic
    d.   receptionist

12. **SECRETAIRE CH. EMPLOI BRANCHE JURIDIQUE 6 ANS D'EXPÉRIENCE**
wants to work in

    a.   accountancy
    b.   personnel department
    c.   law office
    d.   travel agency

4 Métiers: offres - demandes (basic level)

Match up these jobs offers with the jobs wanted.

OFFRES D'EMPLOI

1. **Rennes centre, particulier cherche femme de ménage bonne expérience exigée**
2. **Cherche sécrétaire standardiste connaissance de Rennes et de ses environs souhaitée.Envoyer CV. Ne pas téléphoner**
3. **Recherche chauffeur-livreur pour produits métallurgiques.Envoyer CV.**
4. **Magasin textile femme et sport et loisirs recrute vendeurs (euses) ayant expérience de la vente. Ecrire + photo + lettre**
5. **Entreprise de l'Orne recherche un conducteur de travaux en peinture. S'adresser à HUPOL.**
6. **Recherche cuisinier experimenté près de Rennes**

DEMANDES D'EMPLOI

A **Dactylo employée de bureau cherche place stable à Rennes libre de suite**
B **JF 23 ans possédant, B.A.C.2 ans d'expérience cherche place vendeuse**
C **JF 25 ans cherche place hôtellerie aide-cuisinière.**
D **Jeune homme libre de suite cherche place chauffeur C 1 international**
E **Jeune femme cherche heures de ménage. Sérieuses références. Libre tous les matins**
F. **Peintre OQ sérieux, expérimenté cherche emploi Rennes environs.**

5 Métiers: offres (higher level)

1. **Crêperie-grill recherche jeune fille avec experience pour service salle et préparation à temps partiel. tel.**
2. **Pour début septembre recherche ménuisiers. Ecrire**
3. **Cherche pâtissier libéré obligation militaire, sachant travailler seul. tel.**
4. **Recherche apprentie fleuriste, très motivée, septembre 1989, Rennes centre, bonne présentation. Envoyer CV manuscrit.**
5. **Recherche urgent jeune homme pour SIVP, septembre, octobre, novembre, pour travaux agricoles. Téléphoner heures repas.**
6. **Pour Paris recherche J.F. pour s'occuper 2 enfants, bonnes références exigées, logée, nourrie. Env. CV + photo et téléphone à Mme de Chaumont.**
7. **Recherche mécaniciens VL-PL experimentés avec permis. Garage Davy, Rennes. Tel:**
8. **Société lorientaise recherche sécrétaire trilingue, allemand, anglais. Envoyer photo + CV.**
9. **Recherche coiffeur (se) mixte qualifié (é) débutant (e) s'abstenir, urgent. Ecrire Renée Duclos.**
10. **Entreprise de plomberie-chauffage recherche un plombier-chauffagiste qualifié. Envoyer CV.**

Which ad. would you answer if you were looking for one of these jobs?

a. baker
b. agricultural worker
c. mechanic
d. plumber
e. trilingual secretary

f. waiter/waitress
g. hairdresser
h. carpenter
i. nanny
j. florist

SPEAKING PRACTICE

1 Mon collège (higher level)

Conversation

At basic level you will need to be thoroughly familiar with the names of the subjects you do; time and numbers - for saying how many subjects you take, length of lessons, frequency. You should also be able to express likes, dislikes, preferences - and give an uncomplicated reason for them. Say also how you get to college, how long it takes; if you live far or near from it.

Note   that the French word **collège** means secondary school; and that there is no direct equivalent in French for the concept of 'college' as in Britain. **Lycée** which used to mean grammar school, has, since 1978 meant upper secondary school. **Ecole** means primary school; whereas **une grande école** is a high-powered university, entry by stiff examinations and competition - for this there is no equivalent in English!

At higher level you will need to expand on your answers - initiate some answers, and be able to move easily between tenses; use quantifiers to express nuances. Here is a selection of questions and statements for you to appropriate and personalize.

QUESTIONS	POSSIBLE ANSWERS
Qu'est-ce que tu fais/études/suis comme sujets/matières?	**Je fais/j'étudie/je suis l'histoire. etc.**
Lequel tu préfères? et pourquoi?	**J'aime mieux/je préfère le français etc. Parce que c'est bien/utile/intéressant etc.**
	J'aime bien l'histoire (etc) aussi...
Laquelle tu aimes le moins? et pourquoi?	**C'est l'informatique: c'est très utile mais je la trouve assez difficile.**

Pourquoi tu as choisi de faire le français (etc.)?	Je trouve ça bien/utile... etc.
	J'aime apprendre les langues; je parle déjà l'espagnol/le russe/l'arabe etc.
	Parce que les langues - c'est important; surtout à l'avenir.
	C'est pour mon métier - je voudrais être sécrétaire bi-lingue/je voudrais travailler en France, en Espagne, à l'étranger.
Quel métier voudrais-tu faire/exercer?	Je voudrais être médecin/ingénieur /cadre/.. etc.
	Je ne sais pas encore. Je n'ai aucune idée.
Combien d'heures tu passes à faire des devoirs?	Deux/trois heures tous les soirs.Cela dépend. Très peu.
Où est-ce que tu fais tes devoirs?	A la maison/chez moi - dans ma chambre; dans le salon.
	A la bibliothèque du collège/à la bibliothèque municipale. C'est plus tranquille que de chez moi.
Où est-ce que tu manges à midi?	Je rentre chez moi.
	Je mange à la cantine.
	Je sors au café d'à côté.
Comment tu trouves les repas à la cantine?	Ils sont bons: il y un grand choix pour tous les gôuts/pour tous les régimes; ce n'est pas cher en plus.
	Ils sont mauvais: il y a très peu de choix; il y a toujours une queue.
Qu'est-ce que tu fais pendant la récréation/pendant l'heure du déjeuner/ pendant les heures libres au collège?	Je bavarde/je discute avec mes camarades.Je rattrape sur mes devoirs.Je passe le temps à lire.
	Je me détends - je joue au football/au basket.... etc.
Quel moyen de transport tu prends pour venir au college?	Je viens à pied/à velo. Je prends le bus/le train/ le métro.
	J'habite à côté/pas très loin.
	J'habite assez loin.
	J'ai une voiture/une moto.
Tu mets combien de temps pour arriver au collège?	A peu près 20 minutes/une demi-heure. Cela dépend de la circulation - normalement une vingtaine de minutes.

WRITING PRACTICE

1 Travail saisonnier (higher level)

A French teacher in your school has written to a French friend hoping to arrange summer work for you and another pupil. Below is the reply which the teacher passes on to you. Write a letter in French to the French lady. You should write about 200 words.

Aigueblanche, le 2 mai.

Cher Monsieur,

Je vous prie de m'excuser pour ma négligence à répondre si tard à vos deux lettres. Je vous réponds quant à la proposition concernant vos élèves qui souhaitent venir nous aider dans la ferme pendant l'été de 1988. Je serai bien heureuse de recevoir ces deux jeunes personnes. Vous m'avez dit qu'ils ont travaillé tous les deux en France l'année dernière. Il faut que les élèves m'écrivent pour me dire ce qu'ils ont fait exactement, c'est-à-dire, où ils ont travaillé, pendant combien de temps, quelle sorte de travail, ce qu'ils ont aimé et ce qui ne leur a pas plu. Aussi je voudrais savoir comment ils espèrent passer leurs vacances cette année s'ils viennent à notre ferme dans cette région montagneuse. Peut-être qu'ils ont des questions à me poser.

Ma fille Marie va chez sa correspondante en Allemagne au mois de juillet et Martin, mon fils, s'est cassé la jambe et s'est fait mal au dos dans un accident la semaine dernière. Donc j'ai grand besoin de ces élèves pour nous aider en juillet.

Recevez, Monsieur, mes très cordiales salutations.

Josette.

(courtesy of NISEC)

2. Une journée dans un collège (higher level)

These drawings of lessons in college were made by a former student.

Write a descriptive/narrative story which explains what the lessons are, where they are taking place, what the students are doing. Put in details which are appropriate, and from your own experience, about the content.

LISTENING PRACTICE

1   Le rôle des parents (higher level)

 Mme Gentzbittel speaks about the role of parents in schools.

1.   What part should parents play generally in schools?
2.   In what particular case is she sometimes severe with individual parents?
3.   Give the two examples she uses to show that parents can be excessively demanding of the school.
4.   In what one particular area should parents help to improve the quality of school life?
5.   What two features in the French education system make parents over-anxious for their children?
6.   How does she defend the right of students - children - to determine their success?
7.   What advice does she give to parents, concerning children, concerning teachers?

VOCABULARIES

Basic vocabulary

KEY VERBS

aimer to like		**faire une activité** an activity	
aller to go		**faire une expérience** to do an experiment	
apprendre to learn		**finir** to finish	
arriver to arrive		**gagner** to win	
assister à l'assemblée to go to assembly		**jouer** to play	
avoir to have		**lire** to read	
calculer to calculate		**manquer** to miss	
chanter to sing		**nager** to swim	
chercher to look for		**partir** to leave	
choisir to choose		**passer** to sit (an exam)	
commencer to begin		**penser** to think	
compter to count		**pratiquer un sport** to do a sport	
continuer to continue		**préférer** to prefer	
dessiner to draw		**punir** to punish	
détester to hate		**quitter** to leave	
devenir to become		**regarder** to look	
devoir to have to		**rentrer** to go home	
durer to last		**répondre** to answer	
écouter to listen to		**rester** to stay	
écrire to write		**réviser** to revise	
espérer to hope		**s'amuser** to enjoy oneself	
être to be		**s'ennuyer** to be bored	
étudier to study		**s'entraîner** to train	
expliquer to explain		**savoir** to know/ know how	
faire de la musique music		**surveiller** to supervise	
faire des progrès to make progress		**terminer** to finish	
faire du sport sport		**travailler** to work	
faire ses devoirs to do ones homework		**vouloir** to want	
faire un exercice to do an exercise		**voyager** to travel	

School

m	**allemand** German		*m*	**gymnase** gymnasium	
m	**anglais** English		*f*	**gymnastique** gymnastics	
m	**bac(calaureat)** "A levels"		*f*	**heure du déjeuner** lunch time	
f	**bibliothèque** library		*f*	**histoire** history	
f	**biologie** biology		*f*	**informatique** computer studies	
m	**bulletin** report		*f*	**instruction civique** civics	

m	**bulletin** report		*f*	**instruction civique** civics
m	**bureau** office		*f*	**instruction réligieuse** religious education
m	**camarade** friend		*m*	**italien** Italian
f	**cantine** dining hall		*m*	**jeu** game
f	**chimie** chemistry		*f*	**journée** day
	chouette super		*m*	**laboratoire** laboratory
	classique classical		*f*	**langue étrangère** foreign language
m	**collège** secondary school		*f*	**littérature** literature
	compliqué complicated		*m*	**livre** book
m	**cours commerciaux** business studies		*m*	**lycée** upper secondary school
m	**cours** lesson		*f*	**mathématiques** maths
m	**crayon** pencil		*f*	**matière** subject
f	**cuisine** kitchen			**moyen en anglais** average at English
m	**dessin** art		*f*	**musique** music
m/f	**directeur/trice** headteacher		*f*	**natation** swimming
m	**échange** exchange		*f*	**note** mark
f	**école(primaire)** primary school			**obligatoire** compulsory
f	**éducation physique** *f.* physical education		*m*	**ordinateur** computer
f	**électronique** electronics		*m*	**papier** paper
m/f	**élève** pupil		*f*	**phrase** sentence
m	**emploi du temps** timetable		*f*	**physique** physics
	en avance early		*f*	**piscine** swimming pool
	en retard late		*m*	**professeur** teacher
	en sixième/ cinquième etc. in the first/ second year etc		*f*	**récréation** (morning) break
m	**enseignement** teaching		*f*	**rentrée** back to school
m	**espagnol** Spanish		*m*	**résultat** result
f	**étude** study		*f*	**salle de classe** classroom
f	**études ménagères (arts ménagers) (m)** home economics		*f*	**salle des professeurs** staffroom
m	**étudiant** student		*f*	**salle** room
m	**examen** exam		*f*	**sciences** science
f	**excursion** trip			**secondaire** secondary
m	**exemple** example			**sportif** sporty
	faible en anglais weak at English		*m*	**stylo** pen
f	**faute** fault, mistake		*m*	**tableau** blackboard
	fort en allemand good at German		*f*	**terminale** upper sixth
m	**français** French		*m*	**travail** work
f	**géographie** geography		*m*	**travaux manuels/ pratiques** craft subjects
m	**grec** Greek		*m*	**uniforme** uniform
m	**groupe** group		*f*	**vacances** holidays

Careers, jobs and places of work

	à l'étranger abroad	
m	**agent de police** policeman	
m	**boucher** butcher	
m	**boulanger** baker	
m	**bureau** office	
m	**certificat** certificate	
m/f	**chauffeur/euse** driver	
m	**chômage** unemployment	
m/f	**coiffeur/euse** hairdresser	
m	**commerce** business	
m/f	**cuisinier/ière** cook	
m	**dentiste** dentist	
m	**diplôme** diploma	
m	**docteur** doctor	
m/f	**électricien/nne** electrician	
m	**emploi** job	
m	**employeur** employer	
m	**épicier** grocer	
f	**études** studies	
m/f	**facteur** postman/woman	
f	**ferme** farm	
m/f	**fermier/ière** farmer	
m	**garagiste** garage owner	
m	**garçon de café** waiter	
m	**gendarme** policeman	
m	**hôpital** hospital	

f	**hôtesse de l'air** air hostess
f	**industrie** industry
m/f	**infirmier/ière** nurse
m/f	**journaliste** journalist
m	**magasin** shop
m/f	**mécanicien/nne** mechanic
m	**médecin** doctor
m	**métier** profession
m/f	**musicien/nne** musician
	peut-être perhaps
m	**pilote** pilot
m	**pompier** fireman
m	**porteur** porter
f	**profession** profession
m	**projet** plan
m	**salaire** salary
f	**secrétaire** secretary
m/f	**serveur/euse** waiter/waitrèss
f	**situation** situation, job
m	**travail** work
f	**université** university
f	**usine** factory
f	**vedette** star
m/f	**vendeur/euse** salesman/woman
	vétérinaire vet

Additional higher vocabulary

KEY VERBS

avoir raison/tort to be right/ wrong
faire sa licence to do one's degree
changer d'avis to change one's mind
changer d'emploi to change one's job
conseiller to advise

croire to believe
décider to decide
avoir l'intention to intend
échouer to fail
enseigner to teach
être attiré par to be attracted by
être reçu to pass (an exam)
exercer un métier to follow a profession

fournir to supply, provide
jouer dans une pièce to act in a play
participer to participate
poser une question to ask a question
prendre des notes to take notes

prouver to prove
raconter to tell
réussir to succeed
s'entendre to get on (with people)
s'intéresser à to be interested in
se taire to be quiet
traduire to translate
tricher to cheat

School

f	**année**	year
m	**brevet**	qualification
	capable	capable
f	**chorale**	choir
m	**congé**	leave,holiday
f	**cour**	playground
	dur	hard
f	**durée**	duration,length
f	**formation professionnelle**	training

il vaut mieux	it is better to
f **occasion**	opportunity
f **peinture**	painting
m **pensionnaire**	boarder
f **poterie**	pottery
prochain	next
temporaire	temporary
vraiment	really

Careers, jobs and places of work

m	**acteur**	actor
f	**actrice**	actress
f	**affaires**	business
f	**agence de voyages**	travel agency
f	**agence pour l'emploi**	job agency
m	**animateur**	activities leader
m/f	**apprenti/e**	apprentice
m	**arbitre**	judge;referee
m/f	**architecte/-**	architect
m	**atelier**	workshop
m	**auteur**	author
m	**avenir**	future
m/f	**avocat/e**	lawyer
m/f	**bibliothécaire/-**	librarian
m	**boulot**	work
m	**cadre**	executive
f	**carrière**	career
m/f	**chanteur/euse**	singer
m/f	**chirurgien/nne**	surgeon
m/f	**chômeur/euse**	an unemployed person
m	**commerçant**	tradesman
f	**compagnie**	company
m/f	**comptable/-**	accountant
m/f	**concierge**	caretaker
m/f	**conducteur/trice**	driver

f	**femme de ménage**	home help
f/m	**femme/homme d'affaires**	business woman/man
m/f	**fonctionnaire**	civil servant
m	**hôtelier**	hotelier
m	**ingénieur**	engineer
m	**inspecteur**	inspector
m/f	**instituteur/trice**	primary school teacher
m	**jardinier**	gardener
m	**maçon**	mason
m	**mannequin**	model
m/f	**menuisier/ière**	carpenter;joiner
m	**militaire**	soldier
m	**mineur**	miner
m/f	**opticien/ne**	optician
f	**ouvreuse**	usherette
m/f	**ouvrier/ière**	worker
	P.D.G.	managing director
m/f	**pêcheur/euse**	fisher
m	**pharmacien**	chemist
m	**photographe**	photographer
m	**pilote de course**	racing driver
f	**place**	position; job
m/f	**plombier/ière**	plumber
m/f	**programmeur**	computer programmer

f	**dactylo** typist	
m/f	**danseur/euse** dancer	
m	**décorateur** decorator	
m/f	**dessinateur/trice industriel/le** industrial designer	
m	**douanier** customs official	
	durant during	
m/f	**écolier/ière** schoolboy/girl	
m/f	**étudiant/e** student	

f	**réceptionniste** receptionist
m/f	**réprésentant/e** representative
m/f	**retraité/e** a retired person
m	**stage** course
m/f	**standardiste** telephone operator
f	**sténo-dactylo** shorthand typist
m	**syndicat** union
m	**syndiqué/e** trade-unionist
m/f	**téchnicien/nne** technician

Grammar Section

GRAMMAR SECTION

CONTENTS

Verbs

Articles

Nouns

Adjectives

Adverbs

Making Comparisons, Expressing Superlatives

Demonstrative Adjectives

Demonstrative Pronouns

Pronouns: Possessive Pronouns and Adjectives

Conjunctions

VERBS

Present participle

The impersonal form of the verb, ending in -ing in English and **-ant** in French

Use in these cases:

Tout en mangeant, il a écrit une lettre.	While eating, he wrote a letter.
Je travaille en écoutant la radio.	I work whilst listening to the radio.
En étudiant, on réussit aux examens.	By studying, you pass exams.

The present participle can also be used as an adjective:

son visage souriant	her smiling face
l'équipe gagnante	the winning team

Avoid this English usage of the present participle:

a)   after certain prepositions eg without/before/by trying etc
b)   after certain verbs eg to like/to spend time playing/watching etc

a. **J'ai réussi sans travailler.**	I passed without working.
b. **J'aime jouer aux échecs.**	I like playing chess.
J'ai passé la soirée à lire.	I spent the evening reading.

Past participle

1.   used with the compound tenses

Il a été malade.	He has been ill.
Le bus était déjà arrivé.	The bus had already arrived.

2.   used as an adjective

The past particple can be used as an adjective

Elle a la main blessée.	She has hurt her hand.
les fenêtres cassées.	broken windows.

Infinitive

All verbs are referred to by their infinitive (in dictionaries etc). They cannot be used with personal pronouns.

Use of tenses

The present tense - PRES

The present tense expresses

a.　what is happening now
b.　what happens regularly or sometimes
c.　a permanent or semi-permanent state

Examples

a.	I'm doing my homework.	**Je fais mes devoirs.**
b.	We watch TV on Saturdays.	**Nous regardons la télé le samedi.**
c.	She lives in Edinburgh.	**Elle habite à Edimbourg.**

The future tense - FUTU

The future tense in English is usually expressed by "will" and "shall".

Examples

a.	He will arrive at 8 o'clock.	**Il arrivera à huit heures.**
b.	I shall never smoke.	**Je ne fumerai jamais.**
c.	What will you do next year?	**Que feras-tu l'année prochaine?**

The conditional tense - COND

The conditional tense is recognised in English generally by "would", and sometimes "should", when by the latter preference not obligation is intended.

Examples

a.	I should like to see you again.	**J'aimerais bien te revoir.**
b.	She would go by boat, but she's in a hurry.	**Elle prendrait le bateau, mais elle est pressée.**
c.	He said that he would come.	**Il a dit qu'il viendrait.**
d.	If I lived in the country I'd go for a walk every day.	**Si j'habitais à la compagne je me promènerais tous les jours.**
e.	Would it be possible to send me a brochure on Touron?	**Serait-il possible de recevoir une brochure sur Touron?**

Note   *a) The conditional tense of **devoir** conveys "should" or "ought to".*
       *b) The conditional tense of **pouvoir** often expresses the English "might".*

Examples

a.	You ought to/should do it.	**Tu devrais le faire.**
b.	He might be a policeman.	**Il pourrait être agent de police.**

The imperfect tense - IMPF

The imperfect tense expresses

a.   what was happening

b.   what used to happen

c.   what happened over a period of time and severally

In English look out for "was", "were" and "used to".

Examples

a.	I was sleeping when you knocked.	**Je dormais quand tu as frappé.**
b.	They used to live in Germany.	**Ils habitaient en Allemagne.**
c.	When I was young I used to play tennis a lot.	**Quand j'étais jeune je jouais beaucoup au tennis.**
d.	She visited her family every Sunday.	**Elle rendait visite à sa famille tous les samedis.**
e.	It was excellent.	**C'était excellent.**

Note   ***Penser, croire** and **savoir** are often used in the imperfect in French, where in English it looks like a perfect.*

Examples

a.	They thought it was good.	**Ils pensaient que c'était bon.**
b.	She thought she had found the answer.	**Elle croyait avoir trouvé la solution.**
c.	I didn't know if you would come.	**Je ne savais pas si vous viendriez.**

The perfect tense - PERF

English has many ways of conveying the sense of an action in the past, which can be recognised by "has" and "have", "has been" and "have been", and by "-ed" added to, or radical changes in, the verb.

Examples

a.	They have bought a new house.	**Ils ont acheté une nouvelle maison.**
b.	He has forgotten.	**Il a oublié.**
c.	I washed the car yesterday.	**J'ai lavé la voiture hier.**
d.	She had breakfast in bed.	**Elle a pris le petit déjeuner au lit.**
e.	I have been helping my father.	**J'ai aidé mon père.**

The pluperfect tense - PLUP

The pluperfect tense is recognised in English by "had" and "had been".

Examples

a.	The film had started when I arrived.	**Le film avait commencé quand j'y suis arrivée.**
b.	He had already decided.	**Il avait déjà décidé.**

The past historic - HIST

The past historic is used in narratives in the written language only, generally in newspapers, magazines, novels and the like. You may need to recognise this tense.

Examples

a.	The thief ran off at top speed.	**Le voleur se sauva à toutes jambes.**
b.	She was astonished.	**Elle fut étonnée.**

Question forms

There are three ways of making a statement into a question in French. These apply to all tenses.

a. by intonation, at the end of a statement.
b. by adding **est-ce que** in front of the statement.
c. by turning the verb round (inversion).

Examples

a.	**Vous voulez encore de la viande?**	
b.	**Est-ce que vous voulez encore de la viande?**	Do you want some more meat?
c.	**Voulez-vous encore de la viande?**	
a.	**Il viendra à l'heure?**	
b.	**Est-ce qu'il viendra à l'heure?**	Will he come on time?
c.	**Viendra-t-il à l'heure?**	
a.	**Elle est partie?**	
b.	**Est-ce qu'elle est partie?**	Has she left?
c.	**Est-elle partie?**	

Note   Inversion can also occur when no question is intended
*   a.   after direct speech*
*   b.   after **peut-être** and **à peine***
*   c.   after **où** in a subordinate clause*

Examples

a.	**"Je voudrais vous aider", a-t-il dit.**	"I'd like to help you", he said.
b.	**A peine ai-je terminé, quand...**	I'd hardly finished, when...
c.	**Le village où habitent mes grand-parents est au Pays de Galles.**	The village where my grandparents live is in Wales.

Negatives

Negatives in French are in two parts, positioned on either side of the verb, or round the auxilliary in compound tenses.

Examples

Je n'aime pas faire le ménage.	I don't like doing housework.
Il n'écoutait pas.	He was not listening.
Elle n'a pas oublié.	She has not forgotten.

These are the other negatives -

ne...jamais	never/not ever
ne...rien	nothing/not anything
ne...plus	no more/not any more/no longer
ne...personne	nobody/not anyone
ne...que	only
ne...nulle part	nowhere/not anywhere
ne...aucun	no/not any
ne...guère	scarcely/hardly
ne...ni...ni	neither...nor

Examples

Ils n'ont jamais visité l'Allemagne.	They have never visited Germany.
Je ne vois rien.	I dont see anything.
Elle n'habite plus à Newcastle.	She no longer lives in Newcastle.
Il ne respecte personne.	He respects no-one.
Je ne le trouve nulle part.	I can't find it anywhere.
Il n'y a aucune raison pour y aller.	There is no reason to go there.
Je n'ai guère le temps.	I've hardly got the time.
Il ne mange ni beurre ni fromage.	He doesn't eat butter or cheese.

Note   *a.* **ne...personne**, **ne...nulle part** and **ne...que** *have a different position in compound tenses.*

Ils n'ont trouvé personne.	They found nobody.
Nous ne l'avons vu nulle part.	We didn't see him anywhere.
Je n'ai acheté que deux baguettes.	I only bought two loaves.

b. "Nothing" and "nobody" are frequently subjects in a sentence.

Rien ne me dérange.	Nothing disturbs me.
Personne n'est venu.	Nobody came.

c. These negatives can stand alone.

Never!	Jamais!
Nothing!	Rien!
Nobody!	Personne!

d. Note the following expressions with more than one negative.

Je ne veux plus rien.	I dont want anything any more.
Ils ne font jamais rien.	They never do anything.
Elle n'a jamais parle a personne.	She has never talked to anyone.

Introduction to Timetables

Verbs are set out in five TABLES, as follows:

TABLE 1:   regular verbs. **quitter, finir** and **perdre** are given as examples.

TABLE 2:   shows six groups of verbs which have minor deviations from TABLE 1.

TABLE 3:   lists all the verbs which use **être** in the compound tenses.

TABLE 4:   reflexive verbs. These are given in full.

TABLE 5:   irregular verbs. These are given in full.

Verbs given in full are shown in capital letters.

TABLE 1: regular verbs

One example of each type of regular verbs is written out in full.

QUITTER	- to leave
FINIR	- to finish
PERDRE	- to lose

TABLE 2: verbs with minor deviations form TABLE 1

GROUP 1 Verbs ending in **-eler, -ener, -eter, -ever.**

ACHETER	to buy	**lever**	to lift
amener	to bring, to lead	**mener**	to lead
emmener	to take (someone) away	**peser**	to weigh
geler	to freeze	**se promener**	to go for a walk

One example is written out only in those tenses where the verb differs from TABLE 1 by adding an accent.

GROUP 2 **appeler, jeter** and their compounds

APPELER	to call	**rappeler**	to recall
jeter	to throw	**rejeter**	to throw back

One example is written out only in those tenses differing from TABLE 1, where the final consonant of the stem is doubled.

GROUP 3 verbs ending in **-yer**

appuyer	to press, to lean	**essayer**	to try (on)
balayer	to sweep	**essuyer**	to wipe
employer	to use	**NETTOYER**	to clean
ennuyer	to bore, annoy	**payer**	to pay
envoyer	to send (PRES only)		

One example is written out only in those tenses where the verb differs from TABLE 1.

*Note   verbs ending in -**ayer** can retain the **y** in all tenses.*

GROUP 4   verbs ending in **-ger**

bouger	to move	**manger**	to eat
CHANGER	to change	**nager**	to swim
charger	to load	**obliger**	to oblige
déranger	to disturb	**partager**	to share
diriger	to direct	**protéger**	to protect
échanger	to exchange	**ranger**	to tidy, to arrange
loger	to lodge	**voyager**	to travel

One example is included to show where an extra **e** is required in certain tenses.

GROUP 5   verbs ending in **-cer**

annoncer	to announce	**menacer**	to threaten
avancer	to advance	**prononcer**	to pronounce
COMMENCER	to begin	**remplacer**	to replace
lancer	to throw		

One example is included to show where a **ç** cedilla is required in certain tenses.

GROUP 6   verbs requiring a change of accent in the present tense

considérer	to consider	**protéger**	to protect
différer	to differ	**régler**	to regulate
ESPÉRER	to hope	**répéter**	to repeat
s'inquiéter	to worry	**révéler**	to reveal
pénétrer	to penetrate	**sécher**	to dry
préférer	to prefer		

One example is included to show where the change of accent occurs.

TABLE 3: verbs taking "être" in the compound tenses

aller	to go	(See also TABLE 5)
venir	to come	(See also TABLE 5)
entrer	to go in	(See also TABLE 1)
sortir	to go out	(See also TABLE 5)
arriver	to arrive	(See also TABLE 1)
partir	to leave	(See also TABLE 5)
naître	to be born	(See also TABLE 5)
mourir	to die	(See also TABLE 5)
rester	to stay	(See also TABLE 1)
retourner	to return	(See also TABLE 1)
descendre	to go down	(See also TABLE 1)
monter	to go up	(See also TABLE 1)
TOMBER	to fall	(See also TABLE 1)

Note also these compounds

devenir	to become	(See also TABLE 5)
revenir	to come back	(See also TABLE 5)
rentrer	to go home	(See also TABLE 1)
ressortir	to go out again	(See also TABLE 5)
repartir	to leave again	(See also TABLE 5)
renaître	to be born again	(See also TABLE 5)
redescendre	to go down again	(See also TABLE 1)
remonter	to go up again	(See also TABLE 1)
retomber	to fall down again	(See also TABLE 1)

One example is written out in the two relevant tenses. For all other tenses refer to the TABLES as indicated above.

TABLE 4: *reflexive verbs*

Note   1. *These are verbs which engage an extra pronoun (see full table) to refer to self, or each other.*

Je me réveille à 6 heures normalement.	I usually wake up at 6.
Ils s'écrivent tous les mois.	They write to each other every months.
Vous vous appelez comment?	What's your name?

2. *They can be used transitively (without extra pronoun)*

Je réveille mon frère à 6 h 30.	I wake my brother at 6.30.
J'ai écrit une lettre hier.	I wrote a letter yesterday.
J'appellerai demain.	I'll call tomorrow.

3. *List of verbs often used in the reflexive form.*
One example (se laver) is written out in full.

s'adresser à	to apply	**se faire mal à**	to hurt oneself
s'en aller	to go away	**se fouler**	to twist (ankle)
s'agir de	to be about	**s'habiller**	to dress
s'amuser	to enjoy oneself	**s'informer de**	to find out
s'appeler	to be called	**s'inquiéter**	to worry
s'approcher de	to approach	**s'installer**	to install oneself
s'arrêter	to stop	**s'intéresser à**	to be interested
s'asseoir	to sit down	**SE LAVER**	to wash
se baigner	to go for a swim	**se lever**	to get up
se battre	to fight	**se marier**	to get married
se blesser	to injure oneself	**se mettre en colère**	to get angry
se bronzer	to sunbathe	**se noyer**	to drown
se brosser	to brush	**s'occuper de**	to look after
se brûler	to burn oneself	**se passer**	to happen
se cacher	to hide	**se peigner**	to comb
se casser	to break	**se perdre**	to get lost
se corriger	to correct	**se plaindre de**	to complain
se coucher	to go to bed	**se présenter**	to introduce oneself
se couper	to cut oneself	**se promener**	to go for a walk
se critiquer	to criticise oneself	**se prononcer**	to be pronounced
se débrouiller	to get by/cope	**se rappeler de**	to remember
se demander	to wonder	**se raser**	to shave
se dépêcher	to hurry	**se rendre compte de**	to realise
se déshabiller	to undress	**se renseigner**	to find out

se dire to be said	**se reposer** to rest	
s'écrire to write to each other	**se réveiller** to wake up	
se sentir to feel	**se sauver** to run away	
s'égarer to lose ones way	**se servir de** to use, help oneself	
s'endormir to go to sleep	**se souvenir** to remember	
s'ennuyer to be/get bored	**se taire** to be quiet	
s'entendre to get on with	**se tromper de** to make a mistake	
s'évanouir to faint	**se trouver** to be (situated)	
s'excuser de to apologise	**se voir** to see each other	

TABLE 5: *irregular verbs*

All irregular verbs are written out in full.

TABLE 1: regular verbs

QUITTER *to leave*			je/j'	tu
Infinitive	**quitter**	PRES	quitte	quittes
		COMM	-	quitte!
present participle	**quittant**	FUTU	quitterai	quitteras
		COND	quitterais	quitterais
past participle	**quitté**	IMPF	quittais	quittais
		PERF	ai quitté	as quitté
		PLUP	avais quitté	avais quitté
		HIST	quittai	quittas

FINIR *to finish*				
	finir	PRES	finis	finis
		COMM	-	finis!
	finissant	FUTU	finirai	finirai
		COND	finirais	finirais
		IMPF	finissais	finissais
	fini	PERF	ai fini	as fini
		PLUP	avais fini	avais fini
		HIST	finis	finis

PERDRE *to lose*				
	perdre	PRES	perds	perds
		COMM	-	perds!
	perdant	FUTU	perdrai	perdras
		COND	perdrais	perdrais
		IMPF	perdais	perdais
	perdu	PERF	ai perdu	as perdu
		PLUP	avais perdu	avais perdu
		HIST	perdis	perdis

il/elle/on	nous	vous	ils/elles
quitte	quittons	quittez	quittent
-	quittons!	quittez!	-
quittera	quitterons	quitterez	quitteront
quitterait	quitterions	quitteriez	quitteraient
quittait	quittions	quittiez	quittaient
a quitté	avons quitté	avez quitté	ont quitté
avait quitté	avions quitté	aviez quitté	avaient quitté
quitta	quittâmes	quittâtes	quittèrent
finit	finissons	finissez	finissent
-	finissons!	finissez!	-
finira	finirons	finirez	finiront
finirait	finirions	finiriez	finiraient
finissait	finissions	finissiez	finissaient
a fini	avons fini	avez fini	ont fini
avait fini	avions fini	aviez fini	avaient fini
finit	finîmes	finîtes	finirent
perd	perdons	perdez	perdent
-	perdons!	perdez!	-
perdra	perdrons	perdrez	perdront
perdrait	perdrions	perdriez	perdraient
perdait	perdions	perdiez	perdaient
a perdu	avons perdu	avez perdu	ont perdu
avait perdu	avions perdu	aviez perdu	avaient perdu
perdit	perdîmes	perdîtes	perdirent

TABLE 2: verbs with minor deviations from Table 1

ACHETER	to buy		je/j'	tu
Infinitive	**acheter**	PRES	achète	achètes
		FUTU	achèterai	achèteras
		COND	achèterais	achèterais

APPELER	to call			
Infinitive	**appeler**	PRES	appelle	appelles
		FUTU	appellerai	appelleras
		COND	apellerais	appellerais

NETTOYER	to clean			
Infinitive	**nettoyer**	PRES	nettoie	nettoies
		FUTU	nettoierai	nettoieras
		COND	nettoierais	nettoierais

CHANGER	to change			
Infinitive	**changer**	PRES	change	changes
		IMPF	changeais	changeais
present participle	**changeant**	HIST	changeai	changeas

COMMENCER	to start			
Infinitive	**commencer**	PRES	commence	commences
		IMPF	commençais	commençais
present participle	**commençant**	HIST	commençai	commenças

ESPÉRER	to hope			
Infinitive	**espérer**	PRES	espère	espères

TABLE 3: verbs taking "être" in compound tenses

TOMBER	to fall			
Infinitive	**tomber**	PERF	suis tombé/e	es tombé/e
present participle	**tombant**	PLUP	étais tombé/e	étais tombé/e
past participle	**tombé**			

il/elle/on	nous	vous	ils/elles
achète	achetons	achetez	achètent
achètera	achèterons	achèterez	achèteront
achèterait	achèterions	achèteriez	achèteraient
appelle	appelons	appelez	appellent
appellera	appellerons	appellerez	appelleront
appellerait	appellerions	appelleriez	appelleraient
nettoie	nettoyons	nettoyez	nettoient
nettoiera	nettoierons	nettoierez	nettoieront
nettoierait	nettoierions	nettoieriez	nettoieraient
change	changeons	changez	changent
changeait	changions	changiez	changeaient
changea	changeâmes	changeâtes	changèrent
commence	commençons	commencez	commencent
commençait	commencions	commenciez	commencaient
commença	commençames	commençates	commencèrent
espère	espérons	espérez	espèrent
est tombé/e	sommes tombé/e/s	êtes tombé/e/s	sont tombé/e/s
était tombé/e	étions tombé/e/s	étiez tombé/e/s	étaient tombé/e/s

TABLE 4: reflexive verbs

SE LAVER *to wash*			**je/j'**	**t u**
Infinitive	**se laver**	PRES	me lave	te laves
		COMM	-	lave-toi!
present participle	**se lavant**	FUTU	me laverai	te laveras
		COND	me laverais	te laverais
		IMPF	me lavais	te lavais
past participle	**lavé**	PERF	me suis lavé/e	t'es lavé/e
		PLUP	m'étais lavé/e	t'étais lavé/e
		HIST	me lavai	te lavas

TABLE 5: irregular verbs

ALLER *to go*				
Infinitive	**aller**	PRES	vais	vas
		COMM	-	va!
present participle	**allant**	FUTU	irai	iras
		COND	irais	irais
		IMPF	allais	allais
past participle	**allé**	PERF	suis allé/e	es allé/e
		PLUP	étais allé/e	étais allé/e
		HIST	allai	allas

APPRENDRE - *to learn*
like **PRENDRE**

S'ASSEOIR *to sit down*				
	s'asseoir	PRES	m'assieds	t'assieds
		COMM	-	assieds-toi!
	s'asseyant	FUTU	m'assiérai	t'assiéras
		COND	m'assiérais	t'assiérais
		IMPF	m'asseyais	t'asseyais
	assis	PERF	me suis assis/e	t'es assis/e
		PLUP	m'étais assis/e	t'étais assis/e
		HIST	m'assis	t'assis

il/elle/on	nous	vous	ils/elles
se lave	nous lavons	vous lavez	se lavent
-	lavons-nous!	lavez-vous!	-
se lavera	nous laverons	vous laverez	se laveront
se laverait	nous laverions	vous laveriez	se laveraient
se lavait	nous lavions	vous laviez	se lavaient
s'est lavé/e	nous sommes lavé/e/s	vous êtes lavé/e/s	se sont lavé/e/s
s'était lavé/e	nous étions lavé/e/s	vous étiez lavé/e/s	s'étaient lavé/e/s
se lava	nous lavâmes	vous lavâtes	se lavèrent

va	allons	allez	vont
-	allons!	allez!	-
ira	irons	irez	iront
irait	irions	iriez	iraient
allait	allions	alliez	allaient
est allé/e	sommes allé/e/s	êtes allé/e/s	sont allé/e/s
était allé/e	étions allé/e/s	étiez allé/e/s	étaient allé/e/s
alla	allâmes	allâtes	allèrent

s'assied	nous asseyons	vous asseyez	s'asseyent
-	asseyons-nous!	asseyez-vous!	
s'assiéra	nous assiérons	vous assiérez	s'assiéront
s'assiérait	nous assiérions	vous assiériez	s'assiéraient
s'asseyait	nous asseyions	vous asseyiez	s'asseyaient
s'est assis/e	nous sommes assis/es	vous êtes assis/e/s	se sont assis/es
s'était assis/e	nous étions assis/es	vous étiez assis/e/s	s'étaient assis/es
s'assit	nous assîmes	vous assîtes	s'assirent

AVOIR *to have*

		je/j'	tu
avoir	PRES	ai	as
	COMM	-	aie!
ayant	FUTU	aurai	auras
	COND	aurais	aurais
	IMPF	avais	avais
e u	PERF	ai eu	as eu
	PLUP	avais eu	avais eu
	HIST	eus	eus

BATTRE *to beat*

battre	PRES	bats	bats
	COMM	-	bats!
battant	FUTU	battrai	battras
	COND	battrais	battrais
	IMPF	battais	battais
battu	PERF	ai battu	as battu
	PLUP	avais battu	avais battu
	HIST	battis	battis

BOIRE *to drink*

boire	PRES	bois	bois
	COMM	-	bois!
buvant	FUTU	boirai	boiras
	COND	boirais	boirais
	IMPF	buvais	buvais
b u	PERF	ai bu	as bu
	PLUP	avais bu	avais bu
	HIST	bus	bus

COMPRENDRE - *to understand*
like **PRENDRE**

CONDUIRE *to drive*

conduire	PRES	conduis	conduis
	COMM	-	conduis!
conduisant	FUTU	conduirai	conduiras
	COND	conduirais	conduirais
	IMPF	conduisais	conduisais
conduit	PERF	ai conduit	as conduit
	PLUP	avais conduit	avais conduit
	HIST	conduisis	conduisis

il/elle/on	nous	vous	ils/elles
a	avons	avez	ont
-	ayons!	ayez!	-
aura	aurons	aurez	auront
aurait	aurions	auriez	auraient
avait	avions	aviez	avaient
a eu	avons eu	avez eu	ont eu
avait eu	avions eu	aviez eu	avaient eu
eut	eûmes	eûtes	eurent
bat	battons	battez	battent
	battons!	battez!	-
battra	battrons	battrez	battront
battrait	battrions	battriez	battraient
battait	battions	battiez	battaient
a battu	avons battu	avez battu	ont battu
avait battu	avions battu	aviez battu	avaient battu
battit	battîmes	battîtes	battirent
boit	buvons	buvez	boivent
-	buvons!	buvez!	-
boira	boirons	boirez	boiront
boirait	boirions	boiriez	boiraient
buvait	buvions	buviez	buvaient
a bu	avons bu	avez bu	ont bu
avait bu	avions bu	aviez bu	avaient bu
but	bûmes	bûtes	burent
conduit	conduisons	conduisez	conduisent
-	conduisons!	conduisez!	-
conduira	conduirons	conduirez	conduiront
conduirait	conduirions	conduiriez	conduiraient
conduisait	conduisions	conduisiez	conduisaient
a conduit	avons conduit	avez conduit	ont conduit
avait conduit	avions conduit	aviez conduit	avaient conduit
conduisit	conduisîmes	conduisîtes	conduisirent

CONNAITRE *to know*		je/j'	tu
connaître	PRES	connais	connais
	COMM	-	connais!
connaissant	FUTU	connaîtrai	connaîtras
	COND	connaîtrais	connaîtrais
	IMPF	connaissais	connaissais
connu	PERF	ai connu	as connu
	PLUP	avais connu	avais connu
	HIST	connus	connus

CONSTRUIRE - *to build*
like **CONDUIRE**

CONTENIR - *to contain*
like **TENIR**

CONVENIR - *to suit*
like **TENIR**

COURIR *to run*			
courir	PRES	cours	cours
	COMM	-	cours!
courant	FUTU	courrai	courras
	COND	courrais	courrais
	IMPF	courais	courais
couru	PERF	ai couru	as couru
	PLUP	avais couru	avais couru
	HIST	courus	courus

COUVRIR - *to cover*
like **OUVRIR**

CRAINDRE - *to fear*
like **ÉTEINDRE**

Il/elle/on	nous	vous	ils/elles
connaît	connaissons	connaissez	connaissent
-	connaissons!	connaissez!	-
connaîtra	connaîtrons	connaîtrez	connaîtront
connaîtrait	connaîtrions	connaîtriez	connaîtraient
connaissait	connaissions	connaissiez	connaissaient
a connu	avons connu	avez connu	ont connu
avait connu	avions connu	aviez connu	avaient connu
connut	connûmes	connûtes	connurent

court	courons	courez	courent
-	courons!	courez!	-
courra	courrons	courrez	courront
courrait	courrions	courriez	courraient
courait	courions	couriez	couraient
a couru	avons couru	avez couru	ont couru
avait couru	avions couru	aviez couru	avaient couru
courut	courûmes	courûtes	coururent

CROIRE   *to believe*

		je/j'	**tu**
croire	PRES	crois	crois
	COMM	-	crois!
croyant	FUTU	croirai	croiras
	COND	croirais	croirais
	IMPF	croyais	croyais
cru	PERF	ai cru	as cru
	PLUP	avais cru	avais cru
	HIST	crus	crus

DÉCOUVRIR - *to discover*
like **OUVRIR**

DÉCRIRE - *to describe*
like **ÉCRIRE**

DÉTRUIRE - *to destroy*
like **CONDUIRE**

DEVENIR - *to become*
like **VENIR**

DEVOIR   *to have to*

devoir	PRES	dois	dois
	COMM	-	dois!
devant	FUTU	devrai	devras
	COND	devrais	devrais
	IMPF	devais	devais
dû	PERF	ai dû	as dû
	PLUP	avais dû	avais dû
	HIST	dus	dus

il/elle/on	nous	vous	ils/elles
croit	croyons	croyez	croient
-	croyons!	croyez!	-
croira	croirons	croirez!	croiront
croirait	croirions	croiriez	croiraient
croyait	croyions	croyiez	croyaient
a cru	avons cru	avez cru	ont cru
avait cru	avions cru	aviez cru	avaient cru
crut	crûmes	crûtes	crurent

doit	devons	devez	doivent
-	devons!	devez!	-
devra	devrons	devrez	devront
devrait	devrions	devriez	devraient
devait	devions	deviez	devaient
a dû	avons dû	avez dû	ont dû
avait dû	avions dû	aviez dû	avaient dû
dut	dûmes	dûtes	durent

DIRE *to say*

		je/j'	tu
dire	PRES	dis	dis
	COMM	-	dis!
disant	FUTU	dirai	diras
	COND	dirais	dirais
	IMPF	disais	disais
dit	PERF	ai dit	as dit
	PLUP	avais dit	avais dit
	HIST	dis	dis

DISPARAÎTRE -
like **CONNAÎTRE**

DORMIR *to sleep*

		je/j'	tu
dormir	PRES	dors	dors
	COMM	-	dors!
dormant	FUTU	dormirai	dormiras
	COND	dormirais	dormirais
	IMPF	dormais	dormais
dormi	PERF	ai dormi	as dormi
	PLUP	avais dormi	avais dormi
	HIST	dormis	dormis

ÉCRIRE *to write*

		je/j'	tu
écrire	PRES	écris	écris
	COMM	-	écris!
écrivant	FUTU	écrirai	écriras
	COND	écrirais	écrirais
	IMPF	écrivais	écrivais
écrit	PERF	ai écrit	as écrit
	PLUP	avais écrit	avais écrit
	HIST	écrivis	écrivis

Il/elle/on	nous	vous	ils/elles
dit	disons	dites	disent
-	disons!	dites!	-
dira	dirons	direz	diront
dirait	dirions	diriez	diraient
disait	disions	disiez	disaient
a dit	avons dit	avez dit	ont dit
avait dit	avions dit	aviez dit	avaient dit
dit	dîmes	dîtes	dirent

dort	dormons	dormez	dorment
-	dormons!	dormez!	-
dormira	dormirons	dormirez	dormiront
dormirait	dormirions	dormiriez	dormiraient
dormait	dormions	dormiez	dormaient
a dormi	avons dormi	avez dormi	ont dormi
avait dormi	avions dormi	aviez dormi	avaient dormi
dormit	dormîmes	dormîtes	dormirent

écrit	écrivons	écrivez	écrivent
-	écrivons!	écrivez!	-
écrira	écrirons	écrirez	écriront
écrirait	écririons	écririez	écriraient
écrivait	écrivions	écriviez	écrivaient
a écrit	avons écrit	avez écrit	ont écrit
avait écrit	avions écrit	aviez écrit	avaient écrit
écrivit	écrivîmes	écrivîtes	écrivirent

ENTRETENIR - *to maintain*
like **TENIR**
ENVOYER *to send*

		je/j'	tu
envoyer	PRES	envoie	envoies
	COMM	-	envoie!
envoyant	FUTU	enverrai	enverras
	COND	enverrais	enverrais
	IMPF	envoyais	envoyais
envoyé	PERF	ai envoyé	as envoyé
	PLUP	avais envoyé	avais envoyé
	HIST	envoyai	envoyas

ÉTEINDRE *to put out, to switch off*

éteindre	PRES	éteins	éteins
	COMM	-	éteins!
éteignant	FUTU	éteindrai	éteindras
	COND	éteindrais	éteindrais
	IMPF	éteignais	éteignais
éteint	PERF	ai éteint	as éteint
	PLUP	avais éteint	avais éteint
	HIST	éteignis	éteignis

ÊTRE *to be*

être	PRES	suis	es
	COMM	-	sois!
étant	FUTU	serai	seras
	COND	serais	serais
	IMPF	étais	étais
été	PERF	ai éte	as été
	PLUP	avais été	avais été
	HIST	fus	fus

FAIRE *to do, to make*

faire	PRES	fais	fais
	COMM	-	fais!
faisant	FUTU	ferai	feras
	COND	ferais	ferais
	IMPF	faisais	faisais
fait	PERF	ai fait	as fait
	PLUP	avais fait	avais fait
	HIST	fis	fis

Il/elle/on	nous	vous	Ils/elles
envoie	envoyons	envoyez	envoient
-	envoyons!	envoyez!	-
enverra	enverrons	enverrez	enverront
enverrait	enverrions	enverriez	enverraient
envoyait	envoyions	envoyiez	envoyaient
a envoyé	avons envoyé	avez envoyé	ont envoyé
avait envoyé	avions envoyé	aviez envoyé	avaient envoyé
envoya	envoyâmes	envoyâtes	envoyèrent
éteint	éteignons	éteignez	éteignent
-	éteignons!	éteignez!	-
éteindra	éteindrons	éteindrez	éteindront
éteindrait	éteindrions	éteindriez	éteindraient
éteignait	éteignions	éteigniez	éteignaient
a éteint	avons éteint	avez éteint	ont éteint
avait étient	avions éteint	aviez éteint	avaient éteint
éteignit	éteignîmes	éteignîtes	éteignirent
est	sommes	êtes	sont
-	soyons!	soyez!	-
sera	serons	serez	seront
serait	serions	seriez	seraient
était	étions	étiez	étaient
a été	avons été	avez été	ont été
avait été	avions été	aviez été	avaient été
fut	fûmes	fûtes	furent
fait	faisons	faites	font
-	faisons!	faites!	-
fera	ferons	ferez	feront
ferait	ferions	feriez	feraient
faisait	faisions	faisiez	faisaient
a fait	avons fait	avez fait	ont fait
avait fait	avions fait	aviez fait	avaient fait
fit	fîmes	fîtes	firent

FALLOIR _to be necessary_

			je/j'	tu
	falloir	PRES	-	-
		COMM	-	-
		FUTU	-	-
	-	COND	-	-
		IMPF	-	-
	fallu	PERF	-	-
		PLUP	-	-
		HIST	-	-

LIRE _to read_

	lire	PRES	lis	lis
		COMM	-	lis!
	lisant	FUTU	lirai	liras
		COND	lirais	lirais
		IMPF	lisais	lisais
	lu	PERF	ai lu	as lu
		PLUP	avais lu	avais lu
		HIST	lus	lus

METTRE _to put_

	mettre	PRES	mets	mets
		COMM	-	mets!
	mettant	FUTU	mettrai	mettras
		COND	méttrais	mettrais
		IMPF	mettais	mettais
	mis	PERF	ai mis	as mis
		PLUP	avais mis	avais mis
		HIST	mis	mis

MOURIR _to die_

	mourir	PRES	meurs	meurs
		COMM	-	meurs!
	mourant	FUTU	mourrai	mourras
		COND	mourrais	mourrais
		IMPF	mourais	mourais
	mort	PERF	suis mort/e	es mort/e
		PLUP	étais mort/e	étais mort/e
		HIST	mourus	mourus

Il/elle/on	nous	vous	ils/elles
faut	-	-	-
-	-	-	-
faudra	-	-	-
faudrait	-	-	-
fallait	-	-	-
a fallu	-	-	-
avait fallu	-	-	-
fallut	-	-	-
lit	lisons	lisez	lisent
-	lisons!	lisez!	-
lira	lirons	lirez	liront
lirait	lirions	liriez	liraient
lisait	lisions	lisiez	lisaient
a lu	avons lu	avez lu	ont lu
avait lu	avions lu	aviez lu	avaient lu
lut	lûmes	lûtes	lurent
met	mettons	mettez	mettent
-	mettons!	mettez!	-
mettra	mettrons	mettrez	mettrons
mettrait	mettrions	mettriez	mettraient
mettait	mettions	mettiez	mettaient
a mis	avons mis	avez mis	ont mis
avait mis	avions mis	aviez mis	avaient mis
mit	mîmes	mîtes	mirent
meurt	mourons	mourez	meurent
-	mourons!	mourez!	-
mourra	mourrons	mourrez	mourront
mourrait	mourrions	mourriez	mourraient
mourait	mourions	mouriez	mouraient
est mort/e	sommes mort/e/s	êtes mort/e/s	sont mort/e/s
était mort/e	étions mort/e/s/	étiez mort/e/s	étaient mort/e/s
mourut	mourûmes	mourûtes	moururent

277

NAÎTRE *to be born*

			je/j'	tu
	naître	PRES	nais	nais
		COMM	-	-
	naissant	FUTU	naîtrai	naîtras
		COND	naîtrais	naîtrais
		IMPF	naissais	naissais
	né	PERF	suis né/e	es né/e
		PLUP	étais né/e	étais né/e
		HIST	naquis	naquis

OBTENIR - *to obtain*
like **TENIR**

OFFRIR - *to offer*
like **OUVRIR**

OUVRIR *to open*

	ouvrir	PRES	ouvre	ouvres
		COMM	-	ouvre!
	ouvrant	FUTU	ouvrirai	ouvriras
		COND	ouvrirais	ouvrirais
		IMPF	ouvrais	ouvrais
	ouvert	PERF	ai ouvert	as ouvert
		PLUP	avais ouvert	avais ouvert
		HIST	ouvris	ouvris

PARAÎTRE - *to appear*
like **CONNAÎTRE**

PARTIR *to leave*

	partir	PRES	pars	pars
		COMM	-	pars!
	partant	FUTU	partirai	partiras
		COND	partirais	partirais
		IMPF	partais	partais
	parti	PERF	suis parti/e	es parti/e
		PLUP	étais parti/e	étais parti/e
		HIST	partis	partis

Il/elle/on	nous	vous	ils/elles
naît	naissons	naissez	naissent
-	-	-	-
naîtra	naîtrons	naîtrez	naîtront
naîtrait	naîtrions	naîtriez	naîtraient
naissait	naissions	naissiez	naissaient
est né/e	sommes né/e/s	êtes ne/e/s	sont né/e/s
était né/e	étions né/e/s	étiez né/e/s	étaient né/e/s
naquit	naquîmes	naquîtes	naquirent

ouvre	ouvrons	ouvrez	ouvrent
-	ouvrons!	ouvrez!	-
ouvrira	ouvrirons	ouvrirez	ouvriront
ouvrirait	ouvririons	ouvririez	ouvriraient
ouvrait	ouvrions	ouvriez	ouvraient
a ouvert	avons ouvert	avez ouvert	ont ouvert
avait ouvert	avions ouvert	aviez ouvert	avaient ouvert
ouvrit	ouvrîmes	ouvrîtes	ouvrirent

part	partons	partez	partent
-	partons!	partez!	-
partira	partirons	partirez	partiront
partirait	partirions	partiriez	partiraient
partait	partions	partiez	partaient
est parti/e	sommes parti/e/s	êtes parti/e/s	sont parti/e/s
était parti/e	étions parti/e/s	étiez parti/e/s	étaient parti/e/s
partit	partîmes	partîtes	partirent

PERMETTRE - *to allow*
like **METTRE**

PLAIRE *to please*			**je/j'**	**t u**
plaire		PRES	plais	plais
		COMM	-	plais!
plaisant		FUTU	plairai	plairas
		COND	plairais	plairais
		IMPF	plaisais	plaisais
plu		PERF	ai plu	as plu
		PLUP	avais plu	avais plu
		HIST	plus	plus

PLEUVOIR *to rain*				
pleuvoir		PRES	-	-
		COMM	-	-
pleuvant		FUTU	-	-
		COND	-	-
		IMPF	-	-
plu		PERF	-	-
		PLUP	-	-
		HIST	-	-

POUVOIR *to be able*				
pouvoir		PRES	peux	peux
		COMM	-	-
pouvant		FUTU	pourrai	pourras
		COND	pourrais	pourrais
		IMPF	pouvais	pouvais
pu		PERF	ai pu	as pu
		PLUP	avais pu	avais pu
		HIST	pus	pus

il/elle/on	nous	vous	ils/elles
plaît	plaisons	plaisez	plaisent
-	plaisons!	plaisez!	-
plaira	plairons	plairez	plairont
plairait	plairions	plairiez	plairaient
plaisait	plaisions	plaisiez	plaisaient
a plu	avons plu	avez plu	ont plu
avait plu	avions plu	aviez plu	avaient plu
plut	plûmes	plûtes	plurent

pleut	-	-	-
-	-	-	-
pleuvra	-	-	-
pleuvrait	-	-	-
pleuvait	-	-	-
a plu	-	-	-
avait plu	-	-	-
plut	-	-	-

peut	pouvons	pouvez	peuvent
-	-	-	-
pourra	pourrons	pourrez	pourront
pourrait	pourrions	pourriez	pourraient
pouvait	pouvions	pouviez	pouvaient
a pu	avons pu	avez pu	ont pu
avait pu	avions pu	aviez pu	avaient pu
put	pûmes	pûtes	purent

PRENDRE *to take*			je/j'	tu
	prendre	PRES	prends	prends
		COMM	-	prends!
	prenant	FUTU	prendrai	prendras
		COND	prendrais	prendrais
		IMPF	prenais	prenais
	pris	PERF	ai pris	as pris
		PLUP	avais pris	avais pris
		HIST	pris	pris

PRÉVENIR - *to warn*
like **TENIR**

PRÉVOIR - *to foresee*
like **VOIR**

PROMETTRE - *to promise*
like **METTRE**

RECEVOIR *to receive*				
	recevoir	PRES	reçois	reçois
		COMM	-	reçois!
	recevant	FUTU	recevrai	recevras
		COND	recevrais	recevrais
		IMPF	recevais	recevais
	reçu	PERF	ai reçu	as reçu
		PLUP	avais reçu	avais reçu
		HIST	reçus	reçus

RECONNAÎTRE - *to recognise*
like **CONNAÎTRE**

REPARTIR - *to set out again*
like **PARTIR**

REPRENDRE - *to take again, resume*
like **PRENDRE**

il/elle/on	nous	vous	ils/elles
prend	prenons	prenez	prennent
-	prenons!	prenez!	-
prendra	prendrons	prendrez	prendront
prendrait	prendrions	prendriez	prendraient
prenait	prenions	preniez	prenaient
a pris	avons pris	avez pris	ont pris
avait pris	avions pris	aviez pris	avaient pris
prit	prîmes	prîtes	prirent

il/elle/on	nous	vous	ils/elles
reçoit	recevons	recevez	reçoivent
-	recevons!	recevez!	-
recevra	recevrons	recevrez	recevront
recevrait	recevrions	recevriez	recevraient
recevait	recevions	receviez	recevaient
a reçu	avons reçu	avez reçu	ont reçu
avait reçu	avions reçu	aviez reçu	avaient reçu
reçut	reçûmes	reçûtes	reçurent

RETENIR - *to hold back*
like **TENIR**

REVENIR - *to come back*
like **VENIR**

RIRE *to laugh*			**je/j'**	**t u**
	rire	PRES	ris	ris
		COMM	-	ris!
	riant	FUTU	rirai	riras
		COND	rirais	rirais
		IMPF	riais	riais
	ri	PERF	ai ri	as ri
		PLUP	avais ri	avais ri
		HIST	ris	ris

SAVOIR *to know*				
	savoir	PRES	sais	sais
		COMM	-	sache!
	sachant	FUTU	saurai	sauras
		COND	saurais	saurais
		IMPF	savais	savais
	su	PERF	ai su	as su
		PLUP	avais su	avais su
		HIST	sus	sus

SE SENTIR - *to feel*
like **PARTIR**

SERVIR - *to serve*
like **PARTIR**

SE SERVIR DE - *to use; to help oneself*

SORTIR - *to get out*
like **OUVRIR**

SOUFFRIR - *to suffer*
like **OUVRIR**

il/elle/on	nous	vous	ils/elles
rit	rions	riez	rient
-	rions!	riez!	-
rira	rirons	rirez	riront
rirait	ririons	ririez	riraient
riait	riions	riiez	riaient
a ri	avons ri	avez ri	ont ri
avait ri	avions ri	aviez ri	avaient ri
rit	rîmes	rîtes	rirent
sait	savons	savez	savent
-	sachons!	sachez!	-
saura	saurons	saurez	sauront
saurait	saurions	sauriez	sauraient
savait	savions	saviez	savaient
a su	avons su	avez su	ont su
avait su	avions su	aviez su	avaient su
sut	sûmes	sûtes	surent

SOURIRE - *to smile*
like **RIRE**

SE SOUVENIR - *to remember*
like **VENIR**

SUIVRE *to follow*			**je/j'**	**t u**
	suivre	PRES	suis	suis
		COMM	-	suis!
	suivant	FUTU	suivrai	suivras
		COND	suivrais	suivrais
		IMPF	suivais	suivais
	suivi	PERF	ai suivi	as suivi
		PLUP	avais suivi	avais suivi
		HIST	suivis	suivis

SURPRENDRE - *to surprise*
like **PRENDRE**

TENIR *to hold*				
	tenir	PRES	tiens	tiens
		COMM	-	tiens!
	tenant	FUTU	tiendrai	tiendras
		COND	tiendrais	tiendrais
		IMPF	tenais	tenais
	tenu	PERF	ai tenu	as tenu
		PLUP	avais tenu	avais tenu
		HIST	tins	tins

VENIR *to come*				
	venir	PRES	viens	viens
		COMM	-	viens!
	venant	FUTU	viendrai	viendras
		COND	viendrais	viendrais
		IMPF	venais	venais
	venu	PERF	suis venu/e	es venu/e
		PLUP	étais venu/e	étais venu/e
		HIST	vins	vins

Il/elle/on	nous	vous	Ils/elles
suit	suivons	suivez	suivent
-	suivons!	suivez!	-
suivra	suivrons	suivrez	suivront
suivrait	suivrions	suivriez	suivraient
suivait	suivions	suiviez	suivaient
a suivi	avons suivi	avez suivi	ont suivi
avait suivi	avions suivi	aviez suivi	avaient suivi
suivit	suivîmes	suivîtes	suivirent

tient	tenons	tenez	tiennent
-	tenons!	tenez!	-
tiendra	tiendrons	tiendrez	tiendront
tiendrait	tiendrions	tiendriez	tiendraient
tenait	tenions	teniez	tenaient
a tenu	avons tenu	avez tenu	ont tenu
avait tenu	avions tenu	aviez tenu	avaient tenu
tint	tînmes	tîntes	tinrent

vient	venons	venez	viennent
-	venons!	venez!	-
viendra	viendrons	viendrez	viendront
viendrait	viendrions	viendriez	viendraient
venait	venions	veniez	venaient
est venu/e	sommes venu/e/s	êtes venu/e/s	sont venu/e/s
était venu/e	étions venu/e/s	étiez venu/e/s	étaient venu/e/s
vint	vînmes	vîntes	vinrent

VIVRE *to live*

		je/j'	tu
vivre	PRES	vis	vis
	COMM	-	vis!
vivant	FUTU	vivrai	vivras
	COND	vivrais	vivrais
	IMPF	vivais	vivais
vécu	PERF	ai vécu	as vécu
	PLUP	avais vécu	avais vécu
	HIST	vécus	vécus

VOIR *to see*

		je/j'	tu
voir	PRES	vois	vois
	COMM	-	vois!
voyant	FUTU	verrai	verras
	COND	verrais	verrais
	IMPF	voyais	voyais
vu	PERF	ai vu	as vu
	PLUP	avais vu	avais vu
	HIST	vis	vis

VOULOIR *to want*

		je/j'	tu
vouloir	PRES	veux	veux
	COMM	-	veuille!
voulant	FUTU	voudrai	voudras
	COND	voudrais	voudrais
	IMPF	voulais	voulais
voulu	PERF	ai voulu	as voulu
	PLUP	avais voulu	avais voulu
	HIST	voulus	voulus

il/elle/on	nous	vous	ils/elles
vit	vivons	vivez	vivent
-	vivons!	vivez!	-
vivra	vivrons	vivrez	vivront
vivrait	vivrions	vivriez	vivraient
vivait	vivions	viviez	vivaient
a vécu	avons vécu	avez vécu	ont vécu
avait vécu	avions vécu	aviez vécu	avaient vécu
vécut	vécûmes	vécûtes	vécurent

il/elle/on	nous	vous	ils/elles
voit	voyons	voyez	voient
-	voyons!	voyez!	-
verra	verrons	verrez	verront
verrait	verrions	verriez	verraient
voyait	voyions	voyiez	voyaient
a vu	avons vu	avez vu	ont vu
avait vu	avions vu	aviez vu	avaient vu
vit	vîmes	vîtes	virent

il/elle/on	nous	vous	ils/elles
veut	voulons	voulez	veulent
-	veuillons!	veuillez!	-
voudra	voudrons	voudrez	voudront
voudrait	voudrions	voudriez	voudraient
voulait	voulions	vouliez	voulaient
a voulu	avons voulu	avez voulu	ont voulu
avait voulu	avions voulu	aviez voulu	avaient voulu
voulut	voulûmes	voulûtes	voulurent

ARTICLES

	1 THE	**2** A/AN	**3** SOME/ANY
masculine	**le/l'**	**un**	**du/de l'**
feminine	**la/l'**	**une**	**de la/de l'**
plural	**les**	**des**	**des**

Definite article

The definite article **(column 1)** is used in French, but not in English, in these cases:

J'aime le fromage	I like cheese	meaning "all "cheese
Ouvre les yeux!	Open your eyes!	for parts of the body
Je me lave les mains	I wash my hands	
La reine Elizabeth	Queen Elizabeth	in titles
Le docteur Kildare	Doctor Kildare	
Monsieur le Maire	(Mr) Mayor	
Il apprend l'espagnol	He's learning Spanish	with languages
La France est plus grande que l'Angleterre	France is bigger than England	with countries
Nous allons à la maison des jeunes les vendredi	We go to the youth club on Fridays.	with days of the week

Indefinite article

The indefinite article **(column 2)** is omitted in French in these cases:

Mon père est mécanicien	My father is a mechanic	professions
Ma mère est comptable	My mother is an accountant	
Elle est Française	She is (a) French (woman)	nationality
Il est protestant	He's a protestant	faith
Quelle surprise!	What a surprise!	exclamations

Partitive article

a) The partitive article **(column 3)** is often omitted in English.

b) **du**, **de la** and **des** change to **de** after a negative (except **ne... que**) and before a plural adjective.

c) **de** alone is used after quantifiers, measures and containers.

Examples

a)	**J'écoute des disques**	I listen to records
	Je bois du vin	I'm drinking wine
	Avez-vous de la place?	Have you any room?
b)	**Je n'ai pas de monnaie**	I haven't any change
	Nous n'avons plus de lait	We haven't any more milk
	Il a acheté de grandes bouteilles de limonade	He bought (some) large bottles of lemonade
c)	**beaucoup de gens**	Lots of people
	Il reste combien de temps?	How much time is there left?
	Elle fait trop de bruit	She's making too much noise
	Je n'ai pas assez d'argent	I haven't enough money
	Donnez-moi un peu de riz	Give me a little rice
	Deux paquets de biscuits, s'il vous plaît	Two packets of biscuits, please

NOUNS

Gender

1. All nouns have gender/are either "masculine " or "feminine" *(see Articles)*.
2. Several nouns have special feminine forms:

ami	**amie**	friend
coiffeur	**coiffeuse**	hairdresser
copain	**copine**	friend, mate
cousin	**cousine**	cousin
directeur	**directrice**	headteacher
infirmier	**infirmière**	nurse
instituteur	**institutrice**	primary school teacher
gardien	**gardienne**	warden
jumeau	**jumelle**	twin
paysan	**paysanne**	peasant
serveur	**serveuse**	waiter/waitress
technicien	**technicienne**	technician
vendeur	**vendeuse**	sales assistant
veuf	**veuve**	widower/widow

Number

1. Most nouns add an **s** to form their plural

un arbre	**des arbres**
la pomme	**les pommes**

2. Nouns with these endings form their plurals as follows

journal	**journaux m.**	newspapers
bureau	**bureaux m.**	offices
feu	**feux m.**	fires, traffics lights
chou	**choux m.**	cabbages
bras	**bras m.**	arms
voix	**voix f.**	voices
nez	**nez m.**	noses
ciel	**cieux m.**	skies, heavens
travail	**travaux m.**	works
oeil	**yeux m.**	eyes

Exceptions

bal	**bals m.**	dances
festival	**festivals m.**	fesitivals
pneu	**pneus m.**	tyres
trou	**trous m.**	holes

3. Some nouns are plural in French but not in English

bagages m.	luggage
cheveux m.	hair
devoirs m.	homework
meubles m.	furniture
renseignements m.	information

4. Some nouns are plural in English, but not in French

douane f.	customs
escalier m.	stairs
jean m.	jeans
pantalon m.	trousers
short m.	shorts

ADJECTIVES

TABLES 1-13

Notes   1. *Adjectives follow the noun they describe (exceptions TABLE 16).*
2. *They take the gender and number of the noun they describe.*

TABLES	Singular		Plural		English
	masculine	feminine	masculine	feminine	
1. ending in -**E**	**faible**	**faible**	**faibles**	**faibles**	weak
2. ending in vowels	**connu**	**connue**	**connus**	**connues**	known
	animé	**animée**	**animés**	**animées**	lively
3. ending in -**EUX**	**affreux**	**affreuse**	**affreux**	**affreuses**	awful
4. ending in -**IF**	**actif**	**active**	**actifs**	**actives**	active
5. ending in -**AS, -OS**	**gros**	**grosse**	**gros**	**grosses**	fat
6. ending in other con- sonents	**content**	**contente**	**contents**	**contentes**	pleased
	certain	**certaine**	**certains**	**certaines**	certain
	chaud	**chaude**	**chauds**	**chaudes**	hot
7. ending in -**EL, -IL**	**cruel**	**cruelle**	**cruels**	**cruelles**	cruel
8. ending in -**EN**	**moyen**	**moyenne**	**moyens**	**moyennes**	average
9. ending in -**ON**	**mignon**	**mignonne**	**mignons**	**mignonnes**	sweet (person)
10. ending in -**ET****	**muet**	**muette**	**muets**	**muettes**	dumb
11. ending in -**AL**	**égal**	**égale**	**égaux**	**égales**	equal
12. ending in -**ER**	**étranger**	**étrangère**	**étrangers**	**étrangres**	foreign
13. ending in -**IER**	**régulier**	**régulière**	**réguliers**	**régulières**	regular
** except	**complet**	**complète**	**complets**	**complètes**	complete, full

Use and examples

un coin tranquille	a quiet spot
des gens connu(e)s	well-known people
une rue animée	a busy street
les liaisons dangereuses	dangerous liaisons
un arrêt facultatif	a request stop
la marée basse	low tide
une petite voiture	a small car
une revue mensuelle	a monthly magazine
la taille moyenne	average size
bonne journée!	have a nice day!
ma soeur cadette	my younger sister
les trains internationaux	international trains
une langue étrangère	a foreign language
la semaine dernière	last week

TABLE 14: adjectives with a double/alternative masculine singular

beau	**bel**	**un bel homme**	an attractive man
nouveau	**nouvel**	**le Nouvel An**	New Year
vieux	**vieil**	**un vieil appartment**	an old flat
fou	**fol**	**un fol espoir**	a mad hope
mou	**mol** (rare)	**un mol oreiller**	a soft pillow

TABLE 15: adjectives with a radically different feminine singular

masculine		feminine	
un vin doux	a sweet wine	**la vie douce**	a pleasant life
un homme jaloux	a jealous man	**une femme jalouse**	a jealous woman
mon passe-temps favori	my favourite pastime	**ma leçon favorite**	my favourite lesson
un faux passeport	a false passport	**une fausse addition**	a wrong sum
un poisson frais	a fresh fish	**une boisson fraîche**	a cool drink
un homme malin	a cunning man	**une femme maligne**	a cunning woman

TABLE 16: adjectives which come before the noun.

Examples

autre	**l'autre jour**	the other day
beau	**beau temps**	fine weather
bon	**bon chic, bon genre**	well-bred, with good taste, style, money and connections
grand	**la grande rue**	the main street
gros	**une grosse somme**	a large sum
jeune	**le jeune homme**	the young man
joli	**une jolie maison**	a pretty house
large	**une large rue**	a wide street
long	**une longue journée**	a long day
mauvais	**de mauvaise humeur**	in a bad mood
meilleur	**un meilleur avenir**	a better future
petit	**une petite bouteille**	a small bottle
vieux	**le vieux quartier**	the old quarter

TABLE 17: adjectives which change their meaning when used before or after the noun

ancien	**un ancien collègue**	an old/former colleague
	un livre ancien	an old book
cher	**un cher ami**	a dear friend
	un restaurant cher	an expensive restaurant
curieux	**un curieux personnage**	a strange/odd person/ character
	une personne curieuse	a curious/nosy person
dernier	**le dernier rang**	the last row
	l'an dernier	last year
pauvre	**un pauvre homme**	a poor man (ie piteous)
	un homme pauvre	a poor man (ie impecunious)
prochain	**le prochain train**	the next train
	l'an prochain	next year
propre	**mon propre livre**	my own book
	une maison propre	a clean house
seul	**la seule raison**	the only reason
	un homme seul	a man on his own

TABLE 18: indefinite adjectives

The following adjectives are traditionally called indefinite. This table shows examples of use and meaning; the key notes show their similarity to or difference from adjectives set out in TABLES 1-17.

FRENCH	ENGLISH	EXAMPLES	KEY NOTES
autre	other	**l'autre jour**	gender and number as in TABLE 1.
	another	**une autre personne**	
même	the same	**les mêmes erreurs**	as above
	the very	**le jour même**	
	self	**moi-même**	
quelque	some	**quelque temps**	as above
	a few	**quelques minutes**	
chaque	each	**chaque garçon**	invariable, always in singular

	every	**chaque fille**	
plusieurs	several	**plusieurs fois**	invariable, always in plural
tout	all (the)	**toute la journée**	gender and number as in Table 6.
		tous mes copains	

The following truly indefinite expressions are very useful.

n'importe quel jour	any day, doesn't matter which
n'importe quand	any time, doesn't matter when
n'importe qui	anyone, doesn't matter who
n'importe quoi	anything, doesn't matter what
n'importe comment	any way, doesn't matter how
n'importe où	anywhere, doesn't matter where

ADVERBS

Use them to add colour, variety and style to verbs. Recognise them by their **-ment** ending, equivalent to -ly in English (**franchement** : frankly)

Formation

1.   Add -**ment** to the feminine of adjectives

Adverbs	English	Adjective
certainement	certainly	**certaine**
doucement	gently	**douce**
franchement	frankly	**franche**
exactement	exactly	**exacte**
heureusement	fortunately	**heureuse**
immédiatement	immediately	**immédiate**
naturellement	naturally	**naturelle**

2. Add -**ment** to adjective whose masculine form already ends in a vowel

absolument	absolutely	**absolu**
agréablement	pleasantly	**agréable**
rapidement	quickly	**rapide**
vraiment	truly, really	**vrai**

3. Note this formation for adjectives ending in -**ant**, -**ent**

couramment	fluently	**courant**
évidemment	obviously	**évident**
récemment	recently	**récent**
suffisamment	sufficiently	**suffisant**

Irregular adverbs

Note these exceptions and irregular adverbs

bien	well	**bon**
brièvement	briefly	**bref**
gentiment	kindly	**gentil**
mal	badly	**mauvais**
énormément	enormously	**énorme**
précisément	precisely	**précis**
profondément	deeply	**profond**

Position

In simple tenses (ie **je travaille**) and in compound tenses (ie **j'ai travaillé**) adverbs come as close as possible to the verb they qualify.

Examples

je travaille souvent le soir	I often work in the evenings
j'ai fréquemment travaillé les soirs	I've frequently worked in the evenings
je me suis malheureusement coupé le doigt	I've unfortunately cut my finger

You will find adverbs in other parts of the sentence, to give a different emphasis, but for the purposes of practical communication at GCSE level, remember and use them as in the examples given.

MAKING COMPARISIONS, EXPRESSING SUPERLATIVES

Adjectives: formation

To say something is bigger, taller, more/less/as interesting: add **plus, moins** or **aussi** in front of the adjective, like this:

Masculine sing/pl	Feminine sing/pl	Examples
plus grand/s	**plus grande/s**	**plus grand/e que moi**
plus interéssant/s	**plus intéressante/s**	**plus intéressant/e que l'autre**
moins bon/s	**moins bonne/s**	**une pomme moins bonne que...**
aussi beau/x	**aussi belle/s**	**elle est aussi belle que sa mére**

*Note that **aussi...que** changes to **si... que** after a negative.*

Mon frère n'est pas si grand que ma soeur.

To express superlatives add **le/la/les plus** ... in front (1) or after (2) the noun (see section on *Position of Adjectives*) like this:-

1 **le/s plus grand/s**	**la/les plus grande/s**	**le plus grand succès des années quatre-vingts**
2 **le/s plus long/s**	**la/les plus longue/s**	**le jour le plus long de l'année**

Irregular adjectives

Note - and learn - these frequently used irregulars.

	Comparative	Superlative	
bon	**meilleur**	**le/la meilleur/e**	**la meilleure journée de ma vie**
		les meilleurs	**les meilleurs romans**
mauvais	**pire**	**le/la pire** **les pires**	**le pire exemple**
petit	**plus petit**	**le/la plus petit/e**	**la plus petite voiture**
		les plus petit/e/s	
	moindre	**le/la moindre** **les moindres**	**la moindre chose**

Adverbs: formation

To make comparisions and express superlatives using adverbs: add **plus, moins, aussi** in the same way as for adjectives.

Examples

plus lentement	more slowly/slower
plus rapidement	more quickly/quicker
moins vite	les quicky
aussi doucement que possible	as gently as possible

Irregular adverbs

Note - and learn - these frequently used irregulars.

bien	**mieux**	**le mieux**	well, better, best
mal	**pire**	**le pire**	badly, worse, worst
peu	**moins**	**le moins**	little, less, the least
bientôt	**plus tôt**	**le plus tôt**	soon, sooner, soonest

DEMONSTRATIVE ADJECTIVES

Examples

Singular		Plural		
masculine	feminine	masculine	feminine	
ce	**cette**	**ces**	**ces**	this/that, these/those
cet				

Examples

ce livre/ce livre-ci	this book (here)	note use of **-ci** for emphasis
cet homme	this man/that man	used before nouns beginning with a vowel or silent **h**
cette chemise-là	that shirt (there)	note use of **-là** for emphasis
ces affaires-là	those things (there)	

DEMONSTRATIVE PRONOUNS

Examples

Singular		Plural		
masculine	feminine	masculine	feminine	
celui	**celle**	**ceux**	**celles**	this one/that one, these ones/those ones

Examples

celui de David est...	David's (one) is ...
celles d'Alain sont...	Alan's (ones) are ...
Je voudrais celui-ci, pas celui-là.	I'd like this one, not that one.
Celui qui est assis.	The one who is sitting down.

PRONOUNS, POSSESSIVE PRONOUNS AND ADJECTIVES

Table of pronouns

SUBJ	JE	TU	IL/ELLE	NOUS	VOUS	ILS/ELLES
EMPH/DISJ	moi	toi	lui elle	nous	vous	eux elles
DIR OBJ	me	te	le la	nous	vous	les les
	moi	toi				
IND OBJ	me	te	lui lui	nous	vous	leur leur
	moi	toi				
POSS ADJ	mon	ton	son	notre	votre	leur
	ma	ta	sa	notre	votre	leur
	mes	tes	ses	nos	vos	leurs
POSS PRON	le mien	le tien	le sien	le nôtre	le vôtre	le leur
	la mienne	la tienne	la sienne	la nôtre	la vôtre	la leur
	les miens	les tiens	les siens	les nôtres	les vôtres	les leurs
	les miennes	les tiennes	les siennes	les nôtres	les vôtres	les leurs

Emphatic/disjunctive pronouns

Uses   1. *for emphasis*
           2. *after prepositions*

Examples

1.	**Moi, je trouve ça bien**	I like it (even if you don't)
2.	**Tu viens chez moi?**	Coming round to my place?
	Derrière eux.	Behind them.

Direct object pronouns

Uses   1. *to avoid repetition, replacing the noun*
Position   2. *in front of the verb, except when giving commands. Note that **me** and **te** become **moi** and **toi** after commands.*

Examples

Je le connais bien.	I know him well.
Mes lunettes! Je les ai perdues!*	My glasses! I've lost them!
Regarde-moi!	Look at me.
Donne-les-moi!	Give them to me (Give me them)

*Note   that feminine and plural direct object pronouns agree in number and gender with the past participle in the perfect and pluperfect tenses.

Indirect object pronouns

Uses   *to translate "to me, to her/us" etc: note that English often omits the "to" - think about the meaning!*

Position   *in front of the verb, except when giving commands. Note that **me** and **te** become **moi** and **toi** after commands.*

Examples

1.	**Tu me passes le sel?**	Can you pass me the salt?
	Je te téléphonerai demain.	I'll ring you tomorrow.
2.	**Passe-moi le sel.**	Pass me the salt.
	Écris-moi vite.	Write (to me) soon.

Possessive adjectives

Uses *to show possession*

Note 1. *the gender and number of possessions is important, not the gender and number of the possessors.*
  2. *use **mon, ton, son** (not **ma, ta sa**), when "possessions" begin with a vowel or silent **h**.*

Examples

1.	**Son chien**	His/her dog
	Sa tante	His/her aunt
2.	**Mon amie**	My girlfriend
	Son affaire	His/her business

Possessive pronouns

Uses *to translate "mine, yours, hers" etc*

Ces affaires sont les miennes.	Those things are mine.

Position of object pronouns

When several pronouns are needed together, use in the following numbered order

1	2	3	4	5
me				
te	le			
nous	la	lui		
vous	les	leur	y	en

Examples

La maison? Je la lui ai vendue!	The house? I sold it to him!
Elle me l'a dit.	She told me (it)/said it to me,

Note   1. *in direct commands the pronouns are tacked onto the end of the verb.*
        2. *in negative commands the pronouns remain in front of the verb.*

Donne-le-moi.	Give me it.
Ne le lui donne pas.	Don't give it to him.

Meaning and use of "Y" and "EN"

y   1.   there
     2.   it/them, after verbs taking **à**

1. **La maison des jeunes? J'y vais le vendredi soir.**	The youth club? I go there on Friday evenings
2. **Je ne m'y attendais pas**	I wasn't expecting it.

en   1.   of it/them
      2.   some
      3.   it/them, after verbs taking **de**

1. **Il y en a trois.**	There are three (of them).
2. **Donne-nous-en.**	Give us some.
3. **J'en ai besoin.**	I need it/them.

Indefinite pronouns

		Examples
autre	other (one)	**Non, je prends l'autre, s'il vous plaît.**
chacun/e	each (one)	**Chacun à son gout.**
pas grand'chose	not much	**Je n'ai pas fait grand'chose.**
quelque chose	something	**Quelque chose de bon.**
quelqu'un	someone	**Tu me fais penser à quelqu'un.**
quelques-un/e/s	some	
tout	all/everything	**C'est tout, Madame?** **Merci pour tout.**

Relative pronouns

French	English	Use
1. qui	who, that, which	to link two subject nouns together.
2. ce qui	what, that which	to link two subject sentences together
3. que	whom, that, which	as direct object in second of two sentences.
4. dont	(of) whom, which	as direct object of verb followed by **de**
	whose	as a possessive
5. ce que	what, that which	as direct object in two linked sentences
6. ce dont	what, that which	as direct object sentence, where verb takes **de**, eg **avoir besoin de**

Examples

1.	**Mon frère, qui a vingt ans...**	My brother, who is twenty...
	J'ai perdu mon portemonnaie, qui contenait 50 francs.	I have lost my purse, which had 50 francs in it.
2.	**Ce qui m'intéresse surtout, c'est le cinéma.**	What interests me especially is the cinéma.
3.	**Le livre que j'ai lu hier.**	The book (that/which) I read yesterday.
4.	**Le livre dont je connais l'auteur.**	The book whose author I know.
5.	**Je ne sais pas ce que je ferai plus tard.**	I don't know what I'll do later.
6.	**Ce dont j'ai besoin, c'est une lave-vaisselle!**	what I need is a dish-washer!

Relative pronouns after prepositions

Note   *used mostly in the written language (literary, journalistic etc), infrequently in the spoken form.*

Singular		Plural		
masculine	feminine	masculine	feminine	
lequel	**laquelle**	**lesquels**	**lesquelles**	**which, whom**

Examples

Le bâtiment devant lequel j'ai vu un accident.	The building outside which I saw an accident.
Les personnes avec lesquelles je travaille.	The people I work with.

Note   ***lequel, laquelle*** *etc are also used interrogatively.*

Lequel tu prends?	Which one are you taking?
Laquelle des chemises est-ce-que tu as achetée?	Which one of the shirts did you buy?

CONJUNCTIONS

Uses and examples by notion and function

These are very useful words which provide links between sentences and add pace and style to speaking and writing at higher level.

This list, with examples, provides some of the most frequently used conjunctions.

To express similarity of manner (like, as well as)

comme aussi bien que ainsi que	Je pense comme toi

To express opposition (nevertheless, however, but)

cependant pourtant toutefois mais	Tu as raison, pourtant...

To express consequence (as, since, because, therefore)

comme car parce que puisque donc	Puisqu'il faisait beau, je suis sorti. Il faisait beau, donc je suis sortie.

To express point in time (when)

quand lorsque	Lorsqu'il fait beau, je me promène. Dis-moi quand tu viendras. (note use of future)

To express contemporaneity (whilst, during)

alors que	Alors que vous étiez au cinéma, j'ai fait le ménage.
pendant que	
tandis que	

To express imminence (as soon as)

aussitôt que	Aussitôt que possible.
dès que	Dès qu'il fera beau, je sortirai.

To express choice: possibility; verification (either... or; if/whether)

ou...ou	
soit...soit	Soit aujourd'hui, soit demain.
si	Si tu veux.
c'est-à-dire	Demain, c'est-à-dire le 23 juin.

Answers and Listening Scripts

ANSWERS AND LISTENING SCRIPTS

STARTER KIT

Writing to an office de tourisme

page 40   Their address   Your address
                                                            date

Monsieur, Madame,

Je vous serais reconnaissant/e de bien vouloir m'envoyer un plan de la ville; une liste des hôtels; et tous renseignements complémentaires sur la région. En vous remerciant d'avance, je joins un coupon-réponse international.

Veuillez agréer, Monsieur, Madame, l'expression de mes sentiments les meilleurs.

                    Your signature
                    Your name, printed clearly

Writing to an hotel

page 40   Their address   Your address
                                                            date

Monsieur, Madame,

Pourriez-vous me faire savoir si je peux réserver deux chambres, doubles, une chambre à 1 personne (5 personnes) du 18 août au 23 aôut (inclus)? Je vous serais reconnaissant/e de bien vouloir m'envoyer vos conditions et tarifs.

Dans l'attente de vous lire très prochainement, veuillez agréer, Monsieur, Madame, l'expression de mes sentiments les meilleurs.

                    Your signature
                    Your name (printed clearly)

Writing a holiday postcard

page 41
1. Me voici/nous voici à St. Malo chez des amis.
2. Me voici/nous voici dans un hôtel à Paris, en voyage organisé.
3. Me voici/nous voici dans un camping, pas loin de St. Tropez.
4. Me voici/nous voici dans un gîte près de Macon.
5. Les matins je fais des promenades à pied, l'après-midi je vais me baigner.
6. Le soir je sors/nous sortons manger avec des copains.
7. Je fais/nous faisons des promenades à la campagne en voiture.

Topic Areas

1. Holidays; accommodation and activities

page 51
1   **Quel hôtel?**

1.	A C E G	6.	G
2.	F H	7.	A G
3.	D F	8.	C
4.	B	9.	B F
5.	A	10.	F

page 53
2   **Pension ou location?**

1. A ; C ; B
2. A:- 1 to 3 bedded rooms - some with bathrooms, some with washbasins
   B:- rooms with bathroom : washbasin, shower, WC
   C:-two room accommodation for 4 to 5 people; 3 rooms for six people, all with bathroom facilities, WC, and small kitchen
3. A ; C ; B

page 53   **3**   **Équipment et confort**

	A	B	C
bowls	✓	✓	
caravan hire		✓	
common room		✓	
farm produce		✓	
fishing	✓		
food on site	✓		
games	✓		
horseriding			✓
hot showers		✓	✓
pitch (number)	160	25	6
restaurant nearby	✓		
swimming pool		✓	
water sports	✓		

page 55   **4**   **Section caravaning - camping**

1. 10F50
2. 6F15
3. 10F50
4. pitch for car and caravan; or car and tent; and electricity
5. 59F
6. 59F
7. 63F35
8. 51F65

page 55   **5.   Faites la fête!**

1. Ball games

A   **rugby**
B   **concours de boules** - bowls match
C   **concours de boules**
D   **initiation au golf**
     jeux de croquet et de boules

3. Competitions

A   **concours de pétanque** - bowls match
B   **match water-polo**
     concours de boules
     concours de cartes - card matches
     concours de natation - swimming competitions
C   **concours de boules;**
     concours de cartes

5. Music and dance

A   **danses et chants flamenco** - flamenco songs and dances
     soirée flamenco - flamenco evening
     bal disco - disco dance
B   **soirée dansante** - evening dance
     discothèque
     danse provençales - dances from Provence
C   **grands bals** - grand dances
D   **animations musicales** - music entertainments

2. Water sports

A   **raide de planche à voile** - windsurfing event
B   **match de water-polo**
     jeux piscine - swimming pool games

4. Races

A   **courses de trotinette** - scooter races
     courses aux ânes - donkey races
B   **courses automobile** - car races
     courses de relais - relay races
C   **course de lévriers** - greyhound racing
D   **courses cycliste** - bike races

6. Food and drink

A   **ouverture du restaurant** - restaurant opens
B   -
C   **buvette** - refreshment bar
D   **salon de thé** - tea room

page 58   **6   Les voiles de la liberté**

1. The bicentenary of the French revolution, and the Declaration of the Rights of Man.
2. America; 1976; the Bicentenary of their Independance.
3. Because of its long history - from 900 - of maritime trade.
4. Hundreds.
5. Various events/exhibitions/regattas/displays, European sea-shanty choirs.
6. Vast parking areas provided outside Rouen linked to the quayside by shuttle services.
7. Direct service from Paris to the quayside by special trains.
8. The Bassin Saint Gervais made into a marina for yachts and leisure craft.
9. By cannon fire.
10. The sea.

page 62   **1   Tour du Golfe du Morbihan**

Bienvenue à bord la vedette MONTGOLFIER! Le tour du Golfe durera 4 heures, sans compter l'escale à l'Ile aux Moines - une escale de 2 heures... Le temps de faire un tour à pied, comme les voitures y sont interdites.
Bon un peu d'histoire et de géographie avant notre départ... Le Golfe, qui s'étend sur 100 kilomètres carrés, est parsemé d'une quarantaine d'îles et d'îlots, dont beaucoup appartiennent à des gens particuliers... des propriétés privés. Le mot MORBIHAN veut dire "petite mer" en Breton - MOR c'est la mer; BIHAN, c'est petit. Voilà... Attention à la baignade! Le très étroit goulet à l'entrée du golfe qui ne mesure qu'un kilomètre, provoque de *très* forts courants des marées; celles-ci atteignent une vitesse de 12 noeuds à l'heure... donc, soyez prudents!
Si vous n'êtes pas de passage dans la région, vous aurez déjà remarqué le climat, qui est exceptionnellement doux... ce climat, lié à l'environnement non-pollué, offre un abri aux oiseaux - surtout en hiver - dont certains arrivent de la Lapponie, de la Sibérie... de très loin. Ce même environnement explique, dit-on, la forte concentration de tumulus, de dolmens... des monuments préhistoriques, qui sont d'une renommée mondiale.
Au pourtour du Golfe, à noter la jolie ville d'Auray, où s'est arrêté, en 1777, Benjamin Franklin. Nos amis les Américains et les Anglais sauront que c'est un des fondateurs de l'Indépendance de l'Amérique.

1. four hours
2. two hours
3. 100 square kilometres
4. No cars
5. private property
6. small sea
7. strong and fast currents
8. very mild; unpolluted
9. prehistoric monuments
10. he stayed there in 1777

2 Travel and transport

page 71   **1**   **Titres de transport**

1.	G	5.	C
2.	D,H,K	6.	A,I
3.	B,F	7.	E
4.	J	8.	K

page 74   **2**   **A la gare**

1.	H	6.	C	11.	L
2.	J	7.	G	12.	M
3.	E	8.	I	13.	O
4.	A	9.	B	14.	N
5.	D	10.	F	15.	K

page 75   **3**   **Voyages et excursions en autocar**

1.	B	5.	A
2.	E	6.	B,D
3.	C	7	B,D
4.	D		

| page 76 | **4** | **Une solution: le bus!** |

1. 6am
2. reduced service
3. minibus service
4. at all bus-stops
5. to special **tabacs**
6. if journeys done within one hour

page 77 **5** **Première vague de retours**

1. foreign tourists
2. start of school year soon
3. on Spain - Bordeaux - Paris route
4. RN 10, and A 40
5. Many roadworks
6. wear safety belts, stop regularly, observe speed limits; keep distance

page 78 **6** **Accidents et pannes**

1. at crossroads
2. collision; 2 women
3. knocked over by car
4. at bend in road
5. far right-hand lane
6. warning lights and triangle
7. 1 kilometre at the most
8. it's free
9. send mechanic
10. if repairs take less than 30 minutes

page 82 **2** **Rendez-vous à la gare**

Je n'ai pas réussi à te joindre par téléphone! Voilà pour ton séjour chez nous à York: tu achètes un billet simple en deuxième, à la gare de Paddington. Tu prends le train de 17h 10 (c'est un train rapide/express, et moins cher que le train de 13h 05). Il arrive à 20h 15. Je t'attends/t'attendrai à la sortie. A bientôt!

page 82 **3** **Un petit mot**

1. **je suis arrivé/e**
2. **j'ai pris**
3. **est arrivé**
4. **j'ai changé**
5. **j'ai dû**
6. **j'ai passé**
7. **a mis**
8. **j'ai mis**

page 83   **1   Départs**

1.   **Attention! Attention! Le train de 18h à destination de Paris entre en gare. Attention!**
2.   **On annonce le départ à 17h 11 du train à destination de Poitiers. Attention à la fermeture des portières!**
3.   **Le train de 12h 20 à destination de Bordeaux entre en gare sur la voie numéro 2.**
4.   **Départ imminent à 11h 25 de la correspondance pour Fontenay le Comte.**
5.   **Attention! Attention! Le train de 17h 29 à destination de Bordeaux est annoncé sur la voie numéro 1.**

page 84   **2   Attention! attention!**

1.   **B. Le TGV 861 en Provenance d'Annecy entre en gare.**
2.   **C. Le train de 13h 23 en provenance de Genève et à destination de Paris est annoncé**
3.   **A. Le responsable du groupe ICA est prié de se présenter au Bureau d'Accueil**
4.   **D. Les parents d'Agatha Creutzberg sont priés de se presénter au Bureau d'Accueil**
5.   **F. Assurez-vous de la fermeture des portes. Attention au départ!**
6.   **G. Ce train dessert toutes les gares.**
7.   **E. Appel au service: un porteur est demandé de toute urgence au quai 7.**

3 Environment

page 94   **2   Amis de la nature**

1.   People who like walking, and the countryside
2.   Good comfortable shoes
3.   About two hours
4.   Thursdays are an all day tour
5.   Adults: 10F; children under 13 go free

page 95　**3　La Vallée du Dropt (Dordogne)**

1. Eymet, Biron
2. near Lauzan and Queyssel
3. Queyssel; Villeréal; Montpazier
4. Eymet
5. Eymet, Castillonnes; Montpazier
6. swimming pool at Cabanon
7. on the D288 near Cahuzac
8. best preserved bastide town with fortified gates

page 97　**4　Chantier de fouilles (Bretagne)**

A.　1.　18
　　2.　2 weeks
　　3.　fit for manual work

B.　1.　14 kilometres
　　2.　30 March; 26 September

C.　1.　in a former lighthouse
　　2.　in summer
　　3.　own bedding; tent
　　4.　they do

D.　1.　Saturdays and Sundays
　　2.　7 hours

page 99　**5　Tempête - catastrophe**

1. storm
2. night of 15 - 16 October
3. forests in Brittany
4. 650 million francs
5. unblock roads; retrieve wood; re-forest
6. left without electricity
7. fire brigade; civil organisations; army

page 100   **6   La météo 1 - hiver**

FORECAST	AREA	WHEN
bright spells	**E. Pyrenees and Massif Central**	afternoon
fog	**E. Pyrenees and Massif Central**	morning
overcast	**South East**	-
rain	**Alps**	-
snow	**Alps above 900m**	-
windy	**Brittany**	late evening

page 101   **La météo 2 - été**

1.   sunny again
2.   storms threatening
3.   temperatures above body heat
4.   fine weather again after the storms
5.   30 degrees in the shade
6.   couldn't last - thunderstorms again
7.   get out your umbrellas

page 102   **7   Washington, capitale**

1.   inauguration of President
2.   75% : 10%
3.   crime; drugs; infant mortality
4.   unsympathetic
5.   CIA/FBI/Food & Drug Administration; armament industry; pharmaceuticals
6.   to be near the White House and the networked TV stations
7.   politicians shut doors; civil servants on holiday, theatres close
8.   poverty and bitterness
9.   He drew up the plans for the town
10.   21 per 1000/twice as high as in rest of USA altogether/higher than in some Third World countries
11.   because it has the world's largest library
12.   homicide; drugs
13.   Dupont Circle Square
14.   theft; assault

page 108 **1 Tour de Bordeaux à pied**

...vous m'entendez? oui? Alors, je me présente - je m'appelle Cathérine, je suis professeur d'anglais à Paris, mais je suis d'origine bordelaise; j'ai fait mes études à la faculté de lettres à Bordeaux.

Nous sommes bientôt arrivés, et voilà quelques renseignements sur le tour que nous allons faire. D'abord le car s'arrêtera dans la gare routière pour nous laisser descendre; c'est près de la Place Gambetta. La Place Gambetta... pendant la Révolution on y trouvait l'échafaud...la guillotine...maintenant c'est un petit jardin, aménagé à l'anglaise...dans le style anglais. Puis, nous allons descendre le Cours de l'Intendance, bordé sur les deux côtés d'élégantes maisons du 18e siècle - bien restaurées... refaites... - dont beaucoup se louent, actuellement, comme appartements de luxe. A noter le numéro 57, où mourut en 1828 Goya, le peintre espagnol. Devant le Grand Théâtre nous allons prendre la rue Ste. Cathérine - c'est une rue piétonne; très commerçante: vous y trouverez de grands magasins, des boutiques... bref, tout!

De là nous traverserons la Place du Parlement: une jolie cour entourée de belles maisons... et de restaurants! En passant par de petites rues nous arriverons sur les quais de la Garonne: d'ici vous apercevrez le Pont de Pierre, qui fut - très longtemps - le seul pont de Bordeaux. Plus loin, à gauche, se dressent les deux grandes colonnes qui annoncent l'Esplanade des Quinconces - sorte d'espace verte, très grand... vaste - d'une superficie de 126,000 mètres carrés. Nous remonterons vers le centre pour trouver l'Office de Tourisme. C'est ici que je terminerai le tour guidé, pour vous donner du temps libre - de deux heures. Le car viendra nous prendre à l'Office de Tourisme, à 18h - soyez à l'heure!

Answers

1. TWO from : she's an English teacher in Paris; she was born in Bordeaux;she did her studies at the University of Bordeaux.
2. coach station
3. ONE from : it's an English style garden now; had the scaffold/guillotine during the Revolution
4. as luxury flats
5. Goya died in Bordeaux
6. it's the main shopping street
7. ONE from : it has restaurants; it's a courtyard; it has fine houses
8. it was until recently the only bridge in Bordeaux across the Garonne
9. its size
10. in front of the tourist office
11. two hours
12. 18 h/6pm

4 Shops and shopping

page 118 **1 Le panier garni**

1. tuna, green beans
2. eggs
3. tomatoes, ham, cheese (Bleu d'Auvergne)
4. yoghurts
5. lettuce
6. one week
7. Intermarché

page 119 **2 Où est-ce que je peux acheter..?**

A. 8
B. 2
C. 6
D. 4
E. 8
F. 1, 3
G. 1
H. 7
I. 3
J. 7
K. 1
L. 1
M. 5
N. 1

page 121 **3 Quelle taille?**

1. chest and hip
2. chest
3. hip and waist
4. waist size and overall size
5. order the larger size

page 122 **4 Soldes monstres et prix massacrés**

Grafitti

1. dresses; jumpers; shorts; blouses; men's casual jackets; trousers; jeans
2. 10 August

page 123 **Lovly**

1. closing down
2. ready-to-wear; underwear; knitted wear
3. designer labels/clothes
4. 20%
5. until everything is gone

page 126 **1 A quel étage se trouve..?**

1. Mesdames, messieurs, cette semaine au rayon alimentation offre spécial sur les fruits, les légumes et les fromages. Au rayon alimentation *au sous-sol* du magasin.
2. Messieurs si vous êtes bricoleur, venez au rayon bricolage *au 5e étage.*Les marteaux, les tourne-vis, les scies sont à moitié prix.
3. Mesdames, messieurs, à l'approche de Noël, venez fair un tour à notre boutique cadeaux *au rez de chaussée.* Vous y trouverez des cadeaux originaux pour tous les goûts.
4. *Au 3e étage* à notre rayon des disques vous trouverez tous les derniers disques au hit parade. Une large sélection avec 10% de réduction. C'est à notre rayon des disques *au 3e étage.*
5. Messieurs venez au rayon pour hommes *au 2e étage.* Profitez de nos réductions sur les complets, les vestons, les chemises et les cravates. C'est en janvier seulement.
6. Mesdames venez faire un tour à notre rayon pour dames *au 2e étage.* Cette semaine nous avons une offre spéciale sur tous les manteaux.
7. Mesdames, messieurs - si vous avez des enfants venez voir nos jeux et jouets *au 4e étage*
8. Mesdames, messieurs, pour votre information les toilettes sont *au 5e étage.*
9. Mesdames, allez vite au rayon parfumerie *au rez de chaussée.* Profitez de nos réductions exceptionnelles sur tous les parfums Dior.
10. Et nous avons tout pour l'enfant au *4e étage.* Shorts, chemisiers et jupes à des prix records. Ne manquez pas ces occasions au *4e étage.*

page 127 **2 Je cherche le rayon pour...**

1. Cette semaine au rayon alimentation au 5e étage prix exceptionnels sur la viande de boeuf.
2. Offres limitées sur tous les appareils photos Kodak. Oui, c'est au rayon photo au 4e étage.
3. Tout pour amuser vos enfants à notre rayon jouets au 3e étage.
4. Mesdames, messieurs, avant de quitter le magasin, faites un tour à notre rayon cadeaux - souvenirs au rez de chaussée.
5. Arrivage spéciale de fruits tropicaux. Venez vite au sous-sol et achetez nos bananes, nos mangues et nos fruits de la passion.
6. A notre rayon livres et disques au 6e étage vous trouverez une large sélection de livres de poche, de disques, de cassettes et de disques laser.
7. Messieurs, venez au rayon hommes. Nous avons tout pour l'homme à la mode au rayon hommes au 2e étage.

5 Services

page 136   **1 Quelle boîte?**   **Quel guichet pour?**

1. E   4. F   1. C   4. E
2. A   5. C   2. F   5. A
3. B   6. D   3. B   6. D

page 137   **2 La Poste simplifie l'adresse**

1. bureau distributeur
2. commune
3. destinataire
4. code postal
5. the district area

page 138   **Petits conseils utiles**

1. when phoning from any province to Paris region
2. when phoning from one province to another
3. when phoning from Paris region to any province

page 138   **3 Informations - services**

1. Easter   5. available
2. shut   6. reduced
3. shut   7. additional
4. not available 8. reduced

page 139   **Bloc notes**

a. **médecin de**   e. **police - secours**
   garde   f. **téléphone**
b. **pompiers**   **renseignements**
c. **taxis**   g. **voix de l'Ain**
d. **SNCF ren-**   h. **EDF dépannages**
   seignements

page 139   **4 Pressing de Paris**   **Nettoyage**

1. by weight   unlined skirt, coat, trousers, long-sleeved
2. 1 day   jumper, unlined dress, men's jackets
3. same day

page 141   **5   Le nouveau télégramme**

1. dial 36 55
2. key in 36 56

3. your name, address, phone number: the recipient's name, address, phone number.
4. copy of text sent immediately
5. ask France Telecom to send you one

page 142 **6 Ventes, locations, et dépannages**

B
1. **station Mobil**
2. **Jacqueline**
3. **Dubernet**
4. **cordonnerie**
5. **Jacqueline**
6. **Inter-Services**
7. **Ribault**
8. **Ouest vidéo**
9. **laverie automatique**
10. **Office de Tourisme**

page 144 **7 Pas de vacances pour le Syndicat d'Initiative**

1. what to see; where to stay
2. entertainment; swimming facilties; food
3. money stolen
4. Italy; Canada
5. second half
6. tour of old Bourg, son et lumiére at the church of Brou
7. locals and their friends
8. put up 3 giant screens outside church for continuous slide projection

page 149 **1 Musée Claude Monet**

Si vous avez le temps, je vous recommande vivement d'aller voir ce musée, pas très loin de Paris - à 87 kilomètres, oui, c'est ça, 87 kilométres. Il est ouvert tous les jours, sauf les lundi, de 10 h à 12 h, et ensuite de 14 h à18 h. Les tres beaux jardins sont ouverts sans interruption de 10 h à 18 h. A noter que le musée ainsi que les jardins sont ouverts à partir du ler avril; tout ferme le 31 octobre.

1. Tuesday to Sunday
2. Mondays
3. April - end October
4. 10 h - 12 h
5. 14 h - 18 h
6. 10 h - 18 h
7. 87 kilometres

page 149   **2   Allo, s'il vous plaît!**

Je vous donne les numéros de téléphone - vous les notez? Pour la maison du tourisme c'est le 01 46 18 06. La piscine olympique - voyons, c'est le 12 52 17 44; c'est le (...). Le camping municipal se trouve au 42 03 19 15. Pour le Centre de Loisirs vous faites le 15 47 11 39. Encore une fois? (...). La gare routière ? voyons un peu... c'est le 00 20 99 14. Et enfin, le Casino de la Plage se trouve au 16 41 18 75. (...)

page 149   **3   Pour connaître la ville**

Si vous disposez du temps, je vous propose le tour guidé et commenté, à bord le Petit Train Bleu, départ 10 h tous les jours. Le marché hebdomadaire, très animé, a lieu les mercredi, sur la place principale. Les dimanche matin nous avons également le Marché des Fleurs - très joli, surtout au printemps, vous voyez... et enfin samedi, c'est la Foire Aux vins - expositions, dégustation libre...

1.   flower market   4.   main square
2.   little blue train   5.   Wine Fair
3.   Wednesdays

6 Food and drink

page 154   **Key Speaking Tasks**

MENU CAFETARIA

ITEM

Petit déjeuner anglais (toute la journée)
Saucisse, haricots, frites
Poisson panné, petits pois, frites
Scampis, frites
Plat du jour
Salade niçoise
Melon
Crudités
Jambon en salade
Poulet en salade
Yaourts aux fruits
Gâteau fondant chocolat
Gâteau cassis
Fromages et biscuits
Petit pain
Beurre
Sauces en sachet
Confitures
Biscuits chocolatés
Fruits (orange-pomme)
Céréales (avec lait)
Coca Cola, Diet Coke, Fanta, Lilt
Eaux minérales
Bière "Long Life"
Bière blonde
Laits aromatisés
Vin rouge/blanc (le 1/4)
Jus d'orange/de pomme
Lait frais
Café
Thé

---

page 156 **1 Faites le tour du monde**

1. Russia; England; Germany; Holland; America
2. England; Russia
3. Germany; Holland
4. Germany; America; Russia (fish)
5. bread

page 157 **2 Premier plaisir de la journée**

1. prevents tiredness in the morning and that mid-morning empty feeling; you won't need a large lunch, so you won't feel sleepy in the afternoon
2. helps build, maintain and renew body tissue
3. energy

page 158 **3 Choisir un menu**

a. 6
b. 5
c. 4
d. 3
e. 2
f. 2 and 5 - raspberry
   3 and 4 - blackcurrant
   6 - orange
g. cheese

page 159 **4 La Jonquière**

1. the one called GRILLADES
2. the one called POISSONS
3. six; two
4. salad starters, and hamburger and chips; and their favourite dessert
5. today's special
6. water

page 160 **5 Salade et dessert**

2. salad plate and dessert
3. five
4. rice and green salad
5. tuna and ham

6 Cadre et spécialités

1. Rollin; Isadora
2. Rollin
3. Menestrel
4. Isadora
5. Le Mas
6. Menestrel; Vieil Ecu
7. Menestrel; Lou Pairol
8. Isadora; Closerie; Rollin

7 Les fruits de la Vallée du Rhône

1. they have stones in the middle
2. they have pips
3. they are red fruits
4. cherry blossom, in the spring
5. in wooded high ground / hills
6. between the end of July and August 15

8 Lentilles

1. in cold water
2. unnecessary
3. three measures of water (or two and a half for pressure cooker) to one of lentils
4. 60g dry weight per person
5. drain; season and garnish
6. retains vitamin and mineral contents
7. high fibre content; rich in minerals; high calorific value

1 Râpées de pommes de terre

Ingrédients pour cinq personnes:

1kg de pommes de terre
2 oeufs
sel et poivre

Preparation et cuisson:

"Pêler les pommes de terres, les râper, les faire égoutter quelques minutes dans une passoire.

Les mettre dans un plat creux, casser les oeufs dessus, bien mélanger avec sel et poivre.

Faire cuire par grandes cuillèrées dans un peu d'huile très chaude, quatre minutes sur chaque face.

Servir très chaud".

1.	potatoes	5.	salt and pepper
2.	a few minutes	6.	oil
3.	dish	7.	4 minutes
4.	mix	8.	very hot

page 165   **2   Potée bretonne**

"...la potée bretonne, qu'est-ce que c'est?   Alors, c'est un plat composé; il y a une viande - ça peut être du porc ou du boeuf... euh... normalement c'est du porc.   Ensuite, il y a des légumes - carottes, patates, chou.   Ah oui, il y a des saucisses egalement.   C'est très bon, c'est nourrissant..."

cabbage	✓
cauliflower	
sausage	✓
potatoes	✓
leeks	
carrots	✓
meat	✓

7   Health

page 172   **1   Posologie, présentation**

Headings

1.	PRESENTATION	3.	PRECAUTIONS
2.	POSOLOGIE	4.	INDICATIONS

Symptoms

1. muscular pains
2. toothache
3. earache
4. burns
5. insect bites
6. diarrhoea
7. period pains
8. dry cough
9. throat infections

Instructions

1. swallow
2. do not swallow
3. apply externally
4. take after meals
5. apply the ointment
6. rub in gently
7. dissolve in water
8. warm up

Container, form

1. tin/box
2. ointment/cream
3. bottle
4. sachet
5. drops
6. dressings
7. tablets/pills
8. capsules
9. sugar-coated pills
10. suppositories
11. the mixture

Warnings

1. keep out of reach of children
2. avoid going into the sun
3. avoid prolonged use
4. do not exceed stated dose
5. drinking alcohol not advised
6. do not use on infected cuts

page 173 **2 Premiers soins**

1. remove sting; disinfect the bite; keep watch for several hours in case of allergic reaction
2. contain swelling/bruises by applying a cold spray locally; take something for the pain
3. apply something cold (water, compresses); cover with - but do not rub in - an appropriate cream product; immobilise with bandages

page 174   **3**   **Allo - secours**

1.	**pharmacies ouvertes**	7.	**SOS petite enfance**
2.	**brûlures graves**	8.	**SOS 3e âge**
3.	**SOS médecins**	9.	**police secours**
4.	**pompiers**	10.	**centre anti-poison**
5.	**objets trouvés**	11.	**perte chéquiers**
6.	**SOS explosifs**	12.	**ambulance**

page 174   **4**   **Offrez votre sang**

1. men - 5 times a year' women - 3 times
2. eat before giving blood; avoid fatty foods; take foods high in sugar
3. he represents an upper age limit
4. shows that blood donations analysed; donors informed of irregularities
5. children: shown as knowledgeable and enthusiastic
6. to promote their awareness for later in life

page 175   **5**   **Vivez mieux la mer**

A.   1.   Be fit beforehand
     2.   Don't go off on your own
     3.   Look up the weather forecast
     4.   Make sure your holiday equipment is in good working order
     5.   Don't overestimate your stamina

B.   1.   Stay within supervised areas
     2.   Be careful in deep water or currents
     3.   Swim only after light meal if water at least 20 C

C.   1.   Take care with fire
     2.   take suitable clothing and some food

D.   1.   Make Y shape with arms and body
     2.   Stay on inflatable/surfboard - never try to swim back

page 179   **1   A la pharmacie**

Customer:	**Vous avez quelque chose pour un mal de gorge?**
Chemist:	**C'est pour un enfant ou un adulte?**
Customer:	**C'est pour moi.**
Chemist:	**Est-ce que vous toussez?**
Customer:	**Oui, un peu le matin.**
Chemist:	**Alors, je vous conseille des comprimés ou un sirop.**
Customer:	**Je dois en prendre combien de fois par jour?**
Chemist:	**Les comprimés quatre par jour, et le sirop le matin avant le petit-déjeuner et avant le dîner. Mais il ne faut pas boire d'alcoöl.**
Customer:	**Je vais prendre le sirop. Ça fait combien?**
Chemist:	**41 F, s'il vous plaît, mademoiselle.**
Customer:	**Merci, Monsieur. Au revoir.**
Chemist:	**Au revoir - et si les symptomes persistent, consultez votre médecin.**

1. cough
2. themselves
3. tablets or cough mixture
4. cough mixture
5. 41 F
6. alcohol
7. before breakfast and before dinner
8. consult a doctor

page 179   **3   Chez le médecin**

Patient:	**Je me suis foulé la cheville.**
Docteur:	**Vous êtes très enflé? Montrez-moi, s'il vous plaît... ah oui, en effet. Vous avez mal?**
Patient:	**Oui, beaucoup et je ne peux pas mettre mes chaussures.**
Docteur:	**Vous pouvez marcher?**
Patient:	**Oui, mais ça fait très mal.**
Docteur:	**Je ne crois pas que vous avez la cheville cassée. Je vais vous donner une ordonnance; c'est pour un bandage spécial et de la pommade.**
Patient:	**Merci, Docteur. Il y a une pharmacie près d'ici?**
Docteur:	**Oui Monsieur, tournez à gauche et c'est au coin.**

ANSWERS

1. twisted/sprained ankle
2. wear/put on shoe
3. bandage and ointment (pommade)
4. turn left, on corner

8 Self, house, home & family

page 191   **1   Échange scolaire**

1. 17
2. Tain l'Hermitage
3. brothers
4. one
5. cycling, walking, music, DIY
6. maths and art
7. Italian
8. bank
9. teacher
10. fish
11. penicillin

page 192   **2   Maisons/appartements à louer**

a. 5
b. 2
c. 2, 5
d. 3
e. 4
f. 1
g. 3
h. 8
i. 6
j. 2

page 194   **3   Petits conseils**

1. by turning knob clockwise at night
2. cooks fast; gas-mark 2 or 3 for roasting chicken
3. hot water; it's extremely hot
4. in the garage
5. ask Madame Moreteau who lives opposite
6. put it in plastic bags; then put bags in dustbins in garage
7. every Friday morning
8. late morning and early afternoon

page 195   **4**   **Cherche/vends animaux**

1.   a. 8   b. 6   c. 5   d. 9
2.   ask in the shop
3.   a. make an offer   b. 250f   c. free
4.   horse (1), Boxer puppy (4), budgie (9)
5.   they have handsome parents

page 196   **5**   **"Maisons en Écosse"**

A...   **T'as reçu les brochures de l'agence de voyages?**

B...   **oui..tiens..voilà**

A...   **Alors, qu'est-ce que tu en penses? Regarde cette maison là.... 4 chambres.. pour 8 personnes. Elles est grande, hein?**

B...   **oui, mais c'est peut-être trop grand peut-être. Et cher aussi, £270 par mois.**

A...   **c'est libre en juillet. Ah oui, quand est-ce qu'on veut partir en Ecosse?**

B...   **Eh.. bein... Fin juin les enfants finissent l'école, alors peut-être fin juin début juillet.**

A...   **et puis c'est près de la mer aussi. Tu veux aller nager en Ecosse?**

B...   **non mais parce que quand-même il fait froid, alors c'est pas important ça, la mer.**

A...   **il y a un centre sportif à proximité aussi.**

B...   **oui, ce serait bien pour les enfants parce que,, s'il pleut et...**

A...   **il paraît qu'il pleut beaucoup en Ecosse. Regardons une autre...euh...celle-la serait peut-être mieux pour nous. £180 par mois.**

B...   **c'est moins cher que la première et c'est libre juillet, août, septembre...voyons...euh... 2 chambres, 4 personnes.. mais c'est quand même petit.**

A...   **euh oui...maison isolée, pas de circulation. Et c'est dans les montagnes... ça m'intéresse plus que la mer finalement. On pourrait y faire de belles promenades.**

B...   **mais il y en a d'autres... euh... celle-là, par exemple. Le bungalow moderne... voyons... 3 chambres... euh... 5 personnes... transports fréquents et faciles... mais on aura la bagnole!**

A...   **dans un petit village, pas loin d'Edimbourg. J'aimerais bien voir Edimbourg... le château et tout ça.**

B... **mais c'est cher... £300 par mois, libre début septembre... non ça ne va pas.**

A... **et on pourrait quand-même passer par Edimbourg en route pour celle-ci qui est plus au nord.**

B... **D'accord, si tu veux. On prend celle-ci.**

House A

1.	4	4.	£270
2.	8	5.	near the sea
3.	June and July	6.	sports centre

House B

1.	2	4.	£180
2.	4	5.	in the mountains
3.	July to September	6.	good for walking

House C

1.	3	4.	£300
2.	5	5.	in small village near Edinburgh
3.	beginning of September	6.	good transport

9 Entertainment and leisure

page 207 **1 Allons sortir**

1. H
2. D
3. G
4. C
5. A
6. B
7. I
8. **plein tarif**
9. **demi-tarif**

10. **entrée gratuite**
11. **exposition**
12. leave children unattended; go barefoot; cross gates; annoy the animals; damage plants
13. church of St. Louis; Napoleon's tomb
14. every day
15. 6 pm summer; 5 pm winter

page 209 **2 Découverte de la randonnée**

1. beginners
2. safety course, snow and avalanche conditions; weather forecasts; first aid
3. 6 hours
4. use of equipment; safety rules in practice; getting ready for a downhill; study of terrain (topography)
5. weather conditions

page 210 **3 A vos magnétoscopes!**

1.	C	7.	B	13.	C
2.	B	8.	F	14.	C
3.	F	9.	E	15.	E
4.	A	10.	D	16.	video record the films
5.	F	11.	B		
6.	D	12.	A		

page 211 **4 Les enfants du rock**

1. as gospel singers; in California
2. they began to have hit records
3. Bonnie leaves the group
4. more rock
5. the song included in the film
6. enabled them to reach wider public
7. they were giving a concert in Paris

page 212   **5**   **Télématin**

		TF1	A2
1.	FOOD	**cuisine**	**recette**
	HEALTH	**santé; vivre mieux**	**conseils de forme; diètétique; santé**
	NEWS	**actualité**	**journal; flash d'information**
	MONEY	**journal affaires**	**votre argent**
	SPORT	**sport**	**sport**
	POLITICS	**invité politique**	**édito politique**
	WEATHER	**météo**	**météo**
2.	A2		

page 214   **6**   **Apostrophes**

1. the new Queens of Crime
2. they only speak English

Ruth Rendell

3. thirty
4. sixteen
5. fourteen
6. an ordinary man, has family problems; discussions with his assistant
7. journalist
8. has garden; lawn; greenhouses; pond
9. does gymnastics, aerobics; goes walking, running, swimming
10. sixty

P.D. James

11. in retreat, writing new book
12. in London
13. 350,000 each book
14. a good plot
15. gives social background
16. about London low-life; and middle-class drawing rooms

page 220 **1 Horaires des cours**

Pour les femmes les heures sont le lundi à 17h 30, le mardi à 9h 30; et à 10h le jeudi et vendredi.

Cours enfants - les mercredi après-midi à 15h.

Pour les messieurs seuls nous avons des classes à 17h également les lundi, et les mardi à la même heure.

Cours mixtes... voyons... mardi et mercredi à 18h 30, et les vendredi matin à 10h.

page 220 **2 Le Prince Randolph**

Flegmatique, laconique, monolithique, granitique, il parcourut L'Ouest de son pas souple et allongé, promenant sa longue silhouette racée de Virginien. Il se nommait Randolph Scott, né à l'aube du siècle et mort l'an dernier. Avec au palmarès plus de quatre-vingts films, un par année d'existence. Ses amis l'appelaient familièrement Randy et il règnait dans les coeurs de tous ceux qui vécurent de westerns et d'eau fraîche entre 1940 et 1960.

Il débuta en 1928 et servait, quelque temps, dans des comédies laborieuses. Ses premiers westerns même ne furent pas des réussites.

C'est un cinéaste de série B, Ray Enright, qui, le premier commence à façonner un personnage que Scott ne quittera plus: celui de l'homme laconique, souvent poussé par de secrets motifs et qui cherche obstinément sa voie au milieu des obstacles. Ils tournèrent ensemble cinq films. Des "petits films", comme on dit: mais tous marqués au coin de quelque scène insolite et traversés par la présénce de Randy. Violents, tournés très vite, les uns à la suite des autres, ils confortèrent Scott dans son image de marque. Image que reprit et creusa un autre maître de la série B, un Hongrois en exil, André de Toth. Dans l'espace de six films, inégaux, mais jamais totalement inintéressants, il burina les traits du cowboy solitaire. Il restait à ajouter une touche finale au portrait: celui du vengeur implacable. C'était enfin, après trente ans de métier, l'heure de Bud Boetticher, le temps des chefs-d'oeuvre.

Randy tourna sept films avec l'un des plus talentueux metteurs en scène de sa géneration. Sept films : quatre chefs-d'oeuvre. Le bilan n'est pas mince, pour un ensemble qui s'étend sur quatre ans, entre 1956 et 1960. Disons-le tout net, ces films sont le travail d'une équipe: le metteur en scène, bien sûr mais aussi le scénariste, les acteurs et surtout le producteur, Scott lui-même, qui adopta, avec beaucoup d'intelligence, des méthodes de travail fondées sur la qualité des extérieurs, la solidité du scénario, la force des seconds rôles et la liberté totale du metteur en scène.

Answers

1. at the beginning of the century
2. 1928
3. five
4. laconic; obstinate; driven by hidden motives
5. violent; made quickly
6. six
7. seven; over 4 years (1956 - 1960)
8. that of the implacable avenger
9. team work
10. by having good/quality scriptwriters; locations; supporting actors; and by giving total freedom to his director

10   School, job, work and careers

page 228   **1   Liste des fournitures**

1. Sc physiques = physics; dessin = art; E.M.T. (education manuelle et technique) = technical subjects, eg CDT; E.P.S. (education physique, et sport) = P.E., sport
2. a. Maths; physics; English; extra English; history; geography; CDT; Spanish
   b. history; geopraphy
   c. biology; French
   d. biology; French
3. a. P.E. kit and swimming trunks
   b. nothing; a charge will be made
4. set square; plastic ruler; protractor; compasses; scissors with rounded ends; six colour-pencils; pencil; rubber

page 230   **2   Mme le Proviseur**

1. meetings; member of a youth club association; member of a film censors' group.
2. listens to music; takes bus rides; goes to a train station and watches trains go by.
3. the way they talk; their humour; their spontaneity.

4. a difficult time/a crisis.
5. a role-model; help; because life is super!
6. lack of time; lack of money; poor working conditions.
7. sympathetic/understanding.

page 231 **3 Demandes d'emploi**

1.	b	5.	c	9.	a
2.	d	6.	c	10.	d
3.	a	7.	b	11.	a
4.	b	8.	d	12.	c

page 233 **4 Métiers : offres - demandes**

1.	e	4.	b
2.	a	5.	f
3.	d	6.	c

page 233 **5 Métiers: offres**

a.	3	f.	1
b.	5	g.	9
c.	7	h.	2
d.	10	i.	6
e.	8	j.	4

page 238 **1 Le rôle des parents**

- Quelles sont vos rélations avec les parents d'élèves?

- J'aime travailler avec eux quand ils sont nos partenaires dans la vie du lycée, lorsqu'ils sont en association. A titre individuel, je les respecte, mais je suis très sévère avec eux: je leur envoie pas mal de choses à la figure. Ils ont des exigences exorbitantes dès qu'il se mêlent de pédagogie et ne reconnaissent pas aux profs le droit d'être aussi des êtres humains; après tout, il existe des profs nuls comme il existe des cadres nuls. Alors, pas de panique! Plutôt que de réclamer des exercices supplémentaires, des bacs blancs, les parents feraient mieux de se battre pour une grande sécurite scolaire, pour des loisirs, du sport, une écoute. Il fait remettre les choses à leur place.

- Oui, mais il s'agit de l'avenir de leurs enfants!

- Les parents ne mettent aucune distance entre ce que dit l'enfant et ce qui se passe réellement. Ils formulent une énorme demande face à l'école. Je ne dis pas qu'ils aient complètement tort, mais parfois ils perdent la tête. La réussite de leurs enfants n'est pas la leur. Avant, c'était le règne du "Apprends et tais-toi". Aujourd'hui, heureusement, c'est les enfants qui doivent dire, c'est eux qui savent. Un prof est utile, d'accord, mais pas si décisif que cela. C'est l'emballement du système qui rend les parents fous, la sélection, les concours. J'ai envie de leur dire: laissez vos enfants vivre et leurs profs travailler.

Answers

1. They should be partners.
2. When they start to interfere with teaching methods.
3. i. They want more extra work.
   ii. They want more mock examinations.
4. Sport and leisure activities.
5. Selection; competition
6. She says it's up to the children to make a success; and that teachers are useful but not the final factor.
7. Allow teachers to teach; and allow children to get on with their own lives.